W9-AVK-566

Praise for Randall's Practical Guide to ISO 9000

I encourage not only quality professionals, but students, business professionals, and anyone with an interest in quality system development to purchase this book. Randall's book breaks down in a practical way how to use the most important quality system of this generation.

James P. O'Neil
President and Founder
National Quality Assurance USA, Inc.

[*Randall's Practical Guide to ISO 9000*] is one of the best discussions of the subject I have seen. It will give any interested person a thorough understanding of ISO 9000 and also of the separate but related topic of third party registration.

Radley M. Smith
Director, Automotive Sector
KPMG Peat Marwick Quality Registrar

I found the material thorough and comprehensive. It may well become the standard for the application of ISO 9000. It is easy to read and interesting. I find that the author seems to have captured the essence of the change to ISO very effectively.

Edwin Shecter
Management Consultant
Total Quality Resources

The text provides an extremely useful perspective on ISO 9000. The material is especially well written. Features such as time bombs are going to provide tremendous assistance to corporate QA professionals charged with assisting their organizations in preparing for ISO registration audits. I think Randall's text is an outstanding resource for any organization seeking ISO registration.

Lawrence S. Aft
Professor
Industrial Engineering Technology
Southern College of Technology

This book is a useful handbook for practicing quality systems auditors, quality consultants, and to any employee of organizations who are seeking to implement ISO 9000, or any other quality system for that matter. I will have no hesitation in recommending [this book] to colleagues and clients alike.

David J. Hughes
Managing Director
Lead Assessor, Lead Auditor
Quality Partnerships Limited
Staffordshire, England

My overall impression of the book is that it is a uniquely useful tool to be used for ISO 9000 implementation. It is amazingly easy to read and follow, and I especially like the "Questions to be asked by the Registrar" sections.

Rhonda Fiske
Quality Manager
Tru-Line Manufacturing, Inc.

Randall's Practical Guide to ISO 9000 is a no nonsense guide to the registration process and its implications for a company. It's understandable, easy to read, and will be an invaluable tool for any company choosing the daunting but ultimately rewarding journey toward ISO 9000 quality systems registration.

Mark Morrow
Quality Systems Update Newsletter

Randall's Practical Guide to ISO 9000

Implementation,
Registration,
and Beyond

ENGINEERING PROCESS IMPROVEMENT SERIES

John W. Wesner, Ph.D., P.E., Consulting Editor

Randall's Practical Guide to ISO 9000

Implementation, Registration, and Beyond

Richard C. Randall

ADDISON-WESLEY
An imprint of Addison Wesley Longman, Inc.

Reading, Massachusetts • Harlow, England • Menlo Park, California
Berkeley, California • Don Mills, Ontario • Sydney
Bonn • Amsterdam • Tokyo • Mexico City

Many of the designations used by manufacturers and sellers to distinguish their products are claimed as trademarks. Where those designations appear in this book and Addison-Wesley was aware of a trademark claim, the designations have been printed with initial capital letters.

Due to the constantly changing nature of standards, laws, regulations, statutes, and codes, it is impossible to guarantee absolute accuracy of the material contained herein. The Publishers, Editors, and Author therefore cannot assume any responsibility for omissions, errors, misprinting, or ambiguity contained within this publication and shall not be held liable in any degree for any loss or injury caused by such omission, error, misprinting, or ambiguity presented in this publication.

This publication is designed to provide reasonably accurate and authoritative information in regard to the subject matter covered. It is sold with the understanding that the publisher is not engaged in rendering legal, accounting, consulting, or other professional service. If legal advice, consulting, or other expert assistance is required, the services of a competent professional person should be sought.

The publisher offers discounts on this book when ordered in quantity for special sales. For more information, please contact:

Corporate & Professional Publishing Group
Addison-Wesley Publishing Company
One Jacob Way
Reading, Massachusetts 01867

Library of Congress Cataloging-in-Publication Data

Randall, Richard C., 1959–
    Randall's practical guide to ISO 9000 : implementation, registration, and beyond / Richard C. Randall
        p. cm.
    Includes bibliographical references and index.
    ISBN 0-201-63379-5
    1. ISO 9000 Series Standards.   I. Title   II. Title: Practical guide to ISO 9000.
TS156.6.R35   1995
658.5′62—dc20   95-8178
                                                  CIP

Copyright © 1995 Addison Wesley Longman, Inc.

All rights reserved. No part of this publication may be reproduced, stored in a retrieval system, or transmitted in any form or by any means, electronic, mechanical, photocopying, recording, or otherwise, without prior written permission of the publisher. Printed in the United States of America. Published simultaneously in Canada.

Text design by Wilson Graphics & Design (Kenneth J. Wilson)
Text printed on recycled and acid-free paper

ISBN 0-201-63379-5
2 3 4 5 6 7 8 9 10-MA-99989796
Second printing, October 1996

ENGINEERING PROCESS IMPROVEMENT SERIES

Consulting Editor, John Wesner, Ph.D., P.E.

Global competitiveness is of paramount concern to the engineering community worldwide. As customers demand ever-higher levels of quality in their products and services, engineers must keep pace by continually improving their processes. For decades, American business and industry have focused their quality efforts on their end products rather than on the processes used in the day-to-day operations that create these products and services. Experts across the country now agree that focusing on continuous improvements of the core business and engineering processes within an organization will lead to the most meaningful, long-term improvements and production of the highest-quality products.

Whether your title is researcher, designer, developer, manufacturer, quality or business manager, process engineer, student or coach, you are responsible for finding innovative, practical ways to improve your processes and products in order to be successful and remain world-class competitive. The **Engineering Process Improvement Series** takes you beyond the ideas and theories, focusing in on the practical information you can apply to your job for both short-term and long-term results. These publications offer current tools and methods and useful how-to advice. This advice comes from the top names in the field; each book is both written and reviewed by the leaders themselves, and each book has earned the stamp of approval of the series consulting editor, John W. Wesner.

Key innovations by industry leaders in process improvement include work in benchmarking, concurrent engineering, robust design, customer-to-customer cycles, process management, and engineering design. Books in this series will discuss these vital issues in ways that help engineers of all levels of experience become more productive and increase quality significantly.

All of the books in the series share a unique graphic cover design. Viewing the graphic blocks descending, you see random pieces coming together to build a solid structure, signifying the ongoing effort to improve processes and produce quality products most satisfying to the customer. If you view the graphic blocks moving upward, you see them breaking through barriers—just as engineers and companies today must break through traditional, defining roles to operate more effectively with concurrent systems. Our mission for this series is to provide the tools, methods, and practical examples to help you hurdle the obstacles, so that you can perform simultaneous engineering and be successful at process and product improvement.

The series is divided into three categories:

Process Management and Improvement   This includes books that take larger views of the field, including major processes and the end-to-end process for new product development.

Improving Functional Processes   These are the specific functional processes that are combined to form the more inclusive processes covered in the first category.

Special Process Topics and Tools   These are methods and techniques that are used in support of improving the various processes covered in the first two categories.

Mr. Richard C. Randall is the Southeast Regional Director for National Quality Assurance (NQA), U.S.A.* NQA is accredited by both the U.K. National Accreditation Council for Certification Bodies (NACCB) and the U.S. American National Standards Institute (ANSI)/Registrar Accreditation Board (RAB) as an ISO 9000 Quality System Registrar offering more than ninety different scopes of registration. NQA is one of the world's largest and most successful registrars, with International offices located in Scotland, Northern Ireland, and England. Mr. Randall is a Registered Lead Auditor [qualified through the Institute of Quality Assurance (IQA)—International Register of Certified Auditors (IRCA) program] with expertise in Electronics, Test Houses, Process Industries, and Service Industries.

Prior to NQA, Mr. Randall served as the National Quality Manager for GE Electronic Services, which offers instrument calibration and repair services to the nuclear industry, transportation services industry, telecommunication industry, biomedical/pharmaceutical industry, and a variety of manufacturing industries. At that time the GE Electronic Services quality system was compliant with the Association of American Railroads Specification for Quality Assurance M-1003, MIL-STD-45662A, ANSI/ASQC M-1, and ISO 9002:1987.

Mr. Randall continues to support the Metrology Industry representing NQA in the National Conference of Standards Laboratories (NCSL), where he serves on the "TQM Committee for Calibration Services." This committee is responsible for ANSI/NCSL Z540-1, "General Requirements for Calibration Laboratories and Measuring and Test Equipment," which is in harmony with ISO standards and serves as a basis for the "U.S. Calibration Laboratory Accreditation Program." He is also a member of the American Society for Quality Control (ASQC), where he serves on the ANSI/ASQC M-1/M-2 writing committee.

*The advice and opinions expressed in this guide are strictly those of Mr. Richard C. Randall and do not necessarily reflect the interpretations or policies of NQA, USA.

DEDICATION

To all quality companies and organizations
striving to better themselves,
their product/service, and
their community.

Preface

About This Guide

This guide is intended for those who have experience in the quality industry as well as those who are new to it. This guide is *not* intended to explore the total spectrum of developing a Total Quality Management (TQM) System—that would be well beyond its scope. The reader should realize and appreciate that virtually every individual section of ISO 9000 could easily have a complete book written on its topic. This guide is geared primarily toward discussing the *practical* quality concepts and principles necessary to develop and implement an ISO 9000–compliant quality system. This is accomplished through the use of "real world" examples presented in what I hope you will find an uncomplicated approach.

This book should *not* be considered a substitute for a consultant. No advice or recommendations are given. Only examples and suggested possible approaches toward the general application of ISO 9000 are discussed.

In order to meet U.S. Department of Transportation (DoT), Environmental Protection Agency (EPA), Occupational Safety and Health Administration (OSHA), and other regulatory requirements, many companies have established inefficient dual or multiple programs. Quite often these requirements can be more easily addressed through integrating them into a company's quality program. This guide will explore several of these possibilities, as well as some specific industry and North American Free Trade Agreement (NAFTA) considerations.

I continue to use the word "guide" for good reason. *Your* quality system should be tailored to fit *your* business. Many consultants today are marketing "canned" quality manuals and procedures that they claim meet the requirements of ISO 9000. While these manuals and procedures can be a good starting point, they should not be used "as is." Your business is unique and should be approached as such. I know it can be a big job to go through the processes of flow charting, developing, and documenting your own quality system. But the rewards are well worth the effort. Don't do it *just* to achieve ISO 9000 certification/registration; do it to improve the quality of your organization's product/service.

I have yet to see any two companies use the same approach toward meeting the requirements of ISO 9000.

Notes from the Author

The Title

I've given this book my name with good reason. There is no one "correct" interpretation of the ISO 9000 series. ISO 9000 is not a prescriptive standard, it does not detail the *how*, but rather the *what*. This allows each individual company to define *how* it intends to comply with the standard in a way that best suits that company's method of operation. This book reflects my experience, along with input from respected individuals and groups I consider authorities on quality and ISO 9000.

Interpretation always depends on *how* and *where* you are applying the standard. This book is a practical guide. It should not be viewed as telling you "how to" implement ISO 9000. Rather, it should serve as a source of practical ideas, insight, and guidance as you develop your own approach toward the standard.

ISO 9000

Whenever I use the generic term "ISO 9000," you should assume that I am speaking about the ISO series standard that most suits your application (ISO 9001, ISO 9002, or ISO 9003).

ISO 9000 Registered/Certified

Throughout this guide I will use the phrases "ISO 9000 registered" and "ISO 9000 certified" interchangeably. In reality a company can only be registered/certified to the ISO 9001, 9002, or 9003 standard.

There has also been some controversy over whether it is more proper to use the word "registered" than "certified." This controversy began because in the European Union (EU), when people speak of "certification" they usually mean "product certification," not "quality systems certification." The word "registered" is generally preferred because once a registrar certifies an organization as complying with a standard, the registrar "registers" that company's name and the scope statement in that registrar's public register of certified companies.

It really makes no difference which word you use, provided that it is clear to which type of certification you are referring. To further clarify terminology:

It is the supplier who is "Registered" or "Certified," while the registering bodies themselves should be "Accredited." (An exception to this term is made when referring to calibration and/or testing laboratory accreditation, but this is a different type of system.)

Questions, Comments, and Constructive Criticism

I invite readers to contact me with any questions, comments, and constructive criticism via e-mail.

Users of:	Address e-mail to:
America Online	RCR 9000
Internet	rcr9000@aol.com
CompuServe	>INTERNET:rcr9000@aol.com

Because of my weekly travel schedule I typically pick up my e-mail on weekends. Your patience is appreciated.

Acknowledgments

I would like to extend grateful thanks to the following individuals and organizations:

Mr. James P. O'Neil, President of NQA—U.S.A., Boxborough, MA

Mr. Kenneth J. Legg, Quality Systems Director of NQA—U.S.A., Boxborough, MA

Mr. Stephen J. Marquedant, Operations Director of NQA—U.S.A., Boxborough, MA

Mr. Radley Smith, Director of Automotive Sector, KPMG Peat Marwick Quality Registrar—Detroit, MI

Mr. Jim Van Langen, Vice President, Quality Management Services—SGS International Certification Services, Inc., Hoboken, NJ

Mr. Richard Clements, Chairman of the National ISO 9000 Support Group—Caledonia, MI

Dr. Joe D. Simmons, Chief of the Calibration Program (ret.)—NIST, Gaithersburg, MD

Ms. Maureen A. Breitenberg, Standards Code and Information Program—NIST, Gaithersburg, MD

Mr. Ken Butcher, Technical Advisor to the Laws and Regulations Committee on Weights and Measures—National Conference on Weights and Measures (NIST), Gaithersburg, MD

Mr. James L. Cigler, Program Manager of NVLAP—NIST, Gaithersburg, MD

Mr. Felipe Diez Martinez Day, SECLAC Program Manager—CENAM, Querétaro, Mexico

Mr. Peter J. Key, Deputy Head of NAMAS—London, England

Mr. Peter S. Unger, Vice President of the American Association for Laboratory Accreditation (A2LA)—Gaithersburg, MD

Mr. Wesley McElveen, Director of U.S. Army TMDE—Redstone Arsenal

Dr. John T. Burr, Associate Professor, Quality Systems, Rochester Institute of Technology—Rochester, NY

Ms. Jill A. Swift, University of Miami, "Industrial Engineering Department"—Miami, FL

Mr. Phil Callner, Director of Georgia Tech "Center for International Standards & Quality"—Atlanta, GA

Mr. Lawrence S. Aft, P.E.—Director of "Center for Quality Excellence," Southern College of Technology—Marietta, GA

Mr. Sid Milstein, Executive Vice President & General Manager, GE Test Equipment Management Services—Norcross, GA

Mr. Wayne P. Doucet, National Quality Manager, GE Test Equipment Management Services—Norcross, GA

Mr. Robert E. Burke, Vice President General Manager, Quebecor Printing Federated, Inc.—Providence, RI

Mr. Steven Bergeron, Vice President of Quality and Reliability Assurance, Unitrode Integrated Circuits Corporation—Merrimack, NH

Mr. T.J. Rucker, Laboratory Manager, Johnson Space Center Analysis and Testing Laboratory—Houston, TX

Dr. John W. Wesner, P.E.—Project Leader, Process Integration, AT&T Bell Laboratories (GBCS)—Middletown, NJ

Dr. Katherine Badt, Technical Staff, AT&T Bell Laboratories (GBCS)—Middletown, NJ

Mr. Greg Alia, Quality Manager, Grayson Electronics Co.—Forest, VA

Mr. Gerald Rooks, Director of Quality, Varian Vacuum Products—Lexington, MA

Mr. Ray Edwards, Manager of Quality Engineering, Gilbarco Inc.—Greensboro, NC

Cdr. J.S. Tex Lawson, U.S.N.R. (ret.), Quality Control Manager, Flexible Metal Hose Co.—Tucker, GA

Mr. Chris Jacobsen, Quality Manager, Simmons Machine Tool Corp.—Albany, NY

Mr. Joe DeMiddlear, National Quality Manager, SGS Control Services—Deer Park, TX

Ms. Rhonda B. Fiske, Quality Manager, Tru-Line Manufacturing, Inc.—Decatur, AL

Mr. Ken Giordano, Senior Quality Assurance Engineer, EMC Corporation—Hopkinton, MA

Mr. Francis J. Chinnici, Procurement Quality Manager, CSX Transportation—Jacksonville, FL

Mr. Steve Holladay, President—Management Standards International, Ltd.—Atlanta, GA

Mr. David J. Hughes, Managing Director, Quality Partnerships Limited—Stone, Staffordshire, England

Mr. Edwin Shecter, President of Quality Resources Company—Lawrenceville, NJ

Mr. Larry W. Whittington, President, Whittington and Associates—Marietta, GA

Mr. Jay J. Schlickman, RAB Certified Quality Systems Lead Auditor, Jay J. Schlickman & Associates—Lexington, MA

Mr. Marvin Walker—CQE, The Alpharetta Group (Quality and Management Consulting Services)—Alpharetta, GA

Mr. Gregory G. Scott—Partner, Popham, Haik, Schnobrich & Kaufman, Ltd.—Minneapolis, MN

Ms. Patricia Kopp, ASQC Standards Coordinator

The Institute of Quality Assurance (IQA)

The American Society for Quality Control (ASQC)

The Standards Council of Canada (SCC)

The U.S. Department of Commerce (DoC)

The British Department of Trade and Industry (DTI)

The National Association of Purchasing Management (NAPM), Rail Industry Group

The National Computer Security Association (NCSA)

The National Conference of Standards Laboratories (NCSL)

The NCSL TQM Committee for Calibration Services

I would also like to extend grateful thanks to the following companies for allowing me permission to discuss their creative and insightful approaches toward quality:

Flexible Metal Hose Company
Tucker, GA

GE Test Equipment Management Services
Norcross, GA

Gilbarco, Inc.
Greensboro, NC

Grayson Electronics Company
Forest, VA

Varian Vacuum Products
Lexington, MA

Introduction

How to Use This Guide

Don't try to read this guide in one sitting. Reference it as a handbook while developing each element in your quality system. If you are new to the quality field, focus on one element at a time. As your system evolves and begins to take on its own *signature* personality, you'll find a parallel approach easier to handle.

This guide is structured such that Chapters 3 and 4 correspond with the appropriate ISO 9000 elements. Each section of Chapter 4 will begin with "At a Glance." This overview will contain a very brief summary listing of the requirements from the ISO 9000 section and a small box with check marks indicating which standards (ISO 9001, 9002, and/or 9003) are applicable.

Those that do not apply will be indicated with an **x**. ISO 9003:1994 has all of the same headings, but many areas contain less comprehensive requirements than ISO 9001 and 9002; those will contain an "L." I won't go into detail on these differences because the basic concepts remain the same.

As you read each section you should, as a minimum, have a copy of the relevant ISO 9000 standard (ISO 9001, 9002, or 9003) *and* ISO 9000-2 for reference.

Icons

In an effort to make this guide user-friendly, I've also added icons to "key" specific areas. Here's what the major ones mean.

Quality Manual

Many organizations have documented their quality policy toward ISO 9000 using a Quality Manual. In ISO 9000:1994 the Quality Manual became a requirement. This section will focus on *what* to put in your quality manual.

The National ISO 9000 Users Support Group (see Appendix A for address) recommends that users paraphrase the text from ISO 9000 in their quality manuals. I completely agree with their advice and will focus on this approach. I have prepared a sample quality manual paraphrasing ISO 9001:1994 throughout each section of Chapter 4 as a representative example.

Procedure

ISO 9000 requires a procedure addressing every clause. I've found that companies developing a new quality program tend to "reinvent the wheel" and "paint themselves into corners" with overly restrictive requirements. This section will give you guidance while helping you to avoid some common pitfalls.

Procedures are often compiled into a single manual to facilitate document control. A "Procedure Manual" (a.k.a. "Standard Operating Procedure Manual"—SOP Manual) is a collection of logically grouped procedures used by a functional area. Although ISO 9000 does not specifically require that you develop a procedure manual, this approach is common.

Records

Almost every clause of the standard requires records. This section will list them individually in one place, allowing a quick check to make sure you've addressed them all.

Guidance

This icon will be accompanied with a listing of guidance documents relating to that specific topic or clause of the standard. Although ISO 9004-1 is not intended by its developers to be referenced as a guide in complying with ISO 9001/2/3 (because it goes beyond their minimum requirements), I believe that it contains some very valuable information and guidance worth reviewing. Therefore, I have included references to its appropriate elements. I will also be referencing various industry and military standards that I believe contain useful information and guidance.

The reader must realize that these documents are constantly undergoing revision. I have included the revision level (number, character, date, etc.) of most for specific reference purposes. (If a referenced standard is revised and this book does not indicate the revision level discussed, the book would then appear to be in error.)

If attempting to obtain U.S. Military standards, the reader should also be aware that the U.S. Department of Defense (DoD) has adopted policies to use commercial standards wherever practicable.

DoD Directive 5000.1 (Issued Feb. 23, 1991)

Maximum practicable use shall be made of non-government standards and commercial item descriptions.

DoD Instruction 5000.2 (Issued Feb. 23, 1991)

Non-governmental standards and commercial item descriptions will be used in preference to federal and military specifications and standards whenever practicable.

DoD components will participate in standards development activities of non-government standards bodies, both domestic and international, coordinating on such activity with other federal agencies.

The bottom line here is, if you see a U.S. Military Standard that you would like to have, request it immediately. These standards are being canceled or replaced at a rapid pace.

Questions Your Registrar May Ask

In this area I've placed questions that a registrar may ask during an audit. This section assumes that your document review has already been performed. Your auditor will already have seen how you plan to address the standard and will be attempting to gather objective evidence verifying compliance. You can also derive questions from this section for conducting your own internal audits.

Throughout this guide I will use additional icons relative to the topic discussed to help "key" those areas for future reference. These other icons will be indented and will be used extensively. I won't describe them all, but here are a few of the common ones.

Good Idea

Throughout this guide I will describe how some companies have addressed meeting specific requirements of the standard. Consider these ideas "Best Practices" that you can incorporate into your own quality system. Avoid re-inventing the wheel.

Time Bomb

Many companies leave little time bombs spread throughout their quality system because of oversights. It may take a while, but these problems will eventually be encountered. This section will help you find and defuse those time bombs.

◇ *Phantom Requirements*

There are a few unwritten rules that many auditors consider requirements. These "phantom" requirements are generally questionable and very arguable.

☹ *Bad Idea*

Yes, believe it or not, ISO 9000 allows you to do silly things, too. There are a few instances where these practices make sense, but unfortunately those circumstances aren't very well explained. The standard simply allows you to do them. This section will address them and in some cases even explain where they make sense. Although these practices are acceptable, you're generally better off just to avoid them.

☺ *The Happy Auditor*

Would you like to make life easier for both you and your auditor? Here are some simple practices that will make your auditor happy. Mostly personal opinion.

☠ *Hazardous Material*

Although ISO 9000 does not specifically address hazardous material, this is a serious topic that touches many companies. I recommend including the applicable requirements throughout your quality system under the appropriate ISO 9000 sections. This will help reduce non–value-added redundant systems. It is also an excellent step toward compliance with ISO 14001, "Environmental Management Systems—Specification."

Many quality professionals believe that the next step beyond ISO 9000 compliance is the establishment of a QUENSH Management System. QUENSH stands for QUality/ENvironmental/Safety and Health. Such a system incorporates all of these areas under one system. This is a concept that I support and address, to a limited extent, throughout this guide.

⚔ *Quality Systems Requirements*

In 1994, the Big Three automotive manufacturers (Chrysler, Ford, and General Motors) established a standard entitled *Quality Systems Requirements* (commonly referred to as QS-9000). This standard defines the fundamental quality system expectations of Chrysler, Ford, General Motors, and other subscribing companies for both internal and external suppliers of production and service parts and materials.

Quality Systems Requirements is a harmonization of Chrysler's *Supplier Quality Assurance Manual*, Ford's *Q-101 Quality System Standard*, and General Motors' *NAO Targets for Excellence*. ISO 9001, Section 4, has been adopted as the foundation for this standard.

I will briefly address these additional requirements where appropriate, but most are clearly described in either the *Quality Systems Requirements* itself or the supplemental Reference Manuals [such as the AIAG "Advanced Product Quality Planning and Control Plan" and "Potential Failure Mode and Effects Analysis (FMEA)" manuals].

It should be noted that although *Quality Systems Requirements* is being distributed by the AIAG (Automotive Industry Action Group), it is *not* an AIAG standard. The copyright is held jointly by Chrysler, Ford, and General Motors. Any questions on the content and interpretation of QS-9000 should be addressed to the co-authors, whose names appear on the last page of that document.

I've left a lot of room in the margins. Feel free to make notes on how you might be able to apply these ideas to your own quality system. That's why it's there.

Chapter 1

The Origins and History of ISO 9000

In the Beginning. . . .

As Europe began moving toward the implementation of EC 1992—a single economic marketplace, wherein goods and services would move freely without barriers between countries in the European Community (EC)—it became apparent that standardization and some minimum level of quality assurance was necessary. The "International Organization for Standardization" rose to meet that challenge.

The International Organization for Standardization (ISO) is a Geneva-based worldwide federation. It was founded in 1946 to promote the development of international standards and related activities to facilitate the exchange of goods and services worldwide. ISO is composed of national bodies (currently comprising more than ninety member countries) who normally work together in preparing International standards through Technical Committees (TC). Each member body interested in a subject for which a TC has been established has the right to be represented on that committee. International organizations (governmental and nongovernmental) also participate in the work. The U.S. Representative to ISO is the American National Standards Institute (ANSI).

In 1979, ISO formed Technical Committee ISO/TC 176 on Quality Management and Quality Assurance to develop a single, generic series of quality system standards that could also be used for external quality assurance purposes.

In 1987, based on the work of ISO/TC 176, ISO published the ISO 9000 Standard Series on quality management and assurance. The ISO 9000 series was developed by researching a number of national standards from several ISO member countries including Great Britain's BS 5750 and BS 4891, France's AFNOR Z 50-110, Germany's DIN 55-355, the Netherlands' NEN 2646, Canada's Z-299, and the U.S.A.'s ANSI/ASQC Z-1.15, MIL-Q-9858A, ANSI/ASQC C-1, and ANSI/ASME NQA-1.

Each representative participating in the ISO has taken the ISO 9000 series back to their respective country and, after translation, issued it a designation unique to that country. In the United States, the ISO 9000 series is published by ANSI, in conjunction with the American Society for Quality Control (ASQC). It is referenced as the ANSI/ASQC Q9000 series (this designation was changed with the 1994 revision from the ANSI/ASQC Q90 Series). In the U.K., it is BS EN ISO 9000 (previously BS 5750), and in the European Union it is the EN ISO 9000 series. (The standard had been published previously by the European Community as the EN 29000 Series.)

If you already have a quality system developed to comply with MIL-Q-9858A, 10CFR50 (Appendix B), the Association of American Railroads M-1003 (Section J—Specification for Quality Assurance), or the Canadian CAN3-Z299.1, you will see very little difference between it and ISO 9001. All of these quality standards preceded ISO 9000 in North America. ISO 9000 does *not* contain any new or radical ideas. In fact, ISO 9000 serves as an excellent foundation on which to develop a more comprehensive quality system in compliance with additional standards.

👍 *ISO Acronym Clarification**

"ISO" doesn't stand for anything, although it functions as an acronym when referring to the "International Organization for Standardization."

According to ISO officials, the organization's short name was taken from the Greek word *isos*, meaning "equal." *Isos* is also the root of the prefix "iso," which appears in "isometric" (of equal measure or directions) and "isonomy" (equality of laws or of people before the law). Its selection was based on the conceptual path taken from "equal" to "uniform" to "standard."

In an attempt to make sense of the ISO acronym, many have misconstrued the organization's full name to be the International Standards Organization. One of the most respected newspapers in the United States made this mistake and incorrectly placed periods after each letter of "ISO."

The official explanation may be confusing, but it would have been even more confusing to attempt to create an acronym that would be valid in each of the organization's three official languages—English, French, and Russian.

In French, for example, the organization's name is *Organisation internationale de normalisation*. This would not correspond to the English acronym, IOS, the organization's officials point out.

---

*Reference "ISO: What Does It Stand for Anyway?", *Quality Systems Update*, January 1993.

Is ISO 9000 an International Version of a British Standard?

ISO 9000 was largely based on the BS 5750 series. Therefore, it has gained a reputation for being an international version of that British standard. But where did BS 5750 come from? It has its roots in the U.S. MIL-Q-9858A.

In 1959, the U.S. Department of Defense (DoD) established a Quality Management Program designated MIL-Q-9858. In 1963, it was revised to MIL-Q-9858A—its only revision to date (although it has been amended twice: Amendment 1, dated 7 August 1981, and Amendment 2, dated 8 March 1985).

In 1968, the North Atlantic Treaty Organization (NATO) developed Allied Quality Assurance Publication 1 (AQAP-1) based largely on MIL-Q-9858A. Then, in 1970, the U.K.'s Ministry of Defense (MoD) adopted the provisions of AQAP-1 as its Management Program Defense Standard DEF/STAN 05-8. In 1979, the British Standards Institute (BSI) developed BS 5750 based on DEF/STAN 05.8. Recognizing the popularity of BS 5750/ISO 9000, the MoD later revised DEF/STAN 05-8 to reflect the provisions of ISO 9001–9004 and renumbered them as DEF/STAN 05-21, 22, 23, and 24. So the answer to the original question is both yes and no, depending upon your particular preference.

An Overview of the ISO 9000 Family

ISO 9000 is a generic, baseline family of quality standards written to be broadly applicable to a wide range of varying nonspecific industries and products. With this objective, they establish the basic requirements necessary to document and maintain an effective quality system. These quality systems requirements are intended to be complementary to specific product requirements.

It is this broad objective that is ISO 9000's strength. However, the standard is written so generically that users often have difficulty interpreting and adapting the standard to their specific industry application. The family consists of both "models," which define specific minimum requirements for external suppliers, and "guidelines" for development of internal quality systems.

The cornerstone of the family is "ISO 9000-1: Quality Management and Quality Assurance Standards—Guidelines for Selection and Use." The purpose of this document is to do the following:

- Clarify the principal quality-related concepts and the distinctions and interrelationships among them

- Provide guidance for the selection and use of the ISO 9000 family of International Standards on quality management and quality assurance

The ISO 9000 standards are intended to be used in four situations:

(a) guidance for quality management;

(b) contractual, between first and second parties;

(c) second-party approval or registration; and

(d) third-party certification or registration.

ISO 9000-1 provides general guidance addressing each situation.

The ISO 9000 Models

The "models" are intended to define specific minimum requirements/for external suppliers. If your customer is requiring you to meet the requirements of an ISO standard, they will reference one of these models.

The models are:

ISO 9001:1994   "Quality Systems—Model for Quality Assurance in Design/Development, Production, Installation, and Servicing"

ISO 9002:1994   "Quality Systems—Model for Quality Assurance in Production, Installation, and Servicing"

ISO 9003:1994   "Quality Systems—Model for Quality Assurance in Final Inspection and Test"

ISO 9001 is the most comprehensive model. ISO 9002 is identical to ISO 9001 with the sections addressing Design and Development removed. ISO 9003 is almost identical to ISO 9002 with the sections addressing Production and Installation removed. ISO 9003 is the least comprehensive of the series and is intended primarily for Final Inspection and Test applications.

The ISO 9000 Guidelines

Guidelines are intended to assist the user in expanding the scope of the model selected and consider such factors as the market being served, nature of the product, production, processes, and consumer needs.

The guidelines are:

ISO 9000-1:1994   Quality Management and Quality Assurance Standards—Part 1: Guidelines for selection and use

ISO 9000-2:1993   Quality Management and Quality Assurance Standards—Part 2: Generic guidelines for application of ISO 9001, ISO 9002, and ISO 9003

ISO 9000-3:1991   Quality Management and Quality Assurance Standards—Part 3: Guidelines for the application of ISO 9001 to the development, supply, and maintenance of software

ISO 9000-4:1993   Quality Management and Quality Assurance Standards—Part 4: Guide to dependability program management

ISO 9004-1:1994   Quality Management and Quality System Elements—Part 1: Guidelines

ISO 9004-2:1991   Quality Management and Quality System Elements—Part 2: Guidelines for services

ISO 9004-3:1993   Quality Management and Quality System Elements—Part 3: Guidelines for processed materials

ISO 9004-4:1993   Quality Management and Quality System Elements—Part 4. Guidelines for quality improvement

ISO 9004-5   Quality Management and Quality System Elements—Part 5: Guidelines for the use of quality plans (draft)

ISO 9004-6   Quality Management and Quality System Elements—Part 6: Guidelines to quality assurance for project management (draft)

ISO 9004-7   Quality Management and Quality System Elements—Part 7: Guidelines for configuration management (draft)

Supporting Documents

The ISO 9000 family is still relatively new. However, ISO/TC 176 has recognized the need for supporting documents containing either guidance or additional requirements. The ISO 10000 series has been reserved by ISO/TC 176 for that purpose.

At this time the ISO 10000 series includes:

ISO 10011-1:1990   Guidelines for Auditing Quality Systems—Part 1: Auditing

ISO 10011-2:1991   Guidelines for Auditing Quality Systems—Part 2: Qualification criteria for auditors

ISO 10011-3:1991	Guidelines for Auditing Quality Systems—Part 3: Managing audit programs
ISO 10012-1:1992	Quality Assurance Requirements for Measuring Equipment—Part 1: Metrological confirmation system for measuring equipment
ISO 10012-2	Quality Assurance Requirements for Measuring Equipment—Part 2: Measurement assurance (draft)
ISO 10013	Guidelines for Developing Quality Manuals (draft)
ISO 10014	Guide to the Economic Effects of Quality (draft)
ISO 10015	Continuing Education and Training Guidelines (draft)

Throughout the ISO 9000 family of standards, emphasis is placed on the following points:

- Satisfaction of the customer's need

- The establishment of functional responsibilities

- The importance of assessing (as far as possible) the potential risk and benefits

All of these aspects should be considered in developing and maintaining an effective quality system.

"Vision 2000"

In 1990, an ad hoc task force from ISO/TC 176 was commissioned to prepare a strategic plan for the ISO 9000 series architecture, numbering, and implementation through the year 2000. This task force report has become known as "Vision 2000."

At its October 1990 meeting in Interlaken, Switzerland, TC 176 adopted a two-phase strategy to meet the needs for revision of the ISO 9000 series. The first phase was to meet near-term needs for the first revision. TC 176 would also continue preparing additional standards in quality management, quality assurance, and quality technology. Some will become part numbers to the ISO 9000 series, while others will be in the ISO 10000 series.

Work on the second phase, which began in 1991, includes reaching a goal of universal acceptance while maintaining current compatibility, forward compatibility, and forward flexibility. A chief concern will be market acceptability of the standard.

The ISO 9000:1994 Revision

Directives of the ISO require that all standards be reviewed every five years. Initially introduced in 1987, the ISO 9000 series was revised in 1994. Because of the incredible popularity of the standard, changes were minimal. The majority of the changes were for purposes of clarification, so it is difficult to clearly identify each "new" requirement. It depends largely on how each auditor/company/user interpreted the standard prior to its revision.

Although there are several studies of these changes available, most contain little insight into interpretation or the true intent of these changes. Throughout this guide I will focus on the 1994 revision with practical examples of its application, rather than discussing the changes themselves.

Chapter 2

Implementation

Before deciding to implement ISO 9000, management should define their expectations of what they hope to achieve by developing such a quality system. Simply stated, ISO 9000 compliance is "good business practice." Adopting ISO 9000 should produce the following benefits:

- Improved efficiency of operations
- Optimized company structure and operational integrity
- Improved utilization of time and materials
- Clearly defined responsibilities and authorities
- Improved accountability of individuals, departments, and systems
- Improved communication and quality of information
- Improved records in case of litigation against the company
- Formalized systems with consistent quality, punctual delivery, and a framework for future quality improvement
- Documented systems with useful reference and training tools
- Fewer rejects; therefore, less repeated work and warranty costs
- Rectified errors at an earlier stage; therefore, less scrap
- Improved relationships with customers and suppliers
- Ability to tender for ISO 9000 contracts at home and abroad

The difficulty of implementing ISO 9000 is directly proportional to management commitment. Executive management *must* realize that the quality element plays a key role in the success of the business. The quality system must be "lived" day-to-day. Its success or failure does not rest on the shoulders of the quality manager alone. If a business is not profitable, does management fire the finance manager? Of course not. A successful company is operated through teamwork.

Each company's implementation strategy depends upon many factors:

1. Does the company currently have a quality manager and staff?

2. Does the company currently have a quality system? (And is it based on an existing quality standard?)

3. What is the scope of the business?

4. What is the size of the company (number of employees)?

5. How many locations will be included under the quality program?

Let's examine each question individually, beginning with the flow chart in Figure 2-1.

Scope of Business

What does your business do? If you manufacture and/or design, ISO 9001 is the appropriate standard for you. If you manufacture but subcontract *all* of your design, then ISO 9002 is more appropriate. ISO 9001 is also most appropriate for engineering companies that perform design work only.

If you offer a service, ISO 9002 is most appropriate. Some service companies apply ISO 9001, stating that they "design" their service. In actuality, most still believe that ISO 9002 is more appropriate. The final choice is yours.

I will not discuss ISO 9003 here, because many registrars do not offer registration to that standard.

Now that you've determined which of the ISO 9000 series applies to you, it's time to do some investigation into what other standards exist which you may wish to reference for guidance or incorporate into your quality system. For example:

ISO 9004-2:1991   Quality Management and Quality System Elements—Part 2: Guidelines for services

ISO 10012-1:1992   Quality Assurance Requirements for Measuring Equipment—Part 1: Metrological confirmation system for measuring equipment

Size of Company and Number of Locations

The size of your company will significantly influence both your approach to meeting the requirements of the standard and your implementation strategy. In a small company, many people have multiple job functions. Limited resources may require a little creativity.

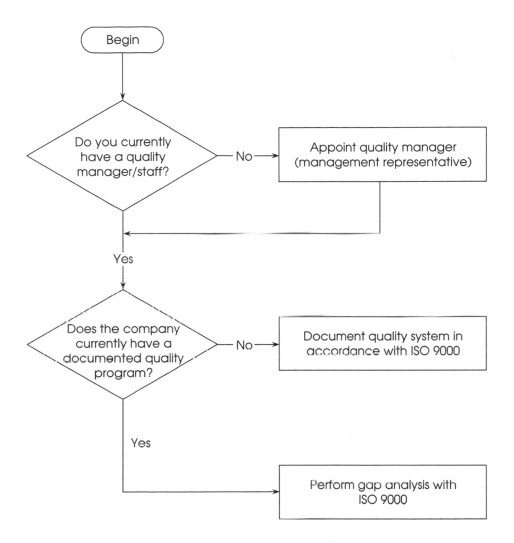

Figure 2-1: Initial Implementation Flowchart

When considering multiple locations, you should consider the amount of flexibility that each location requires. Some businesses need a certain degree of flexibility in order to satisfy various regional customer requirements. (A friend in the U.K. once told me that iced tea to the English is like warm beer to an American.)

When developing your procedures, build in that flexibility. Instead of stating "This, and this way only, is the way in which things are done," describe each approach or method used and allow each location the choice or flexibility (provided that each method meets the requirements of ISO 9000).

For example, several different individuals may be authorized to perform contract reviews:

Contract reviews shall be performed by the Regional Manager, Local Sales Representative, or Local Production Coordinator.

Different methods of indicating that a contract review has taken place may be appropriate because of different resources. The following example is one where not all locations have access to a computer production scheduler.

Contract reviews shall be indicated by one of the following:

- *The reviewer inputting the "job" into the computer production scheduler (this will result in a printed "Work Order" identifying the person who accepted/reviewed the order in the upper right hand corner)*

- *The reviewer completing and signing the "Contract Review" checksheet (form CR431)*

- *The reviewer signing and dating the actual contract itself*

The possibilities are virtually endless. My point is that both a single quality manual and a single procedure manual can easily apply to multiple facilities in various regions.

The following chapters will guide you through the actual implementation, but you will need an implementation plan.

The Implementation Plan

1. Obtain management commitment:

    - Define the company "Quality Policy"

    - Establish realistic, measurable quality objectives in the company business plan

    - Secure the necessary resources to achieve stated quality objectives

2. Gain support from staff:

    - Meet with all supervisors and managers to announce quality objectives and discuss this implementation plan

    - Provide quality awareness and an overview of ISO 9000

    - Require each department and function to become active in its appropriate industry-related organization (reference Appendix A; optional— but it greatly reduces the number of times the wheel is reinvented)

- Require each department and function to attend training and certification courses offered by their appropriate industry-related organization (reference Appendix A; optional—but this, too, will increase long-term efficiency)

- Announce quality objectives and implementation plan to employees

3. Develop a documented quality manual [a quality (policy) manual, without procedures, usually consists of 25–35 pages]:

- Paraphrase ISO 9000 while tailoring to meet your specific business needs and requirements, as necessary

- Involve individual department supervisors and managers in the review process

- Submit quality manual to executive management for review and approval

4. Develop procedures for "Writing a Standard Operating Procedure" and "Writing a Work Instruction":

- Involve individual department supervisors and managers in the review process

- Review and approve

5. Develop procedures and work instructions:

- Meet with all of the supervisors and managers responsible for the following job functions (as applicable):

Project management	Quality/reliability assurance
System engineering	Sales/marketing
Software engineering	Purchasing
Manufacturing engineering	Document control
Component engineering	Technical publications/ training
Test engineering	Field service
Production/manufacturing	Warehouse/ transportation

- Distribute the final quality manual, along with procedures for "Writing a Standard Operating Procedure" and "Writing a Work Instruction."

Then assign each job function or area responsibility for developing their related procedures. (The best ideas will typically come from the staff performing the work functions.) Obtain commitment dates and develop a timeline.

Note: The Quality function normally develops procedures for:

4.1	Management Responsibility
4.2	Quality System
4.13	Control of Nonconforming Product
4.14	Corrective and Preventive Action
4.17	Internal Quality Audits
4.20	Statistical Techniques

However, this, too, can vary from one company to another.

6. Verify progress and status:

- Adjust commitment dates and schedules (timeline) as necessary
- Provide "mentoring" to those areas or departments having difficulty
- Reassess adequacy of resources

7. Review and approve procedures and work instructions:

- Verify compliance with company quality manual (which in turn is in compliance with ISO 9000)

8. Develop and implement training on quality program:

- Meet with Training function to develop a training program
- Distribute appropriate procedures and work instructions to each function
- Schedule training for each department (including internal auditors)
- Hold in-house seminars
- Complete and document training

9. Conduct internal audits:

- Schedule internal audits
- Conduct internal audits of each department and function
- Initiate corrective action with follow-up audits where necessary

10. Management review:

- Assess the effectiveness of quality system (were quality objectives met?)

- Review and revise quality objectives (maintain quality system)

With an ISO 9000 quality system in place, you now have the option of considering certification/registration. It is to be hoped that you will begin to explore the possibilities of continuous improvement through developing a more comprehensive "Total Quality Management" (TQM) system.

Chapter 3

Definitions

At a Glance

9001	9002	9003
✓	✓	✓

For definitions refer to ISO 8402, except for the following words:

product—which may include the following:

- Hardware

- Software

- Processed material

- Service

tender—which is also referred to in the U.S. as a proposal or quote

contract; accepted order—can be established by any means (including verbal, EDI, formal contract, etc.)

📖 *Quality Manual*

While no policy toward the definitions clause of the standard is required, it is an important element to review for purposes of application. Many companies have developed their own internal terminology. You'll find that ISO 9000 consultants and auditors will be speaking the language of the quality profession as it is defined in the various terminology standards (see Guidance).

If you insist on continuing to use your own internal terminology, you'll find yourself constantly giving explanations and acting as an interpreter. More than one noncompliance has been issued because of a breakdown in communication. Rarely is there any added value to using customized internal terminology. I suggest using standardized industry/quality language and terminology wherever applicable.

This has more advantages than is apparent on the surface alone. As you develop partnerships with your suppliers, you should strive to eliminate and prevent errors caused by miscommunication and misunderstanding. Using standardized industry terminology can certainly help in achieving that goal.

QS-9000 states in its introduction that

> *The words "shall," "will," and "must" indicate mandatory requirements. The word "should" indicates a preferred approach. Suppliers choosing other approaches must be able to show that their approach meets the intent of Quality System Requirements.*

I believe that this is an important clarification that should be viewed by all organizations as applying not only to *QS-9000*, but also to ISO 9000.

▤ *Procedure*

Many procedures contain a section entitled "Definitions." While this is acceptable, it can generate a great deal more difficulty than is apparent on the surface. If a definition changes (it happens), the task of reviewing each and every procedure and work instruction may be overwhelming. This approach is most often used by small companies who want each procedure to stand alone.

Larger companies or organizations will typically prepare a single procedure addressing only special definitions and/or reference other sources for definitions.

☞ *Guidance*

For further guidance, refer to the following:

ISO 8402:1994, Quality Management and Quality Assurance—Vocabulary

ISO 3534-1:1991, Statistics—Vocabulary and Symbols
Part 1: Probability and General Statistical Terms

ISO 3534-2:1993, Statistics—Vocabulary and Symbols
Part 2: Statistical Quality Control

ISO 3534-3:1985, Statistics—Vocabulary and Symbols
Part 3: Design of Experiments

ISO 5127-1:1983, Documentation and Information—Vocabulary
Part 1: Basic Concepts

ISO 10209-1:1992, Technical product documentation—Vocabulary
Part 1: Terms Relating to Technical Drawings: General and Types of Drawings

ISO/IEC Guide 2:1991, General Terms and Their Definitions Concerning Standardization and Related Activities

ISO/IEC Guide 30: 1992, Terms and Definitions Used in Connection with Reference Materials

ANSI Z94.0-1989, Industrial Engineering Terminology

ANSI/ASQC A1-1987, Definitions, Symbols, Formulas, and Tables for Control Charts

ANSI/ASQC A2-1987, Terms, Symbols, and Definitions for Acceptance Sampling

ANSI/ASQC A3-1987, Quality Systems Terminology

ANSI/AWS A3.0-89, Standard Welding Terms and Definitions (Adopted by the U.S. DoD)

ANSI/IEEE 100-1992, Standard Dictionary of Electrical and Electronics Terms

ANSI/IEEE 729-1983, Standard Glossary of Software Engineering Terminology

ASTM E 456, Terminology Relating to Quality and Statistics

ASTM D 996, Terminology of Packaging and Distribution Environments

MIL-STD-109B, Quality Assurance Terms and Definitions

MIL-STD-1309D, Definitions of Terms for Testing, Measurement and Diagnostics

NCSL Glossary of Metrology-Related Terms (August 1994)

✍ Note

Another handy booklet is the "Acronym List" prepared by the National Conference of Standards Laboratories (NCSL) TQM Committee on Calibration System Requirements. While primarily intended to assist the committee in developing ANSI/NCSL Z540-1, it lists virtually every quality-related acronym known (both national and international) along with its definition. This list is available for sale from the NCSL (see Appendix A for address and telephone number).

Canadian Standards

CAN/CSA-Q640, Quality—Vocabulary (ISO 8402)

Chapter 4

Standards Requirements

4.1 Management Responsibility

At a Glance

9001	9002	9003
✓	✓	L

Executive Management must do the following:

- Define and document a quality policy

- Ensure that this policy is understood, implemented, and maintained at all levels of the organization

- Define and document the responsibility, authority, and interrelation of personnel who manage, perform, and verify work affecting quality

- Identify resource requirements and provide adequate resources, including the assignment of trained personnel, for management, performance of work, and verification activities, including internal quality audits

- Appoint a member of its own executive management as a "Management Representative"

- Review the quality system at defined intervals sufficient to ensure its continuing suitability and effectiveness

> **QUALITY MANUAL**
>
> 1 MANAGEMENT RESPONSIBILITY
>
> 1.1 Quality Policy
>
> ABC Company is committed to achieving the following objectives for quality:
>
> 1. maintain and continuously improve the quality of our products and services;
>
> 2. improve the quality of our own operations, so as to meet continually all of the customer and other stakeholders' stated or implied needs;
>
> 3. provide confidence to management and employees that the requirements for quality are being fulfilled and maintained, and that quality improvement takes place;
>
> 4. provide confidence to our customers and other stakeholders that the requirements for quality are being, or will be, achieved in the delivered product or service;
>
> 5. ensure that all quality system requirements, including ISO 900X, are being fulfilled.

📖 Quality Manual

ISO 9001/2/3, clause 4.1.1, "Quality policy," begins as follows:

> *The supplier's management with executive responsibility for quality shall define and document its policy for quality, including objectives for quality and its commitment to quality. The quality policy shall be relevant to the supplier's organizational goals and the expectations and needs of its customers.*

Developing a company quality policy should be something individual and unique to each company. I can give you no guidance other than to approach this task with determination and sincerity. Don't set aside ten or fifteen minutes during your Monday morning staff meeting to develop your quality policy.

This could take all day, or longer. Make sure that *all* of the senior management are involved in this process. It is part of senior management's job to provide leadership. To do this they must have a shared vision of organizational goals. A quality policy can be included in your mission statement.

You must also define your "objectives for quality," which may be included in your quality policy, mission statement, or described separately. ISO 9000-1 provides guidance in clause 4, "Principal concepts." If we paraphrase the "key objectives and responsibilities for quality" given, we can easily develop the text shown in clause 1.1, "Quality policy," of the sample quality manual.

✍ Note

Remember to state which quality standard(s) your company intends to comply with (ISO 9001, 9002, 9003 along with any others, as appropriate) in your quality objectives.

How do you know what the expectations and needs of your customers are? If your answer is "gut feeling," then you *don't* have an answer. Just because customers buy your product doesn't necessarily mean it meets their expectations and needs. Many companies complain that their quality is limited by that of their suppliers. How would you feel to learn that your customers considered you a necessary evil rather than a partner in quality?

☺ The Story of the Frog Princess

The whole issue of customer expectations brings to mind the story of "The Frog Princess." Long ago in Europe there once was an old peasant who went out each night to search for frogs. He enjoyed cooking and eating their legs. One night as he reached down to catch a frog he was startled to hear it cry out!

"Please, kind sir, I am no ordinary frog! I am actually a beautiful princess who was turned into a hideous frog by an evil old witch. Just one kiss will return me to my human form, and I will repay you with sexual favors!"

The old man thought for a moment, then began to place the frog into his sack. The frog princess was overcome by a wave of terror, afraid that the old man must be deaf to refuse such an offer. She shouted, "Didn't you hear what I said?" The old man looked down at her and responded, "Yes, but at my age I would rather have a talking frog." What do your customers really need/want?

◇ Quality Policy Authorization

It is an unwritten rule that a company's quality policy must be signed and dated by the most senior management and be a separate controlled document. Some auditors even insist that it be on letterhead and that it be included in the quality manual as a separate document (sometimes called a "Commitment Page"). These "requirements" are most often voiced by auditors from the "old school." They typically have difficulty accepting "paperless" systems where such a signature is not possible (except as a graphic image at best).

While a company's quality policy should be issued by the senior management, there are several ways to indicate authorization. In the case of a paperless system, proper security levels should indicate authorization. As to the quality policy being a separate document on letterhead, no such requirement exists in *any* standard that I am aware of.

European companies typically state their quality policy as a part of their quality manual. In a broader sense, the entire quality manual is generally considered a company's policy toward quality. With this approach, the quality policy is "authorized" when the quality manual is approved because it's a part of that manual.

◇ *Quality Policy vs. Mission Statement*

Some auditors want to see a clearly defined quality policy by that title. Most auditors would consider a quality policy contained in a mission statement to be meeting the intent of ISO 9000, but there are a few auditors who disagree. They view these two concepts as being distinct and separate. Although it certainly is a good idea to have a company mission statement, you may wish to ask a potential registrar what his or her interpretation is toward this point. Of course, you could just play it safe and describe your quality policy under the heading of "Quality Policy."

☝ *Union Involvement*

If you have union employees, regardless of your present labor–management relationship, union officials should be made aware from the very beginning of the company's interest in implementing ISO 9000. They should be an integral part of the effort, made to feel like a part of the process, not an afterthought. Unions certainly understand that competition abroad is a critical topic. They can be powerful allies if given the opportunity.

💣 *Slogans*

According to the results of "The Rath & Strong Personal Initiative Survey" (released in February 1994), "All the slogans, vision statements, pushing, and cajoling in the world can't force an organization's employees to take the personal initiative needed to effect change. In fact, these activities may do just the opposite."

The Lexington, MA–based management consulting company arrived at this conclusion after polling almost 200 senior executives from Fortune 500 manufacturing and service companies regarding which activities foster superior performance results for an organization.

This is old news to those who subscribe to the quality philosophies of W. Edwards Deming. Deming's teaching centered around fourteen points for success. His tenth point is:

* *Eliminate slogans, exhortations, and targets for the work force.*

Slogans never helped anybody do a good job. In fact, I believe that the number of slogans a company has is directly proportional to management's lack of understanding the real problems with which they are confronted.

It seems that whenever poor management doesn't know what else to do, they create a slogan. In many companies, whenever a new slogan is introduced to the work force, it is viewed as management telling them that they aren't working hard enough or smart enough. In other words, transferring the blame for poor results from management to the work force. In many instances these slogans are associated with "flavor of the month" programs.

If you've had a history of such programs, then you will find much greater difficulty in employee acceptance of a new quality policy and program. It will initially be viewed as just another "flavor of the month" program. Don't expect your employees to jump on the bandwagon just because you tell them to. It may take several months for them to truly believe you're serious this time.

Procedure

Your procedure manual should detail your method(s) of quality policy deployment:

* **How** your quality policy will be communicated to "all levels of the organization"
* **What** means will be used to communicate the quality policy
* **Who** will be responsible for ensuring that this communication takes place
* **How** the company will determine the effectiveness of this communication
* **How** the quality policy will be maintained

Many companies have created ingenious methods of communicating their quality policy throughout their organization. Here are a few examples:

* Training sessions
  (group, teleconference, computer, CD-interactive ROM, etc.)
* Staff meetings
* Posting on notice boards and other conspicuous locations throughout the facility (offices, meeting rooms, break rooms, cafeterias, remote locations, etc.)

- Articles in company newsletters
- Videos
- Cards (sometimes printed on the backs of business cards)
- Printed on payroll checks
- Pamphlets/self-study booklets

Many of these methods can also be used to communicate necessary information about ISO 9000 to your staff at the same time. Questions to be answered could include these:

- What is ISO 9000?
- Which ISO 9000 Standard is most appropriate for your business?
- Why is ISO 9000 important to your business?

Employees may not be able to state the company quality policy verbatim, but they should know and understand the key concepts.

Don't forget about indoctrination and orientation of new employees. If you use temporary employees, you should address at which point you will indoctrinate them to your quality policy. Many companies employ temporary workers for a year or more.

♀ *Varian Associates*

Varian Associates, Lexington, MA, printed their company quality policy on business cards and distributed them to all of their employees. The General Manager occasionally walks through the facility asking employees if they know what the quality policy is and if they have their card with them. If they do, they receive immediate recognition (free lunch, free dinner for two, gift certificates, etc.).

This action on the part of senior management strongly communicates two important points:

1. This program is for real (it's not a "flavor of the month" program), and

2. Senior management is willing to put their money where their mouth is.

♀ *Departmental Mission/Quality Statements*

Gilbarco Incorporated, Greensboro, NC, has taken their quality policy to another level. After the company quality policy and mission statements were developed, each individual department developed a focused "Departmental Mission Statement" to support the company's statements. For example, the drafting department incorporated in its mission statement a definition of what quality means to them. This personalizes the company quality policy and gives greater ownership to the individual departments.

QUALITY MANUAL

1.2 Organization

1.2.1 Responsibility and Authority

The responsibility, authority, and interrelation of personnel who manage, perform, and verify work affecting quality shall be defined and documented, particularly for personnel who need the organizational freedom and authority to:

(a) initiate action to prevent the occurrence of any nonconformities relating to product, process, and quality system;

(b) identify and record any problems relating to product, process, and quality system;

(c) initiate, recommend, or provide solutions through designated channels;

(d) verify the implementation of solutions;

(e) control further processing, delivery, or installation of nonconforming product until the deficiency or unsatisfactory condition has been corrected.

Quality Manual

When developing your quality manual, consider paraphrasing the standard throughout this section. Wording should closely resemble text from the standard to avoid distorting the intent. Specific details should be contained in your procedures. Some minor tailoring may be required in subclause (e), ". . . processing, delivery, or installation . . . ," but remember, you only need to state policy in your quality manual.

Procedure

Your procedure manual should begin by defining the senior management positions and describing their authority and responsibilities (this could also be contained in your quality manual). For example:

General Manager
The General Manager for ABC Company has ultimate authority and responsibility for this quality system and is the highest level of management for resolving quality issues within ABC Company. The General Manager will designate and empower a Quality Manager with the authority to establish, assure implementation, and maintain this quality system.

While sales and marketing are a vital part of any organization, at first glance ISO 9000 seems to place little emphasis on their role. Upon further review you will see that sales will generally be involved in "contract review," and both sales and marketing may provide "Design input." Because these groups are not as directly involved as production or engineering, their responsibilities toward the quality system should be more focused. For example:

Sales Manager
The Sales Manager is responsible for ensuring that the ABC Company sales force is cognizant of the ABC Company quality system and properly trained in areas pertinent to performing their function.

Senior management staff (regardless of actual title) could include, but is not limited to, the following:

- General Manager (highest level of management overseeing quality system)
- Quality Manager
- Production Manager
- Engineering Manager
- Service Manager
- Sales Manager
- Marketing Manager
- Purchasing Manager
- Personnel Manager
- Finance Manager

Titles will change from one company to another, but this should be a good indication of whom to include. Another approach would be to include or refer to short-form job descriptions.

Q *The Quality Element*

Generally a quality structure would report directly to the Quality Manager. You may wish to define the Quality Manager as in the following example:

Quality Manager
The Quality Manager shall have organizational freedom and authority to establish, assure implementation, and maintain this quality system. The Quality Manager shall have access to the highest level of management in resolving quality issues and shall be empowered with "stop work" authority.

You should define all additional quality functions, their authority and responsibilities. Some titles to consider:

- Quality Representative (not to be confused with Management Representative)

- Alternate Quality Representative

- Inspector

- Internal Auditor

"Quality Representative" is a very popular title used to describe those in various departments or remote locations acting as an extension of the Quality Manager. "Alternate Quality Representatives" typically assist the local Quality Representative with equal authority and responsibility. Alternate Quality Representatives are usually selected in the same manner as the primary Quality Representative.

In a large organization with several people involved in the quality element, you should define the authority for delegation throughout all levels. For example:

The Quality Manager may delegate authority throughout the QA chain of command, but shall retain overall responsibility. Local Quality Representatives and Alternate Quality Representatives will report directly to the Quality Manager for all quality matters.

If you use temporary employees, consider whether they would ever be allowed to be inspectors or even Quality Representatives.

💣 *Alternate Quality Manager*

Don't forget to appoint an alternate in case of absence of the Quality Manager. This is a common oversight.

👤 *Other Functions*

At this point you should describe all other functions responsible for quality (Inspectors, Internal Auditors, etc.). This can be done in generic terms, with specific responsibilities detailed in individual job descriptions.

⊞ *Organization Charts*

Organization charts are a great way to show the interrelation of personnel who manage, perform, and verify work. While you may certainly place an organization chart in your Quality Manual, it should be an overview reflecting the more stable upper structure (Figure 4.1-1). A more detailed version should be in your procedure manual(s).

Clearly, you don't want to be in a position of updating all of your Quality Manual every time you restructure. Leave that level of detail for the more flexible procedure manual(s). Avoid using or including the names of individuals. Limit organizational charts to position titles alone so as to reduce the number of updates. Also, ensure the consistent use of titles in the organization chart, Quality Manual, Procedure Manual, and Work Instructions.

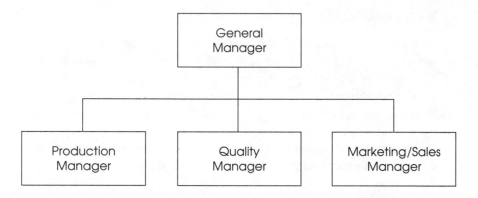

Figure 4.1-1: Organization Chart

♀ *Functional Organization Charts*

In a small company, you may have more functional responsibilities than people. In that case, simply create a "Functional Organization Chart." This chart would show all of the functions and how they interrelate, also allowing you to explain how one person may perform several different job functions.

⬦ *Required Organization Charts*

Organization charts are so prevalent that some auditors actually consider them to be the *only* way in which to communicate the interrelation of personnel. While ISO 9000 obviously does not specifically require organization charts, you would be well advised to use them.

☹ *Overly Simplistic Organization Charts*

While you should try to keep organization charts focused on the interrelation of key personnel, don't oversimplify. An organization chart can be oversimplified to the point that it is no longer of use (Figure 4.1-2).

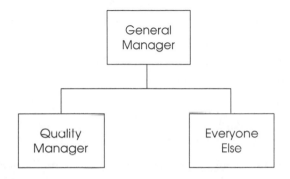

Figure 4.1-2: Oversimplified Organization Chart

QUALITY MANUAL

1.2.2 Resources

ABC Company will identify resource requirements and provide adequate resources, including the assignment of trained personnel, for management, performance of work, and verification activities including internal quality audits.

📖 *Quality Manual*

The details as to how you meet this requirement should be contained throughout your procedure manual(s). The quality manual need only state a policy consistent with ISO 9000.

📑 *Procedure*

Your procedure manual should define the following:

- **Who** (by job title) will identify resource requirements for each area or project

- **How** resource requirements for each area or project will be identified

- **Who** (by job title) is responsible for requesting, acquiring, and verifying that adequate resources are provided

- **How** adequate resources are requested, acquired, and verified

- **Who** is responsible (by job title) for assigning trained personnel for management (usually a Human Resource Department working in conjunction with senior management)

- **Who** is responsible (by job title) for assigning trained personnel for performance of work (usually a Human Resource Department working with middle and/or front line management)

- **Who** is responsible (by job title) for assigning trained personnel for verification activities including internal audits (usually the Quality Department working with various levels of management)

- **How** trained personnel are assigned for management, performance of work, and verification activities including internal quality audits

All of the details you define here are subject to verification by your ISO 9000 auditor (if seeking registration).

"Resources" includes the following:

- Equipment

- Facilities

- Raw materials

- Production capability

"Production Capability" includes the availability of the following:

- Trained personnel

- Adequate manpower/time

- Adequate support functions

> Q U A L I T Y   M A N U A L
>
> **1.2.3** Management Representative
>
> ABC Company's management with executive responsibility will appoint a member of ABC Company's own management who, irrespective of other responsibilities, will have defined authority for
>
> (a) ensuring that a quality system is established, implemented, and maintained in accordance with this quality manual, and
>
> (b) reporting on the performance of the quality system to ABC Company's management for review and as a basis for improvement of the quality system.
>
> Responsibilities of the management representative may also include liaison with external parties on matters relating to ABC Company's quality system.

Quality Manual

I interpret someone appointed by "the supplier's *management* with executive responsibility," that person being "a member of the supplier's own management who, irrespective of other responsibilities, shall have defined authority for" quality, as being a "Quality Manager." The actual title for this person is irrelevant, but I suggest establishing a title with the word "quality" in it. This demonstrates your commitment to achieving your quality policies and objectives. If you're going to have a focused "Customer Service Manager," have that person reporting to your Quality Manager.

It should be noted that a small company may not have the additional resources to have a full-time Quality Manager. (I'll let you define the word small.) In such instances, it is common for someone responsible for production to also be responsible for quality. While some auditors see this as a conflict of interest, in many instances it cannot be avoided.

Regardless of your specific organizational structure, the management representative *must* be a member of the company's executive management.

Who Is Your Management Representative?

While many auditors are content with quality system "authority" defined, others actually demand to see the title "Management Representative" (perhaps the next revision of the standard should include ". . . regardless of title").

Because of this uncertainty, I suggest that in your Quality Manual you clearly state *who* (by title) serves as your management representative.

☹ *ISO Coordinators and/or ISO Representatives*

Some companies have decided to create a position titled "ISO Coordinator" or "ISO Representative" to act as the management representative. The thinking is that the current Quality Manager probably has his or her hands full already with the existing quality program. The "ISO Coordinator" can assist in modifying the program to meet the requirements of ISO 9000, help interface with other departments, interact with the registrar, then step aside after the company achieves registration.

While this approach may work well for some companies, I find that for many it does not. In too many instances, the "ISO Coordinator" has no experience in the field of quality (the position is often political) and is placed in a position of directing an experienced quality manager. This immediately creates resentment. Those positive aspects of this approach, such as interfaces and relationships established between the various departments, generally vanish with the "ISO Coordinator."

Instead of assigning your quality manager a temporary "ISO Coordinator," I suggest allowing your quality manager to redirect some work functions to others. Perhaps you should even assign additional resources. Use consultants strategically to assist in additional training and other immediate short-term tasks. Your quality manager already has a base of knowledge to start with, so your learning curve should be shorter by sticking with this individual. Give him or her the authority necessary to perform the assigned responsibilities. Allow the quality manager to establish long-term relationships with these other departments. One last comment. Assigning your quality manager to an "ISO Coordinator" will certainly rob him or her of the pride associated with achieving the accomplishment of ISO 9000 registration.

🗐 *Procedure*

Your procedure should detail the following:

- **Who** appoints the management representative
- **How** such appointments are made

While the management representative is normally appointed by the general manager (or equivalent), there are other possibilities. The authority and responsibilities of the management representative should also be defined in this section.

✈ *Multiple Locations*

If your company has multiple locations under the same quality system, it may be necessary to have multiple management representatives. I'm not talking about your facility across the street. Closely located facilities may be served by the same management representative. However, facilities in other states, districts, or provinces would probably need their own management representative.

This can be handled in a variety of ways. A single national quality manager could serve as the national management representative, with local quality representatives acting as the local management representative. Whatever approach you choose, be sure to describe it in your related documented procedures.

💣 *Team Management Representatives*

Some companies experimenting with self-directed work forces have attempted to designate a team as being their management representative for quality and reporting directly to executive management. Most registrars do *not* interpret this approach as meeting the intent of ISO 9000. Many experts in self-directed work force training and management agree—this is far beyond the scope of such an approach toward labor management. (Many companies have confused employee empowerment with employee abandonment!) This may have contributed to the clarification that the management representative be a member of a company's own executive management in the 1994 revision of ISO 9000.

◇ *Can the President or CEO be the Management Representative?*

This is a common question among small companies. I believe that one should look at the intent of the standard. For a very small company, I believe that the president can indeed be the management representative. However, as companies grow in size it becomes increasingly difficult for the president or CEO to be effective in that role. If you choose to take the position of the president or CEO being the management representative, be prepared to justify that decision.

> QUALITY MANUAL
>
> **1.3** Management Review
>
> ABC Company's management with executive responsibility shall review the quality system at defined intervals sufficient to ensure its continuing suitability and effectiveness in satisfying the requirements of this quality manual and ABC Company's stated quality policy and objectives. Records of such reviews shall be maintained.

Quality Manual

You should define the details (such as minimum management review intervals) in your procedure manual. If you choose to state a specific management review interval in your quality manual, be realistic and state it as a minimum. Typically, once per calendar year is sufficient. Then set a more frequent management review cycle in your procedure manual as a "target."

Procedure

The management review is typically documented in the form of "meeting minutes." The review should be given (or coordinated) by the management representative (quality manager, quality representative, quality director, etc.) to senior management (CEO, president, director, division manager, etc.) of the group, division and/or location(s) that the quality system includes. Some management reviews are presented to a "review panel." If this is the case, it is your senior management, not the quality manager, who should select this panel. A "review panel" should include representatives from support functions (e.g., technical services, marketing, research, development, finance) because changes in procedures or resources may be required for corrective action.

While the standard does not state a specific frequency for these reviews, it does require you to define intervals. Most registrars expect to see a minimum of one management review per calendar year. However, more frequent reviews are preferred. Quarterly reviews are typical.

As a minimum, the management review should address *corrective actions* (ref. ISO 9001/2/3, clause 4.14.3d) and *internal audits* (ref. ISO 9001/2/3, clause 4.17, Note 20). The review may also include, but is not limited to, the following additional topics:

- A review of minutes from the last meeting (outstanding action items)
- Follow-up internal audit activities
- Suitability of internal audit schedule

- ISO 9000 registrar audits (surveillance visits)/responses
- Customer audit(s)/responses
- Customer satisfaction survey results
- Customer complaints/issues/resolutions
- Warranties (type, root cause, trend analysis, etc.)
- Adequacy of existing quality policy and objectives
- Adequacy of existing documented quality system
- Vendor rating/performance evaluations/timeliness (JIT on-time delivery)
- Cost of waste/rework/scrap/warranties
- Cost of quality (sum of costs of prevention, appraisal, and failure)
- Measurement assurance and calibration
- Training needs/issues
- Organizational structure/staffing
- Statistical data/needs/trend analysis/process capability (C_p) analysis

A great deal of data communicated through the management review can be restructured into bar graphs, pie charts, Pareto analysis, etc. The overall *effectiveness* of the quality system is often determined by observing trends.

I suggest that you develop a standard format for such management reports so they may be continuously improved as you add data. You may also consider combining reports from other areas, such as "Health and Safety," into the management review.

You may, of course, call such reviews anything you like. I suggest, however, that you stick with the title "management review" because that is what an auditor would ask to see. It helps if your employees recognize it by that name.

The last sentence of the clause requires that you maintain records (meeting minutes) of your management reviews. Meeting minutes should contain

- The date of the meeting
- A list of attendees
- A brief description of each topic covered
- Action items, as applicable, assigning responsibility and due dates

You may also include attachments of related reports and relevant data. Some more progressive management reviews are expanded to include a forward-looking plan for the next quarter or year, along with a summary of the results from the past period.

Future business developments that may be considered include, but are not limited to, the following:

- Changes in customers or customer requirements
- Introduction of new technology
- Changes in resources
- Growth
- Contraction of business
- Economic changes
- Changes in business focus

This area is certainly open to creativity.

Multiple/Remote Locations

Companies with multiple locations served by a central headquarters should have local or regional management reviews performed separately and copied to their headquarters for inclusion into a "global" management review reflecting the status of the total system, including the branch locations. These local reviews can cover many of the same topics mentioned earlier, but may also include explanations relating to the results of data collected on a central computer system. E-mail may also be used as a means for remote locations to transmit periodic management reviews to headquarters.

In small companies, it is common for the quality representative to be in daily contact with senior management. In these instances, senior management is constantly aware of the status of the quality system through informal reviews. This may also be true in small satellite operations connected to a central headquarters. This is the situation at GE Test Equipment Management Services. They have developed a "Local Management Review" form listing issues commonly discussed with check blocks to quickly and easily document such activities. (See Figure 4.1-3.)

Quality Systems Requirements

QS-9000 has added the following clauses:

4.1.4, Business Plan (not subject to third-party audit)

4.1.5, Analysis and Use of Company-Level Data

4.1.6, Customer Satisfaction

While clause 4.1.4, "Business Plan," is not subject to third-party audit, it does require companies to "utilize a formal, documented, comprehensive business

---

GE Capital
Test Equipment Management Services

Local Management Review

Areas Reviewed: (This form is for guidance ONLY, and is NOT required for the review process)

☐ Customer Complaint Log   ☐ Nonconformance Log   ☐ Customer Notifications

☐ Recurring Defective Parts   ☐ Subcontractor Issues   ☐ Internal Audit/ Follow-up

☐ Qualification Form Update   ☐ Training Issues   ☐ Customer Audit(s)/ Response

☐ Other _____

_____

_____

Attendees: (In addition to District Manager)

Name:_____ Title:_____

Name:_____ Title:_____

Name:_____ Title:_____

Meeting Minutes: (Specific details of Management Review)

_____

_____

_____

_____

_____

_____

Action Items: (As appropriate—Include commitment dates and attach any necessary supporting documents)

_____

_____

_____

_____

District Manager/Supervisor Signature:

Name: _____ Date:____/____/____

MgtRev 10-92

Figure 4.1-3: "Local Management Review" Form
Used by GE Test Equipment Management Services

plan." I believe that any company developing a "Management Review" procedure should consider the following question:

Does your quality system effectively meet measurable objectives defined in the business plan?

These measurable objectives can, and should, extend beyond the minimum requirements of ISO 9000.

Although not specifically stated in QS-9000, it appears that "Analysis and Use of Company-Level Data" and "Customer Satisfaction" are intended to be elements of the management review.

💣 *Are You Managing by Fear?*

No quality initiative can succeed if fear is present. Those familiar with the quality philosophies (fourteen points) of W. Edwards Deming will recognize his eighth point:

• *Drive out fear so that everyone can work effectively.*

While fear may not be used, or condoned, by executive management as a motivator, it may be used by front-line supervisors and employee co-workers (through peer pressure). How can executive management identify that this is happening so that it can be addressed? Fear is often a hidden force, but there are several ways in which executive management can recognize its existence. For example:

• Low scores on employee attitude surveys or few employee suggestions

• A chronic lack of questions at meetings

• Multiple approval signatures required on purchase orders

• Multiple approval signatures required for document approval and control

• Extensive dress rehearsals for internal management presentations (management reviews)

• Memos that justify actions

• Padded estimates

• Lack of teamwork

At least one indicator can be directly identified in the management review itself:

• A high number of customer returned goods relative to a low number of documented customer complaints

When fear is present, no one wants to be the bearer of bad news. If, upon further investigation, inspection and test results are found clustered near the lower acceptance limit with few falling outside tolerance, this may also indicate the presence of fear. The inspector probably didn't want to be the bearer of bad news, so marginal items were passed.

Another indicator:

- A low level of scrap relative to an excessive amount of repair and/or rework

Many companies closely monitor scrap with little attention given to the time and effort expended on repair and/or rework. When fear is present, an excessive amount of repair and/or rework may be taking place simply to keep "Scrap Reports" below required or imagined limits or targets.

Once the presence of fear is recognized, only management can take action to drive it out of the workplace. As Joseph M. Juran observed, 80% of all nonconformities are controllable by management. It's up to management to eliminate barriers and create a positive, productive working environment.

 ## Records

The requirements of Section 4.1 generally relate to documented policies and procedures. The only record specifically addressed is for the "Management Review." This record should identify the following:

- **When** the management review was conducted
- **Who** was involved (present)
- **What** factors were considered (results of internal audits, corrective actions, etc.)
- **What** conclusions were reached
- **What** actions were taken (if any were deemed necessary)

☞ Guidance

For further guidance, refer to:

ISO 9000-2:1993, Quality Management and Quality Assurance Standards—Part 2: Generic guidelines for application of ISO 9001, ISO 9002, and ISO 9003
Section 4.1—"Management responsibility"

ISO 9004-1:1994, Quality Management and Quality System Elements—Part 1: Guidelines
Section 4.1—"Management responsibility"

ISO 9004-2:1991, Quality Management and Quality System Elements—Part 2: Guide to quality management and quality systems elements for services
Section 5.2—"Management responsibility"

ᘯ *Questions Your Registrar May Ask*

Many of the questions a registrar may have regarding this area would normally be addressed during the documentation review. However, here are some questions that may be asked during the assessment to verify that your employees understand the "documented" quality system.

4.1.1 Quality Policy

☑ What is your quality policy? What are your quality objectives?

☑ Where is your quality policy, including objectives for quality and commitment to quality, documented?

☑ How is the quality policy relevant to the company's organizational goals and the expectations and needs of its customers?

☑ Who is responsible for ensuring that your company quality policy and objectives are communicated to all levels of the organization?

☑ How are your quality policy and objectives communicated to all levels of the organization?

☑ How do you ensure that the quality policy is understood at all levels of the organization? Can you provide evidence that demonstrates this?

4.1.2.1 Responsibility and Authority

☑ Is the responsibility, authority, and interrelation of personnel who manage, perform, and verify work affecting quality defined? Where is this documented?

☑ Who in your company has the organizational freedom and authority to initiate action to prevent the occurrence of any nonconformities relating to product, process, and quality system? Where is this defined and documented?

☑ Who in your company is authorized or responsible for identifying and recording any problems relating to product, process, and quality system? Where is this defined and documented?

☑ What are the designated channels through which those with organizational freedom and authority may initiate, recommend, or provide solutions to any quality problems? Where is this defined and documented?

☑ Who in your company is authorized or responsible for verifying the implementation of solutions? Where is this defined and documented?

☑ Who in your company is empowered with the organizational freedom to control further processing, delivery, or installation of nonconforming product ("stop work" authority) until the deficiency or unsatisfactory condition has been corrected? Where is this defined and documented?

4.1.2.2 Resources

☑ Where are resource requirements identified? How is this documented?

☑ How are resource requirements determined to be adequate? Who makes this determination?

☑ Who is responsible and authorized for assigning trained personnel for:

- management?
- performance of work?
- verification activities (inspection and testing)?
- performing internal quality audits?

☑ How is the assignment of personnel accomplished? Where is this defined and documented?

4.1.2.3 Management Representative

☑ Who is your management representative? Where is this documented?

☑ Is the management representative a member of executive management?

☑ Has an alternate been designated in case of absence of the management representative?

4.1.3 Management Review

☑ Who reviews the quality system to ensure its continued suitability and effectiveness in satisfying the requirements of ISO 9000 and the company's stated quality policy and objectives? How is a determination as to the effectiveness of the quality system made?

☑   Is that individual a member of management with executive responsibility?

☑   How often are management reviews required to occur? Where is this defined and documented?

☑   How are management reviews recorded (documented)?

☑   When was your last management review? May I see it?

4.2 Quality System

At a Glance

9001	9002	9003
✓	✓	L

You must do the following:

- Establish, document and maintain a quality system

- Prepare a quality manual covering the requirements of ISO 9001/2/3

- Prepare documented procedures consistent with the requirements of ISO 9001/2/3 and your stated quality policy

- Effectively implement the quality system and its documented procedures

- Define and document how the requirements for quality will be met

- Ensure quality planning is consistent with all other requirements of your quality system and is documented in a format to suit your method of operation

> QUALITY MANUAL
>
> **2.0** QUALITY SYSTEM
>
> **2.1** General
>
> ABC Company has established, documented, and maintains a quality system as a means of ensuring that product conforms to specified requirements. ABC Company has prepared a quality manual covering the requirements of ISO 9001:1994.

Quality Manual

The earlier ISO 9001/2:1987 only required that you have a documented quality system covering the quality system requirements of the standard. This ambiguity resulted in many companies creating overly complex quality systems that were difficult to assess for compliance with the standard. This was due, in part, to the U.S. approach of writing a quality manual containing both policy and limited procedures, supplemented by a more detailed procedure manual with work instructions. Many U.S. quality manuals receive nonconformances because of conflicts between these two manuals. This confusion has been further compounded by inexperienced quality managers writing quality manuals in their own words rather than paraphrasing text directly from the standard. A great deal is usually lost in the translation.

Paraphrasing the Standard

The National ISO 9000 Support Group recommends that companies write their quality manual paraphrasing as much of the original wording contained in ISO 9000 as possible. In fact, this can be done with minimal tailoring to almost every clause of the standard (as demonstrated in the sample quality manual).

Some consultants and quality experts are giving advice contradictory to this. However, one can easily argue that the wording in the standard has been very carefully thought out. If more than eighty countries can agree on this wording, it must be pretty good. Why change it? Of course you should adapt and tailor it to your specific application, but don't reinvent the wheel.

If your quality system complies with additional standards, I suggest the same approach. Simply add their requirements to the appropriate clauses. Lay out your quality and procedure manuals to correlate with the applicable clauses of the quality standard you consider most important. Given the current trends in both industry and government, however, you may be better served to follow the ISO 9000 structure. This is certainly true for commercial manufacturers.

Most companies seeking ISO 9000 registration consider that to be the most important standard. Your registrar *will* appreciate it if your manual's contents follow the numbering sequence of the ISO 9000 standards (as in Figure 4.2-1). In fact, many registrars send out a cross-reference matrix for you to complete and submit along with your manuals for their review prior to the assessment.

Far too often, companies overcomplicate their quality manual. When an auditor asks where you address a particular topic, your employees should be able to readily locate that area of the manual. If too much time is spent hunting for the

---

ABC Company

Table of Contents

Section	Description	Page
	Statement of Policy/Mission Statement/Approval	i
	Introduction/Company History	ii
	Table of Contents	iii
1.0	Management Responsibility/Organization	1
2.0	Quality System	4
3.0	Contract Review	6
4.0	Design Control	7
5.0	Document and Data Control	11
6.0	Purchasing	12
7.0	Control of Customer-Supplied Product	14
8.0	Product Identification and Traceability	15
9.0	Process Control	16
10.0	Inspection and Testing	18
11.0	Control of Inspection, Measuring, and Test Equipment	19
12.0	Inspection and Test Status	21
13.0	Control of Nonconforming Product	22
14.0	Corrective and Preventive Action	23
15.0	Handling, Storage, Packaging, Preservation, and Delivery	25
16.0	Control of Quality Records	26
17.0	Internal Quality Audits	28
18.0	Training	29
19.0	Servicing	30
20.0	Statistical Techniques	31

Rev. A
3-Oct-94   Page iii

Figure 4.2-1: An Example of an "Auditor-Friendly" Table of Contents from a Corporate-Level Quality Manual

appropriate areas (see example in Figure 4.2-2), your employees become frustrated, and your auditor concludes that they have not been fully trained or indoctrinated to the quality system.

If you follow the appropriate clauses from ISO 9000, and if an auditor asks an employee where you address "purchasing," for example, and the employee does not immediately know, he or she can ask which section of the standard that is. Learning that it is Section 4.6, they should know to turn to Section 6 in their manual. This same approach is valid for procedure manuals.

Even when a section doesn't apply, such as "Design Control" in ISO 9002/3, the section can still be listed for continuity, stating:

> *The ABC Company quality system does not currently include design control.*

Some companies with inexperienced quality managers have found their quality manuals restricting them, rather than liberating them to explore continuous improvement. This can easily be avoided by limiting the quality manual to reflect the broad quality system while reserving specific details for the procedure manual(s) and work instructions.

✍ Note

If you choose to paraphrase the standard, I should point out that some ISO 9000 auditors prefer to see the word "shall" replaced with "will," "are," "has," or "is." Others, such as myself, have no preference.

💻 *Paperless (On-line) Quality Manuals*

Some companies have chosen to create their quality manual as a computer "online" document. There are both advantages and disadvantages to this approach. The primary disadvantages are

- *All* employees must have at least "read-only" access to the system

- It is difficult to provide your customers a controlled copy

The second problem can be overcome by allowing those customers access to your system via modem with a "read-only" security-level access. If this is not a concern, then enjoy the advantages of immediate updates and document control via security access. The advantages almost always outweigh the disadvantages.

⊞ *Grayson Electronics' Paperless Quality System*

Grayson Electronics, Forest, VA, has their quality manual in a "Word for Windows" document on their computer network. Everyone who has access to a computer has access to the quality manual as well as related procedures. Their

ABC Company

Table of Contents

Figure 4.2-2: An Example of an "Auditor-Unfriendly" Table of Contents from a Corporate-Level Quality Manual

network has security levels *and* "Word for Windows" allows you to password-protect (encrypt) a document, so the manuals are available with "read-only"/ "print-only" access. Grayson's document control policies state that only those documents residing in the computer are controlled. All others are considered for information purposes only and are uncontrolled.

☹ *Multiple Quality Manuals*

ISO 10013, "Guidelines for developing quality manuals" (currently in draft form), defines the following terms:

(a) Quality manual—"A document stating the quality policy and describing the quality system of an organization" (ISO 8402).

(b) Quality management manual—"A document stating the quality policy and describing the quality system of an organization which is for internal use only."
Note—The quality management manual may contain proprietary information.

(c) Quality assurance manual—"A document stating the quality policy and describing the quality system of an organization which may be used for external purposes."
Note—A quality assurance manual would normally contain no proprietary information and may be used for customers and third-party assessors.

It is not intended that you develop multiple quality manuals. These terms are listed simply to describe the different approaches that could be used in developing a quality manual.

While a "quality assurance manual," described in (c) above, is the most popular approach, the "quality management manual" described in (b) is an ideal choice for small companies who do not intend to distribute their quality manual outside of the company. Some consultants are recommending the use of both a "quality management manual" and a "quality assurance manual." I know of no registrar who requires or expects to see both manuals. One will suffice!

Small companies will often include their procedures in their quality manual rather than create a separate procedure manual. This guide focuses on the approach of having both a "quality manual" (policy or system description) and a "procedure manual" simply because that is the most popular approach for medium to large companies.

Combining the two manuals into one is perfectly acceptable. In fact, ISO 10013 states in clause 4.2, "Quality manuals":

A quality manual should consist of, or refer to, the documented quality system procedures intended for the overall planning and administration of activities which impact quality within an organization.

When a company takes this approach, the quality manual contains quality system–oriented policy statements in one paragraph, followed immediately by procedures in the next. This approach greatly minimizes the number of documents that must be controlled. However, as a company grows, so does the complexity of its operations. The larger companies don't follow this approach because the size of this single document eventually becomes unmanageable. Another reason that companies generally prefer the two-manual approach is that the level of detail contained in the procedure manual may be such that the information is considered proprietary and confidential.

References

The last sentence of ISO 9001/2/3, clause 4.2.1, states:

The quality manual shall include or make reference to the quality-system procedures and outline the structure of the documentation used in the quality system.

As discussed earlier, the quality manual can include procedures. However, this is not typical of medium to large companies. A literal interpretation of this sentence could mean adding specific references at the end of each section. For example:

For details relating to purchasing refer to:
ABC Company Standard Operating Procedure 6, "Purchasing"

This approach takes a conservative interpretation of the standard and is generally preferred by ISO 9000 auditors. Such a literal interpretation may work great for many companies, but could be restrictive and difficult for others. This requirement may also be met through the use of a single matrix.

The last sentence in this clause of the standard also requires you to "outline the structure of the documentation used" in the quality system. This can be stated in your quality manual using the following example:

The ABC Company Quality System is a means by which the ABC Company Quality Policy is implemented. The quality system is documented in the following structure:

Level 1
ABC Company Quality Manual (Policies / Quality System Description)

Level 2
ABC Company Standard Operating Procedure Manual(s)
(Quality, Financial, Personnel, Engineering, Hazardous Materials, Safety, etc.)

Level 3
ABC Company Work Instructions
(Machine / Equipment / Operator Instructions, Drawings, Schematics, etc.)

Level 4
Records
(Evidence of Compliance with this Quality System—i.e., Completed Forms, Technical Data, etc.)

The number and nature of subdocuments may vary for each company, but the concept remains the same. I would also suggest continuing this section with the following paragraph.

The ABC Company Quality System may be supplemented by various industry, military, and international standards, methods, and procedures from sources which include, but are not limited to, the following:

•*ANSI (American National Standards Institute)*

•*ASQC (American Society for Quality Control)*

•*ASME (American Society of Mechanical Engineers)*

•*IEEE (Institute of Electrical and Electronics Engineers)*

•*AWS (American Welding Society)*

•*ASTM (American Society for Testing and Materials)*

•*GIDEP (Government Industry Data Exchange Program)*

•*ISO (International Organization for Standardization)*

•*NCSL (National Conference of Standards Laboratories)*

Procedure

Since you have already addressed the structure of your quality system in your quality manual, I suggest that you use this section in your procedure manual to describe how each set of documents is to be written (the layout and physical structure). You may even have examples in this section.

Topics may include the following:

- The physical layout and appearance of headers
- The use of footers
- Required section headings
- Numbering schemes for documents
- Use of the company logo on manuals, procedures, and work instructions
- Specifications for fonts to be used (style, point size, etc.)
- Standard conventions for flow charts (if used)

If you are having individual departments create and write their own procedures, this should be one of the first procedures that you write and put into place so that this effort is standardized.

✍ *Note*

Standardized conventions for flow charts have been established by several different countries and/or organizations. However, most are now adopting ISO 5807:1985, "Information processing—Documentation symbols and conventions for data, program and system flowcharts, program network charts, and system resources charts."

♡ *The KISS Principle*

ISO 10013, clause 4.1, "Documented quality system procedures," states:

> *Documented quality system procedures should form the basic documentation used for the overall planning and administration.*

One of the most important aspects that I can emphasize in writing text is the KISS principle: *Keep It Short and Simple*. Use straightforward words and terms. Do not use documentation to demonstrate a vast and sophisticated command of your native language. Avoid using "committee language." Too often companies don't take advantage of using pictures, flow charts, pictograms, and cartoons to clarify ideas and concepts. Remember that these are documents written to enable co-workers to perform their tasks more efficiently and consistently.

Many courses describing how to develop and write procedures instruct you to include sections for *definitions* and *responsibilities*. This is a good idea *if* you plan for each procedure to stand on its own independently of others. Such an approach is common for large companies, where individual departments have no significant need for ready access to the procedures used by other departments.

If, however, all of your procedures are issued in a single manual, these sections may prove redundant with no added value (particularly in small companies). You may, instead, simply have one procedure addressing nothing but *definitions* (Glossary) and another addressing *responsibilities*.

Another approach is to place all definitions and responsibilities in your quality manual and include the following statement in each procedure.

All definitions and responsibilities not explained here are detailed in the ABC Company Quality Manual.

As you can see, the array of choices is extensive. Each company or organization should take the approach that works best for it.

QUALITY MANUAL

2.2 Quality System Procedures

ABC Company has prepared documented procedures consistent with the requirements of ISO 9001:1994 and the company's stated quality policy. The range and detail of the procedures that form part of this quality system depend on the complexity of the work, the methods used, and the skills and training needed by personnel involved in carrying out the activity. Documented procedures may make reference to work instructions that define how an activity is performed.

Quality Manual

I would like to focus on the last paragraph of this clause in ISO 9001/2/3. This statement is much more significant than it first appears. It allows you to address issues such as these:

- Illiterate employees and/or employees who speak a different "first" language
- Use of flow charts as procedures or work instructions
- Use of "pictograms" or "cartoons" as procedures or work instructions
- Use of videos as procedures or work instructions
- Work procedures on computer or Interactive CD-ROM (multimedia)
- Apprenticeship for work processes performed by "craftsmen" or "artists"

The type of procedures or work instructions you develop should be appropriate to the industry, the complexity of the work processes, and the technology used. (You will notice in the sample quality manual that I have incorporated note 7 from ISO 9001/2/3, clause 4.2.2.)

Many businesses have difficulty in documenting processes that involve an art or craft. Similarly, many ISO 9000 auditors have difficulty verifying compliance with the standard as processes rely more heavily on the judgment (skill) of these artists and craftsmen.

Workers who, for example, are painting images on furniture often utilize documented procedures that are general in scope with inspection criteria relying heavily on subjective judgment. Methods to ensure reduction of variability (the key concern here) should be described.

Procedure

Some consultants are proclaiming that ISO 9000 auditors are expecting to see a procedure for each specific job task. This is *not* necessarily the case. One procedure can address multiple job tasks.

For example, the following procedures can be combined into a single procedure:

- Reworking defective material

- Repairing defective material

- Regrading defective material

In fact, you really only need twenty procedures: one addressing each section of the quality system requirements in the appropriate ISO 9000 standard. (Of course you can expand and build on top of this.) Procedures are generally supported by specific work instructions that describe detailed job tasks.

Paperless (On-line) Procedures

Some elements of your operation may be better suited to have access to computer "on-line" procedures. Areas best suited for this are those where people perform their primary job function at a computer terminal. For example: Purchasing and Contract Review (Order Entry). Some companies have chosen to have all of their procedures "on-line." In fact, if purchasing is done through a computer program, the actual procedure for that process (purchasing) could be contained in the "Help" screens.

The Holy Hand Grenade of Antioch

A common question is "How detailed should the documented procedures or work instructions be?" The answer will vary for each company, depending upon the complexity of the processes and level of detail contained in their training program. However, there should be a balance. Generally speaking, the more detailed the training program, the less detail required in documented procedures or work instructions, and vice versa, with consideration given to the process itself.

A good example of too much detail in relation to a process can be found in the movie *Monty Python and the Holy Grail.* In scene 21, King Arthur's search for the Holy Grail has led him and his men to the cave of Kyre Banorg. There they are confronted by a most foul, cruel, and bad-tempered fluffy white bunny rabbit who guards the entrance to the cave.

After a bloody frontal assault ends with the loss of three men, Arthur is forced to consider other options.

LANCELOT: We have the Holy Hand Grenade.

ARTHUR: Yes, of course! The Holy Hand Grenade of Antioch! 'Tis one of the sacred relics Brother Maynard carries with him! Brother Maynard! Bring up the Holy Hand Grenade!
How does it, uh . . . how does it work?

KNIGHT #1: I know not, my liege.

KNIGHT #2: Consult the Book of Armaments!

MAYNARD: Armaments, Chapter Two, Verses Nine to Twenty-one.

BROTHER: "And Saint Attila raised the hand grenade up on high, saying, 'Oh, Lord, bless this thy hand grenade that with it thou mayest blow thy enemies to tiny bits, in thy mercy.' And the Lord did grin, and people did feast upon the lambs, and sloths, and carp, and anchovies, and orangutans, and breakfast cereals, and fruit bats, and large—"

MAYNARD: Skip a bit, Brother.

BROTHER: "And the Lord spake, saying, 'First shalt thou take out the Holy Pin. Then, shalt thou count to three, no more, no less. Three shalt be the number thou shalt count, and the number of thy counting shalt be three. Four shalt thou not count, nor either count thou two, excepting that thou then proceed to three. Five is right out. Once the number three, being the third number, be reached, then lobbest thou thy Holy Hand Grenade of Antioch towards thy foe, who being naughty in my sight, shall snuff it.'"

MAYNARD: Amen.

ALL: Amen.

ARTHUR: Right! One . . . two . . . five!

KNIGHT #1:   Three, sir!

ARTHUR: Three!

[boom]

The *key* word here is balance. The more training you give your employees, the less detailed your work procedures or work instructions need to be. Many work processes are so uncomplicated that a simple flow chart is enough to describe the procedure or work instructions.

Industry Procedures/Specifications/Standards

There are an incredible number of procedures, specifications, and standards already written and available from government, military, and various industry organizations. In many instances you can find a document relating to an area that you're concerned with and simply reference it for direction and guidance in your procedure.

For example, in your procedure describing "packaging":

For additional information refer to:

- *ASTM D 3950, "Strapping, Plastic (and Seals)"*
- *ASTM D 3951, "Standard Practice for Commercial Packaging"*
- *ASTM D 3953, "Strapping, Flat Steel, and Seals"*
- *ASTM D 4675, "Selection and Use of Flat Strapping Materials"*
- *MIL-STD-129M, "Marking for Shipment and Storage"*
- *MIL-STD-147D, "Palletized Unit Loads"*

These documents contain a wealth of good information, but may require steps beyond your capability or need. You may want to simply have these documents available to supplement your existing procedures. To take advantage of their information while not being held to their requirements, you can follow such references with:

> *These standards and procedures are listed here for guidance and reference only. Full compliance is* not *required.*

Some auditors may cringe at my making such a suggestion (which renders the entire statement unauditable). But allow me to explain with the following example. If you have an extensive line of products, it may not be practical to have a procedure or work instruction for packaging each and every item.

Using these procedures and standards for guidance and reference (*along* with training on those items that are common) will allow your shipping staff to adapt to new situations as they occur while ensuring that the quality of the product is maintained, thus meeting the intent of the standard.

If you reference or use a document, you must have it available. At the very least you will benefit from referencing these documents for information while developing your own procedures. A listing of many sources is contained in Appendix C.

🖥 *Paperless (On-Line) Procedures*

When designing "on-line" procedures, you should avoid trying to force the typical $8\frac{1}{2} \times 11$ paper version onto the wider, shorter terminal screen (portrait vs. landscape). Several "off-the-shelf" packages for developing "on-line" documentation are available. Don't reinvent the wheel. If you already use a customized software package, consider having your programmers embed the appropriate procedures into its "Help" function.

📄 *Quality Bulletins*

There will be instances when you will need to do one of the following:

- Communicate emergency changes to existing quality procedures

- Expedite interim applications of new, pending quality procedures

- Communicate one-time or limited-use instructions or information relative to the quality system

This information can be communicated through a "Quality Bulletin" (a.k.a. "Quality Alert"). (See Figure 4.2-3.) I suggest that you allow yourself this option by detailing the preparation and distribution of quality bulletins in your "Quality System" procedure.

ABC Company
Quality Bulletin

SUBJECT:

Number: _____
Date: _____
Page: _____ of _____

DISTRIBUTION:

Supersedes No. _____
Dated: _____

_____
Quality Manager

☐ Retain this bulletin until further notice.
☐ This bulletin will be invalid after (date)_____ .
☐ This bulletin will be incorporated into Quality
Procedure No. _____ by (date) _____ .

C:\QUALITY\FORMS\QB-994.DOC

Figure 4.2-3: Sample of Quality Bulletin Form

QUALITY MANUAL

2.3 Quality Planning

ABC Company has defined and documented how the requirements for quality will be met. Quality planning will be consistent with all other requirements of the quality system and will be documented in a format to suit the company's method of operation. ABC Company will give consideration to the following activities, as appropriate, in meeting the specified requirements for products, projects, or contracts:

(a) the preparation of quality plans;

(b) the identification and acquisition of any controls, processes, equipment (including inspection and test equipment), fixtures, resources, and skills that may be needed to achieve the required quality;

(c) ensuring the compatibility of the design, the production process, installation, servicing, inspection, and test procedures, and the applicable documentation;

(d) the updating, as necessary, of quality control, inspection, and testing techniques, including the development of new instrumentation;

(e) the identification of any measurement requirement involving capability that exceeds the known state of the art, in sufficient time for the needed capability to be developed;

(f) the identification of suitable verification at appropriate stages in the realization of product;

(g) the clarification of standards of acceptability for all features and requirements, including those that contain a subjective element;

(h) the identification and preparation of quality records.

Quality plans may be in the form of a reference to the appropriate documented procedures that form an integral part of this quality system.

Quality Manual

I am often asked to define a "quality plan." Here again is a function that companies have already been performing, to some extent, but calling it something else. Some companies call it a "production plan," "project plan," "service plan," or "product tracking sheet."

Let's put it into financial terms and look at how these plans relate to a "quote." To arrive at a cost estimate someone had to evaluate the job, and in doing so, certain quality considerations were taken into account.

The purpose of that evaluation was probably the following:

- To ensure the specifications can be met (you can perform the work)

- To determine whether any regulations or codes apply and can be met

- To determine whether any special processes are required

- To determine the resources needed (raw material, parts, machinery, tools, inspection and test equipment, special skills, number of employees, etc.)

- To determine the necessary steps in the process to complete the job

- To ensure the necessary documented procedures and instructions are available

- To determine when and where testing and inspection activities are required

- To determine the total time necessary to complete the job

Someone had to gather and review all of this information in order to arrive at a price to tender (quote) the job in order for the company to be profitable. After acceptance of the "estimate" included in a formal quote, you probably go through still more functions in performing the job.

For example:

- Assigning responsibility for the job

- Determining which quality records will be generated during the course of performing the work

- Scheduling the job

All of this information constitutes a basic "quality plan."

The standard requires that you address a series of stated subclauses, "as appropriate." Your auditor will be attempting to verify that you have addressed these requirements as they apply. The best approach toward addressing "quality plans" in your quality manual may be to paraphrase as much text as possible from the standard itself with minimal tailoring (as in the sample quality manual).

A quality plan can be product-specific, project-oriented, or generic. A service-oriented company, such as a testing or calibration laboratory, may have a single generic quality plan that applies to their entire operation. This will work because the only significant variation in the process is detailed in each specific test method or calibration procedure. This example might also be applicable to a high-volume "job shop" with short duration. The structure and detail in which a quality plan is prepared depends largely on the type of business to which it will be applied.

◇ *Corporate-Level Quality Planning*

Some companies have struggled with this clause because they have incorrectly interpreted it such that it would apply to corporate-level quality system planning. Clearly, this was not intended by ISO 9000. Quality planning must only be directed toward meeting the specified requirements for

- Products (service, hardware, processed material, software, or a combination thereof)
- Projects
- Contracts

This interpretation is reinforced by noting those other areas in the standard where quality planning is mentioned (refer to ISO 9001/2, clauses 4.9c, 4.10.1, 4.10.2.1, 4.10.3a, 4.10.4, 4.12, and 4.13.2). The context is consistent. Any other form of quality planning would be beyond the scope of ISO 9000.

Procedure

Your procedure must address, in detail, the actual preparation of quality plans. Unfortunately, the specific points required in the standard are out of sequence and therefore difficult to follow. While your auditor will appreciate them appearing in your quality manual as they are in the standard, I suggest they be restructured in your procedure manual following the actual sequence of events.

This procedure should contain the following steps:

1. Procure, examine, and derive requirements from the accepted quotation (tender) or contract relating to the job being planned:

    - Reviewing standards of acceptability for all features and requirements including those containing a subjective element that must be clarified
    - Considering any quality standards, legal requirements, regulations, or codes that apply
    - Ensuring the compatibility of the design, the production process, installation, servicing, inspection, and test procedures, and the applicable documentation

2. Determine the necessary documented procedures, instructions, drawings, and schematics required

3. Determine the resources needed (i.e., raw material, parts, machinery, tools, test fixtures, jigs, templates, number of employees):

- Including the identification and acquisition of any controls, processes, inspection equipment, fixtures, total production resources, and skills that may be needed to achieve the required quality

- Identifying suitable verification at appropriate stages in the product realization

- Identifying any measurement requirement involving capability that exceeds the known state of the art in sufficient time for the needed capability to be developed

- Updating, as necessary, quality control, inspection, and testing techniques, including the development of new instrumentation

4. Examine the production operations, sequences, test and inspection points required, (considering any design, special processes or servicing required):

- Identifying and defining responsibility for the preparation of quality records

Those ISO 9002 companies offering only services would, of course, tailor this procedure accordingly.

✍ Note

ISO is currently developing a guidance document which will specifically address the use of quality plans:

> ISO 9004-5 "Quality Management and Quality System Elements—
> Part 5: Guidelines for the use of quality plans" (draft)

◇ In What Shape Should Quality Plans Appear?

While "Quality Plans" are required, as stated in the first sentence of ISO 9001/2, clause 4.2.3, and defined, it is still unclear in exactly what shape or form a quality plan is intended to appear. As we see in the note under clause 4.2.3, quality plans "may be in the form of a reference to the appropriate documented procedures that form an integral part of the supplier's quality system." In ISO 9004-1, clause 5.3.3, "Quality Plans," the statement is made that "a quality plan may be a part of a larger overall plan" and "quality plans may be included or referenced in the quality manual, as appropriate."

Does this mean that, for some operations, the quality plan could be contained in the quality manual, procedure manual, or a combination of both, along with work instructions? I believe that it does. This approach would be most valid for companies providing defined services or highly focused manufacturing operations.

Some companies may wish to use a "Quality Plan Checklist" (Figure 4.2-4) to determine whether their existing systems serve as an adequate "generic quality plan." Such checklists may be completed by the Sales Department or the Quality Department (function) as a part of the contract review. In those cases where a complete "new" quality plan is not required, minor changes may be needed in the existing system(s).

Quality Plan Forms

Quality plans may be prepared using a standard form. If you choose to use this approach, your procedure should describe *how* to complete your form. I have created a sample "Quality Plan" form for illustrative purposes (Figures 4.2-5 and 4.2-6). Although this form may be used as a template in creating your own, I must stress that yours could be considerably different and still meet the requirements of the standard.

Refer to Figure 4.2-5. While the upper portion is self-explanatory, I have added a couple of fields that would apply to a specific job. This is an example of how many companies actually create a quality plan for each job in the form of a "work order." Those fields are:

- Quantity

- Contract number (this could also be a job number or work order number)

- Completion due date

Similar formats are used by production planning software packages (MRP systems). These fields could be eliminated, allowing the quality plan to be valid for multiple jobs or orders. When this happens, they are more often referred to as a standard "production plan" or "service plan."

The lower columns would be completed as follows:

The "NO." column ① would contain the sequence number.

The "MFG. OPER. PROC. NO." column ② would contain the manufacturing operation procedure number. This column could be tailored to represent any type of procedure appropriate to the operation. The name could also be changed to reflect a "work instruction" or "service procedure number." When an inspection or test operation is taking place, this column could represent the "inspection or test procedure number."

The "INSP. / TEST POINT NO." column ③ would contain the inspection/test point number. This column could be tailored to represent a specific physical inspection/test location/area.

The "MANUFACTURING OPERATION PROCESS/ATTRIBUTES TO BE VERIFIED & METHOD" column ④ should contain a brief description of

ABC Company	C:\QUALITY\FORMS\QP-0894.DOC

Quality Plan Checklist

PROGRAM OR PROJECT:	CONTRACT NO.
PART OR ASSY. NAME:	QUANTITY:
DRAWING NUMBER:	COMPLETION DUE DATE:

Y / N	Criteria
	Are any additional controls, processes, equipment (including inspection and test equipment), fixtures, resources, and/or skills needed to achieve the required quality? If so, list below:
	Are the design; production processes; installation, servicing, inspection and test procedures; and the applicable documentation all compatible? If not, then what changes are necessary?
	Is any updating of quality control, inspection, and testing techniques, including the development of new instrumentation, necessary? If so, describe below:
	Is any measurement capability that exceeds the known state of the art required? If so, what capability needs to be developed?
	Is any additional verification (i.e., inspection and testing) needed in the realization of the product? If so, at what stage(s)?
	Have standards of acceptability for all features and requirements been clarified, including those which contain a subjective element? If not, what remains to be clarified?
	Are any additional quality records required? If so, identify them.

Prepared By:	Date: / /

Figure 4.2-4: Sample "Quality Plan Checklist" Form

Figure 4.2-5: Sample "Quality Plan" Form

the operation taking place and/or the actual attributes being measured. In the case of inspection activities that are conducted using a drawing or schematic for the attribute values, your procedure would already be listed in column ②. You need only reference the activity, for example: "First article inspection."

NO.	MFG. OPER. PROC. NO.	INSP./ TEST POINT NO.	MANUFACTURING OPERATION PROCESS / ATTRIBUTES TO BE VERIFIED & METHOD	INSPECTION /TEST EQUIPMENT	EST. HRS. PER POINT

ABC Company

Quality Plan

CONTINUATION SHEET

C:\QUALITY\FORMS\QP-2694.DOC

PLAN NO. _____

PAGE: _____ OF _____

Figure 4.2-6: Sample "Quality Plan" Continuation Sheet

The "INSPECTION/TEST EQUIPMENT" column ⑤ should list the inspection or test equipment required. This can be done by simply listing a generic description, model numbers, or, in a small company where equipment is numbered, the specific instrument I.D. The approach you take should be defined in this procedure.

The "EST. HRS. PER POINT" column ⑥ should contain an estimate of the man-hours anticipated per activity. While this is not a requirement, cycle times are often a consideration. This column is *not* intended to be used for establishing quotas.

Additional columns could be added for other purposes. For example: A column could be added for the inspector to sign off, indicating that the production run had passed each inspection. But, for that matter, you really don't need another column. You could simply state in your procedure that each inspection point "passed" would be indicated by the inspector initialing or stamping the area beside that requirement. In either case, you are reducing paper by keeping everything together. This one document becomes a quality plan, a work order, and an inspection record.

The example shown in Figure 4.2-7 is a partially completed quality plan for a metal fabrication operation. The "—" marks indicate that field as being not applicable to a particular process. The numbers under the "MFG. OPER. PROC. NO." column refer to specific procedures. Notice how some of the procedures are actually applicable to many parts of an operation. For example: procedure #9-3 addresses loading a CNC program into the blanking machine, loading the material for the production run, running the first piece for "First Article Inspection," and, after inspection, resuming operation to complete the order. Procedure 9-3 may actually contain specific work instructions as subdocuments to procedure #9—which just happens to correspond to ISO 9000, clause 9, "Process Control." I want to emphasize that it is *not* necessary to have a different procedure addressing each one of these steps.

Notice procedure #15 for allocating and moving material. This procedure most likely addresses "Handling and Storage." Procedure 10, of course, addresses "Inspection and Testing."

Someone familiar with the metal fabrication business may question why I did not include an inspection activity at the beginning to ensure that the #10 gauge stainless steel sheet metal allocated was correct. In that industry, different gauges of material typically appear very similar, and mistakes can be common. If I have an effective ISO 9001–compliant quality system, the material would have been purchased from an approved source (ISO 9001/2, clause 4.6.2), inspected upon receipt (ISO 9001/2, clause 4.10.2), and properly identified as acceptable (ISO 9001/2, clauses 4.12 and 4.8). So, to answer that question, it had already been checked. Redundant checking would be unnecessary, but could be performed if required by your quality system.

Under the "Inspection/Test Equipment" required column, I've listed instruments by their I.D. number. The reason I chose this approach was simply because of the limitation in the column width.

NO.	MFG. OPER. PROC. NO.	INSP./ TEST POINT NO.	MANUFACTURING OPERATION PROCESS/ ATTRIBUTES TO BE VERIFIED & METHOD	INSPECTION /TEST EQUIPMENT	EST. HRS. PER POINT
1	15	—	#10 gauge stainless steel sheet metal is allocated.	—	.25
2	15	—	Material is moved to "blanking" area.	—	.10
3	9-3	—	Program #45 is loaded into CNC "blanking" machine and material is loaded for process. First piece is run.	—	.25
4	10	1	First article inspection performed.	#53	.10
5	9-3	—	Complete operation (510 pieces).	—	5
6	15	—	Pieces moved to "breaking" area.	—	.10
7	9-5	—	Load die configuration #45 into "break" press. First piece loaded and formed.	—	.5
8	10	2	First article inspection performed.	#55	.10
9	9-5	—	Complete operation (510 pieces).	—	2.0
10	15	—	Pieces moved to "spot welding" area.	—	.10

Cont.

Figure 4.2-7: Partial "Quality Plan" Example

Under the "Estimate of Man-Hours per Point" column, I used numbers indicating the percentage of an hour. This is common for computer-based production planning systems. This column is optional and could actually be replaced by something else more significant to your operation.

⚲ *Heavy Manufacturing/Cranes*

If you're involved in heavy manufacturing, your employees probably use overhead cranes on a daily basis. These cranes typically have their maximum weight capability posted beside them, but if you don't know how much an item weighs, this is meaningless. Some quality plans include a column stating the weight of each part and the anticipated total weight of the assembly during each phase of manufacture. Armed with this information your work force can ensure that these limitations are not exceeded.

⚒ *Quality Systems Requirements*

QS-9000 strongly recommends referencing the AIAG "Advanced Product Quality Planning and Control Plan" when developing a quality plan. The QS-9000 standard also contains additional requirements for the use of "Cross-Functional Teams," "Feasibility Reviews," and "Control Plans."

📂 *Records*

Depending on how you approach this requirement, a "quality plan" could be a document, a record, or both.

☞ *Guidance*

For further guidance, refer to:

> ISO 9000-2:1993, Quality Management and Quality Assurance Standards—Part 2: Generic guidelines for application of ISO 9001, ISO 9002, and ISO 9003
> Section 4.2—"Quality system"

> ISO 9004-1:1994, Quality Management and Quality System Elements—Part 1: Guidelines
> Section 5.3—"Documentation of the quality system"

> ISO 9004-5, Quality Management and Quality System Elements—Part 5: Guidelines for the use of quality plans (draft)

> ISO 10013, Guidelines for Developing Quality Manuals (draft)

✍ *Note*

One company that is familiar with ISO 9000 and has experience in developing "on-line" quality manuals and procedures is

> Interleaf, Inc.
> P.O. Box 61098
> New Bedford, MA 02746-9961
> 1-800-955-5323

Industry-Specific Guidance

> ISO/IEC Guide 49, Guidelines for Development of a Quality Manual for Testing Laboratories

ᘒᗢ *Questions Your Registrar May Ask*

Most of the questions a registrar may have regarding this area would normally be addressed during the documentation review. However, here are some questions that may be asked during the assessment, as appropriate.

4.2.1 General

☑ How does the quality system ensure that product conforms to specified requirements?

4.2.2 Quality System Procedures

☑ How was the quality system and its documented procedures implemented?

4.2.3 Quality Planning

☑ Do you have quality plans? How are they documented and formatted? Where is this defined and documented?

☑ Who is responsible for preparing quality plans? Where is this defined and documented?

☑ Who reviews and approves each quality plan? How is approval indicated?

☑ How are quality plans updated? Who is authorized to make such revisions?

☑ How is the identification and acquisition of any controls, processes, equipment (including inspection and test equipment), fixtures, resources, and skills that may be needed to achieve the required quality accomplished?

☑ How do quality plans ensure compatibility of the design, the production process, installation, servicing, inspection, and test procedures, and the applicable documentation?

☑ How do quality plans identify the need for updating of quality control, inspection, and testing techniques, including the development of new instrumentation, as necessary?

☑ How are quality plans developed and scheduled to identify any measurement requirement(s) involving capability that exceeds the known state of the art, in sufficient time for the needed capability to be developed?

☑ How do quality plans identify suitable verification (inspection and test points) at appropriate stages in the realization of product?

☑   How do quality plans address the clarification of standards of acceptability for all features and requirements, including those that contain a subjective element?

☑   How do quality plans address the identification and preparation of quality records?

4.3 Contract Review

At a Glance

9001	9002	9003
✓	✓	✓

You must do the following:

- Establish and maintain documented procedures for contract review and for the coordination of these activities

- Review, before submission of a tender, or at the acceptance of a contract or order (statement of requirement), the tender, contract, or order to ensure

  (a) that the requirements are adequately defined and documented;

  (b) that any differences between the contract or accepted order requirements and those in the tender are resolved; and

  (c) that you have the capability to meet contract or accepted order requirements

- Identify how an amendment to a contract is made and correctly transferred to the functions concerned

- Maintain records of contract reviews

Q U A L I T Y   M A N U A L

3.0 CONTRACT REVIEW

3.1 General

ABC Company has established and maintains documented procedures for contract review and for the coordination of these activities.

📖 *Quality Manual*

Contract review is a very important activity, as your company lawyer would certainly agree. Whether or not papers are exchanged, every job you perform results in a contract. And every contract contains terms and conditions. If your standard terms and conditions do not apply, either the customer's terms apply, or the law supplies terms to complete the contract.

In either case, you will have substantially increased contractual obligations. Understand what it is that you are reviewing and accepting. Establish a policy toward handling contracts that suits your business while reducing unnecessary legal risks.

📑 *Procedure*

I suggest that you involve your company lawyer in writing and/or reviewing this procedure. If you have a small company that cannot easily afford a company lawyer for such tasks, then I suggest you contact the Small Business Administration. There are programs, such as SCORE, in which retired professionals assist small business at no charge.

> Service Corps of Retired Executives (SCORE)
> 409 3rd Street S.W.
> Washington, DC 20024
> Tel: 1-800-634-0245
>   (202) 205-6762
> Fax: (202) 205-7636

> **QUALITY MANUAL**
>
> **3.2** Review
>
> Before submission of a tender, or at the acceptance of a contract or order (statement of requirement), the tender, contract, or order will be reviewed to ensure that:
>
> (a) the requirements are adequately defined and documented (where no written statement of requirement is available for an order received by verbal means, ABC Company will ensure that the order requirements are agreed before their acceptance);
>
> (b) any differences between the contract or accepted order requirements and those in the tender are resolved;
>
> (c) ABC Company has the capability to meet contract or accepted order requirements.

📖 *Quality Manual*

The primary reason for contract review is to ensure that you can, in fact, perform the work while meeting the expectations of your customer. You want to avoid a breach of contract. But what is breach of contract?

Each of the following is a breach of contract:

- Failure to complete the work

- Failure to complete the work on time (within the original time plus any extensions provided for in the contract)

- Failure to *meet the specifications*

- Supplying *defective workmanship or materials*

- Supplying *used material or parts* without telling the customer

- Supplying equipment that *infringes a patent*

▤ *Procedure*

First, you must have a procedure for contract review. Remember that a contract can take many different forms. It can appear as a formal contract, a purchase order, verbal orders, etc. Contracts can cover the following:

- A single shipment
- Multiple shipments
- An order received against an annual forecasted volume
- A release against an annual contract (blanket purchase orders)

Depending on your business, this review can take place at several different levels. Give particular thought as to *who* will be authorized to review and approve contracts and *how* the completion of such reviews will be documented. Contract review may be delegated to several different individuals, perhaps because they handle different product lines or services.

▤ *Tenders*

If you submit tenders (a formal offer—often a bid, proposal, quote, or estimate), are they reviewed prior to issue? They should be, because once a tender is accepted it would be considered a contract. Next, you must document the coordination of the contract review activities. You should develop an infrastructure that facilitates direct communication and teamwork among your sales, marketing, and production functions. Realize, however, that this is often easier said than done.

What Are You Reviewing Orders For?

Both quoted and unquoted (unsolicited) orders must be reviewed to ensure the following:

- That the requirements are adequately defined and documented
- That you have the capability to meet contract or accepted order requirements

In reviewing and processing an order, several issues should be addressed:

The essential requirements of each order:

- Quantity
- Price
- Payment terms

- Specifications
- Quality requirements (quality standard invoked, if any)
- Special requirements (if any)
- Government regulations
- Documentation
- Billing requirements (method)
- Packaging requirements
- Delivery points (including method)

The production schedules for multigrade or multiproduct plants must also take these factors into account:

- Stock levels
- Storage capacities
- Forecasted sales demands
- Maintenance shutdowns

The point in the delivery process at which responsibility for maintaining the quality of product passes from the supplier to the purchaser or other party must be identified. In the case of consignment stocks, responsibility for maintenance of quality must also be defined and agreed upon in the contract.

The supplier and purchaser must agree upon special purchaser requirements beyond the supplier's standard specification. The quality system or quality plan must ensure that such special requirements are communicated to all personnel involved in processing the order.

✍ Note

Do not be misled by the absence of certain provisions from a customer's purchase order. If the purchase order is silent about any of these:

- Delays
- Implied warranties
- Damages
- Consequential damages

you may be responsible for delays (even if beyond your control), for implied warranties, and for consequential damages, under the statutes of your state or province.

Request for Quotation (RFQ)

Your procedure should also address how you respond to an outside "Request for Quote" (RFQ) or "Request for Proposal" (RFP). Sometimes you may be required to submit your proposal on the customer's form. The customer's form is always based on the customer's terms. These would normally require some modification or, alternatively, acceptance of increased risk on your part.

Such quotations can be handled in a variety of ways:

1. If you wish to quote only to your standard terms, a statement can be added to the bid form, such as:

   Exception is taken to conditions _____ through _____ of the bid form. This proposal is subject to the conditions set out by ABC Company Form ABC-002 (1/94), a copy of which is attached.

2. If you wish to submit a price only and negotiate contract terms later if your price turns out to be attractive, you can also state "taking exception to the customer's terms," or you can quote as in 1, above.

3. You can take exception to some of the proposed terms, and add some of your terms, as appropriate.

4. If the risks are acceptable, you can use the customer's form without taking any exceptions. (This would be an unusual case.)

✍ Note

While none of this is specifically addressed in ISO 9000, I have explored it here in order to give you insight as to *what* your procedure on "Contract Review" could be expanded to cover.

Review and Approval of Tenders

The individual preparing and issuing a routine proposal, quote, or tender (typically a sales representative) is normally responsible for ensuring that the tender is properly reviewed. Approval is usually indicated by signing and dating all copies of the proposal, quote, or tender (multipage carbonless transfer forms are common).

The procedure would usually state:

If the individual preparing a proposal/tender has any concerns regarding the technical or quality requirements of a proposal/tender, that individual is responsible for ensuring that the appropriate technical and/or quality personnel are consulted prior to approval and issue of the proposal/tender."

It is also common practice for a copy of all proposals (quotations) issued to be contained in a "Quote Log Book" for reference.

☺ *Standard Terms and Conditions*

Most companies have standard terms and conditions for performing work. These terms and conditions of sale are normally printed on the back of quotation forms, acknowledgments, and invoices. They usually address issues such as these:

- Payment
- Warranty
- Limitations of liability
- Protection against unreasonable secrecy obligations

Use of "Special" Terms or Conditions

There will be occasions when you will not want to use one or more of your standard conditions. You should then state this on the face of the quotation and specify the terms you do not want to use. For example, if equipment is altered or customized to customer specifications with no established historical performance, you may choose to not warrant the work.

In another example, if you patch a transformer, or if you repair equipment that does not have proper over-voltage or over-temperature protection, you may not want to warrant the material or workmanship that you provide. In such cases it is necessary to specify that your standard condition (in this case your standard warranty) does not apply. Alternatively, you may wish to modify your terms and conditions for certain orders.

This situation typically arises in "**RUSH**" orders or special processes. To avoid the standard warranty you should add an appropriate provision to the quotation, such as:

> *Since only one coil of the transformer is being replaced and all impurities accordingly cannot be removed, no warranty applies to this work.*

Or,

> *Since this equipment has not been baked as recommended, no warranty will apply.*

Or simply,

> *This work is not warranted. All services are accepted "As is."*

I have addressed these changes here rather than clause 4.3.3, "Amendment of contract," because at this point no contract yet exists.

Resolving Differences in the Tender (Proposal/Quote)

An obvious question is "How can you resolve differences in the tender (quote) if the people reviewing the contracts don't have copies of the quotes?" If you keep a "Quote Log Book," as mentioned earlier, you should keep it current and in the same area as those personnel reviewing contracts. If all of your quotations are on your computer system, this can be more easily accomplished.

Verbal orders

Sub-clause (a) of this clause states:

> *Where no written statement of requirement is available for an order received by verbal means, the supplier shall ensure that the order requirements are agreed before their acceptance.*

If you take orders by writing them on an order form, I suggest adding the following statement into your contract review procedure:

> *Verbal orders shall be transferred onto a standard written form suitable to the work scope and maintained in the relevant customer job file.*

If you typically take orders by entering them into a computer, then state something like:

> *Verbal orders shall be entered into a computer system suitable to the work scope and maintained in the relevant customer job file.*

Other means of recording verbal orders include audio tape, video tape, and computer multimedia (audiovisual). When any of these is used, the customer must be informed and aware that the discussion is being recorded. These alternative approaches are discouraged because they are so easily altered. However, there are valid reasons for using each approach.

Acknowledgments (Confirming Orders)

Many companies have established the practice of sending written "Acknowledgments" (a.k.a. "Confirming Orders") to their clients, particularly when they place orders verbally. Another good practice is to include the following statement in your standard terms and conditions on your acknowledgment form:

> *Except in particulars specified by the Buyer and expressly agreed to in writing by the Seller, the products (services) furnished hereunder shall be produced in accordance with the Seller's standard practices and procedures.*

This can make contract reviews significantly easier in that now all changes must be documented. This level of documentation leaves many people concerned because this simply is not the way most companies in the U.S. conduct business. They wonder how their customers will perceive this change.

Other companies' experiences have shown that some customers (typically those that are not ISO 9000–compliant) may complain about the new formalization. Others (typically those that are ISO 9000–compliant) will prefer to deal with your company because they understand the underlying principles behind formalizing these processes.

Credit Checks (Verification)

Many companies will perform a credit check of a potential customer prior to accepting an order. (This can include credit card verification in commercial or retail sales.) This is not a requirement of ISO 9000, but if it is your practice, it should be included in your documented "Contract Review" procedure.

Delivery Delays

In the U.S. it has almost become common practice for a customer to demand what a supplier perceives as an unreasonable delivery date. In many instances the customer knows that the stated delivery date is unattainable, but justifies the practice by expecting all of their suppliers to be late on delivery. The supplier's sales force agrees to this date in order to win the contract, knowing that the terms cannot be met. Sales then passes this unattainable time scale to production. Shortly after the due date has passed, the customer begins to call the supplier expediting the order.

This is a practice that *must* end. Customers should establish reasonable delivery dates and require their suppliers to be accountable for meeting those expectations. Both customers and suppliers should include "on-time delivery" as a measure of subcontractor performance.

All of this having been said, we must recognize that, even under ideal conditions and with best intentions, delays are going to occur. Another good practice is to include the following statement in your "Standard Terms and Conditions of Sale":

> *In the event of any delay in Seller's performance due to fire, explosion, strike, or other differences with workmen (employees, subcontractors, contract labor, etc.); shortage of utility, facility, material or labor, delay in transportation, breakdown or accident; compliance with or other action taken to carry out the intent or purpose of any law or regulation; or any cause beyond the Seller's reasonable control, Seller shall have such additional time within which to perform this contract, as may be reasonably necessary under the circumstances and shall have the right to apportion its production among its customers in such a manner as it may consider equitable.*

Again, this is an area where your company legal counsel can provide the best input.

Catalog Orders

This area is often forgotten. If you normally take orders where standard catalog numbers are referenced, then be sure to adequately address this area. If referenced at order entry, the catalog becomes a part of the contract review. Although catalogs are normally not considered controlled documents in the sense of maintaining "receipt acknowledgments" from customers, they must be formally issued to those individuals taking orders. They must also be revision-controlled. In many instances it is acceptable for obsolete catalogs (clearly marked "Obsolete") to be available for reference by those individuals taking orders.

⚑ When ISO 9000 Is Invoked by Your Customer

ISO 9000 has several requirements that must be specified before they are applicable. They may be specified in your quality system, at your discretion, or in your customer's contract or purchase order. ISO 9000 simply requires that you have the ability to meet these added requirements when, where, and to the extent that they are specified. They are found in the following areas of ISO 9000:

- Customer verification of subcontracted product (4.6.4.2)
- Product traceability (4.8)
- Technical data pertaining to measuring devices (4.11.1)
- Nonconforming product accepted with or without repair by concession (4.13.2b)
- Delivery to destination (4.15.6)
- Availability of quality records (4.16)
- Servicing (4.19)

Ensure that your contract review addresses these topics. Many companies act proactively toward these requirements by developing a policy toward each in advance.

Blanket Purchase Orders

If you are working under blanket purchase order(s) that were accepted prior to your adopting ISO 9000, be sure to reopen and review those P.O.s before you undergo an ISO 9000 audit. Since new work may arrive under these purchase orders, your registrar would want to ensure that you have reviewed the orders. This is a common oversight.

> **QUALITY MANUAL**
>
> **3.3** Amendment to Contract
>
> ABC Company will identify how an amendment to a contract is made and correctly transferred to the functions concerned within the organization.

Quality Manual

I suggest leaving this clause vague in the quality manual, with detail contained in your procedure(s).

Procedure

In this procedure be sure to give enough detail describing the following:

- **Who** is authorized to amend a contract

- **How** to amend a contract

- **Who** is responsible for communicating changes to contracts

- **How** changes in a contract are communicated to the appropriate function(s)

- **When** a contract can be amended

Delivery Delays

Even when efforts are made, in good faith, to meet contract delivery dates, there will be times when these due dates cannot be met. When this first becomes apparent, you should contact your customers and agree upon a revised delivery date. The customer may wish to accept a partial delivery while awaiting the remainder. In any event, the contract should be amended to reflect these changes.

Contract Change Order Form

The commercial construction industry has for years had what they called a "Contract Change Order Form" used specifically for documenting last-minute changes in a design. (In the U.K. the same form is called a "Contract Variation Instruction" or "Request.") This document is typically a multiform pad used by workers and site foremen to document requests for last-minute changes in a construction project. This form may be used to document changes that are needed when an architect has mistakenly specified something substandard to local building codes. In other instances, the subcontractor may feel that the architectural plan is not in harmony with commonly accepted good building practices. In such an instance, he may document the concern and request a change from the customer or the customer's architect. This, in essence, is a request to change or amend the contract. The same concept can easily be applied to a variety of industries.

Communication of Contract Changes

Changes in contracts can be communicated by various means. The following list is just a few:

- Memos (including e-mail with receipt acknowledgment)
- Quality bulletins (quality alerts)
- Updated (revised) procedures
- Updated (revised) work instructions
- Updated (revised) drawings or schematics
- Updated (revised) quality plan

QUALITY MANUAL

3.4 Records

Records of contract reviews will be maintained. Channels for communication and interfaces with the customer's organization in these contract matters will be established where possible.

Quality Manual

I suggest that details surrounding contract review records be contained in your procedure(s). In the *sample* quality manual, I have incorporated the note concerning "channels of communication." This is optional and should not be viewed by an ISO 9000 auditor as a requirement.

 # Procedure

In this procedure, describe how to document that "before submission of a tender, or at the acceptance of a contract or order (statement of requirement), the tender, contract, or order" is reviewed. This can include tenders (quotations), formal contracts, purchase orders, verbal orders, EDI (Electronic Data Interchange) orders, etc. Let's discuss each type individually.

Tenders (Proposals/Quotations)

Tenders (quotations) are normally reviewed prior to delivery by the salesperson who is negotiating with the customer. This review is often indicated by that person, or some other authority, signing the tender. Computer-generated tenders may simply indicate the salesperson's initials.

Formal Contracts

Formal contracts usually require each party's signature of acceptance. Just make sure that the individual who signs the contract accepting the order has defined (documented) authorization to do so.

Purchase Orders

You probably receive most of your business via purchase orders. In small companies providing commercial products or services, this is typically documented by having an authorized person date and initial the purchase order, indicating that it has been reviewed and is accepted. This is then typically followed by a confirming order sent to the customer. Copies of confirming orders (if used) should be maintained as quality records to show further evidence of contract review and acceptance.

As companies attempt to streamline operations and processes, another approach is rapidly becoming popular. Orders are typically entered into a computer for production planning, with access to the order entry screen password-protected. The contract review procedure is then written to state that only authorized individuals can enter orders, and each order must be reviewed prior to entry. The computer system then captures the user's ID and associates it with the entered order. The user's ID is typically entered automatically into a field on the order entry screen, other systems record the user's ID into an "audit log." In either case, you now have a documented record of the contract review. As an added plus, a quick review of security levels or areas can serve as a listing of who is authorized to review contracts.

Another popular means of documenting contract reviews is to use a "Contract/Order Review Form." Although this form is not a requirement of ISO 9000, it can be useful in some industries, particularly in the initial evaluation and analysis of a contract or order. The sample in Figure 4.3-1 could be tailored to reflect your specific industry needs and business practices.

Verbal Orders

As previously discussed, many companies transfer verbal orders onto a standard written form or into a computer system suitable to the work scope. If this is the case, then documenting acceptance is discussed above. Other possibilities include audio tape (highly discouraged), video tape, or computer multimedia (audiovisual—also highly discouraged). When any of these are used, the contract can receive immediate review and approval in the same medium.

EDI (Electronic Data Interchange)

Companies using EDI typically operate under a formal contract with the customer. If this is not the case, you still have options. Here are a few examples:

- Save those files to a disk marked "EDI Orders Reviewed and Accepted"

- Print those files onto paper so that a review can be documented

- Handle the order the same as if it were a verbal order

"Paperless" systems tend to make companies more creative in meeting this requirement.

Complete the procedure by addressing where accepted contracts or orders will reside. Generally these records will be maintained by the sales manager or the order entry department.

 ## Records

Records should include the following, as applicable:

- Tenders (quotes/proposals)

- Formal contracts

- Documented verbal contracts

- Purchase orders

- Blanket purchase orders (including EDI agreements)

- Nondisclosure agreements

- Confidentiality agreements

ABC Company

Contract / Order Review

Customer:	Contract / Order No.:	Contract Type:
Product Description:	Start Date:	End Date:

Are the requirements adequately defined and documented? ☐ YES   ☐ NO
Requirements differing from those in the tender resolved? ☐ YES   ☐ NO
Capable of meeting contract / order requirements? ☐ YES   ☐ NO

IDENTIFY ANY SPECIAL OR UNUSUAL QUALITY RELATED REQUIREMENTS
(USE EXTRA SHEETS IF NECESSARY)

Special Instructions:

Special Equipment / Fixtures / Gauges:

Special Test Equipment:

Advanced Metrology Techniques:

Special or Unusual Skills:

Workload / Manpower:

Other:

Reviewed by:	Date:	Accepted ☐ Rejected ☐
C:\Quality\Forms\CR-994.DOC		

Figure 4.3-1: Sample Contract/Order Review Form

Related forms may include the following (if used):

- Acknowledgments (confirming orders)
- Contract/order review forms
- Contract/order change forms
- Invoices

☞ *Guidance*

For further guidance reference:

> ISO 9000-2:1993, Quality Management and Quality Assurance Standards—
> Part 2: Generic guidelines for application of ISO 9001, ISO 9002, and ISO
> 9003
> Section 4.3—"Contract review"

ᏻ *Questions Your Registrar May Ask*

4.3.1 General

☑ What constitutes a contract/order?

☑ How are contract review activities coordinated? Where is this defined (documented)?

☑ What is your system for receiving incoming orders/contracts? Are personnel (phone operators, mailroom personnel, fax room personnel, etc.) instructed as to how to recognize orders and where to direct them?

☑ How are orders/contracts segregated and routed to reach the correct department (i.e., sales person, catalog sales, custom design, or specialized products)?

4.3.2 Review

☑ Do you review tenders (quotations) prior to issue?

☑ Who is authorized to review tenders (quotes)? How can I verify the individual who reviewed a quote was authorized?

☑ Do you issue verbal quotations? How are they recorded?

☑ Are personnel who review contracts/orders/quotations trained to ensure that:

(a) the requirements are adequately defined and documented; where no written statement of requirement is available for an order received by verbal means, the order requirements are agreed before their acceptance;

(b) any differences between the contract or accepted order requirements and those in the tender (quote) are resolved;

(c) the company has the capability to meet contract or accepted order requirements?

☑ How are situations resolved where customer requirements are not adequately defined? Is this detailed in a documented procedure?

☑ How are differences between the contract or accepted order requirements and those in the tender (quote) resolved? Is this detailed in a documented procedure?

☑ How is it determined whether the company has the capability to meet contract or accepted order requirements? (For example, how is availability of ordered products and ability to meet requested delivery dates verified?) Is this process detailed in a documented procedure?

✍ Note

Some auditors may ask to review historical records of product shipment comparing the requested and accepted delivery dates with the actual shipping dates. (How are back-orders or partial shipments handled?)

☑ If you were to receive an order for a number of items that clearly could not be produced in the required time scale, what would you do?

☑ Who is responsible for reviewing contracts/orders? Where is that responsibility defined?

☑ How can I verify that a specific contract/order/quotation was reviewed by someone who was authorized?

☑ Have all of your existing blanket purchase orders been reviewed as required by this clause?

☑ How do you communicate contract requirements to the necessary functions (design, production, etc.)? How are special contract requirements communicated to the necessary functions?

4.3.3 Amendment to Contract

☑ How are amendments to contracts made? How would I be able to identify who amended one and when it was amended (revised)?

☑ Who is authorized to amend (revise) contracts/orders? Where is this defined?

☑ What controls are in place to ensure that amendments to contracts are correctly transferred to the functions concerned? Can you demonstrate that system to me using an example where this was necessary?

4.3.4 Records

☑ What type of record is established to provide evidence that the contract review was carried out and the results?

☑ How are records of contract reviews maintained? Who is responsible for maintaining those records? Where are those records maintained?

4.4 Design Control

At a Glance

You must do the following:

9001	9002	9003
✓	✗	✗

- Establish and maintain documented procedures to control and verify the design of the product in order to ensure that the specified requirements are met

- Prepare plans for each design and development activity

- Assign design and development activities to qualified personnel equipped with adequate resources

- Define organizational and technical interfaces between different groups that have input into the design process, and ensure that the necessary information is documented, transmitted, and regularly reviewed

- Ensure that design-input requirements relating to the product, including applicable statutory and regulatory requirements, are identified, documented, and their selection reviewed for adequacy

- Ensure that document design output is expressed in terms that can be verified against design-input requirements

- Ensure that, at appropriate stages of design, formal documented reviews of the design results are planned and conducted

- Perform design verification, at appropriate stages of design, to ensure that the design-stage output meets the design-stage input requirements

- Perform design validation to insure that product conforms to defined user needs and/or requirements

- Ensure that all design changes and modifications are identified, documented, reviewed, and approved by authorized personnel before their implementation

> QUALITY MANUAL
>
> **4.0** DESIGN CONTROL
>
> **4.1** General
>
> ABC Company has established and maintains documented procedures to control and verify the design of each product in order to ensure that the specified requirements are met.

📖 Quality Manual

When developing your quality manual, I suggest paraphrasing as much original text from each clause of the standard as possible, incorporating the associated "Notes," with specific details contained in your procedure manual.

As written, the standard appears to focus only on the design of new products and their evolution (design changes and revisions). However, these requirements are also applicable to the reconfiguration or modification of existing designs. One way to determine this difference is to ask the following questions:

- Is the drawing or part number revised? (Only ISO 9001, clause 4.4.9 applies)

- Is a new drawing or part number issued? (All of ISO 9001, clause 4.4 applies)

Whether a product is designed, reconfigured, or modified for one customer or to become a standard "catalog" item makes no difference. The requirements of the standard do not make such a distinction. This entire section can easily be paraphrased with minimal tailoring.

📄 Procedure

This procedure could simply be an overview of all of the procedures that affect the design and development process. The following is a very brief example:

ABC Company has developed a comprehensive Design Control System consisting of the following Standard Operating Procedures (SOPs):

> *SOP 4.1—General (this procedure)*
>
> *SOP 4.2—Design and development planning*
>
> *SOP 4.3—Organizational and technical interfaces*
>
> *SOP 4.4—Design input*
>
> *SOP 4.5—Design output*

> *SOP 4.6—Design review*
>
> *SOP 4.7—Design verification*
>
> *SOP 4.8—Design validation*
>
> *SOP 4.9—Design changes*
>
> *These procedures shall be followed throughout the design process along with applicable industry standards and codes.*

Since specific designs don't typically have associated work instructions, your standard operating procedures (SOPs) could include not only the *who*, *what*, *when*, and *where*, but also the *how.* You can easily expand beyond this example (perhaps even adding a flow chart).

QUALITY MANUAL

4.2 Design and Development Planning

ABC Company will prepare plans for each design and development activity. These plans will describe or reference these activities, and define responsibility for their implementation. The design and development activities will be assigned to qualified personnel equipped with adequate resources. These plans will be updated as the design evolves.

Procedure

In this procedure, focus on providing detail describing plans for design and development:

- **Who** will prepare plans for each design and development activity
- In **what** format these plans will appear
- **When** and **how** these plans will be initiated, reviewed, updated

In large companies this usually involves cross-departmental teams working within defined Project Management guidelines. If designs are to be assigned to development teams:

- **What** qualifications must the team members have?
- **What** equipment and resources will they require?
- **Who** is responsible for each design and development activity?

Assignment to "qualified personnel equipped with adequate resources" should include considerations such as these:

- Assignment of responsibilities (Responsibility Matrix, Deployment Charts, etc.)
- Job descriptions
- Training
- Expertise availability

Plans describing design and development activities should recognize that the design processes may apply to various organizations within the operation in differing styles and time frames. Some activities may even be subcontracted. These plans should address all relevant aspects of the design process.

Updating plans as the design evolves should include scheduling considerations such as these:

- Critical dates, major milestones (PERT, Gantt charts, etc.)
- Availability and coordination of resources
- Sequential and parallel work schedules
- Design reviews
- Market readiness review

Design and development planning should address all of the requirements contained in this section of the standard.

☺ *Deployment Charts*

A deployment chart combines two ideas: *what* happens in a process or project, and *who* is responsible for each step. These charts show the major steps of a process, much like a top-down flow chart, along with each person, group, or team responsible. These charts can be constructed around virtually any task or project, including design and development planning (activity assignment).

To construct a deployment chart, list the major steps of a project or process vertically, then list the individuals, groups, or departments involved along the top, as shown in Figure 4.4-1. Then mark each step in the appropriate columns, denoting who is responsible for that step. You can also expand this idea and use different symbols to represent the different roles at each stage.

For more information on the use of deployment charts and working with teams, refer to "The Team Handbook," available (in English or Spanish) from Joiner Associates at (800) 669-8326 (U.S. only) or (608) 238-8134.

Deployment Chart for Project: A316-94

Task	J. Doe	F. Cole	S. Green	K. Foche	Marketing	Test Lab
Design Input	P	S	A	-	S	-
Design Output	P	-	S	A	S	A
Design Verification	A	-	S	A	A	P
Design Validation	A	-	S	A	A	P

Legend: P = Primary Responsibility   A = Advisory Role
         S = Support Role   - = Not Applicable

Authorized By: _John Smith_   Date: _10/27/94_

Figure 4.4-1: Deployment Chart

QUALITY MANUAL

4.3 Organizational and Technical Interfaces

Organizational and technical interfaces between different groups that have input into the design process will be defined, and the necessary information documented, transmitted, and regularly reviewed.

Procedure

Organizational and technical interfaces must be established for the design process. Although your organizational structure may remain the same, regardless of the specific design project, technical interfaces (specific individuals) often change. Therefore, some flexibility may be necessary. Organizational and technical interfaces should be defined (by title) with sufficient authority and responsibility for their role in the design process. Organizational and technical interfaces often include representatives from the following groups, as appropriate:

Project management   Quality/reliability assurance

System engineering   Sales/marketing

Software engineering   Purchasing

Manufacturing engineering	Document control
Component engineering	Technical publications/training
Test engineering	Field service
Production/manufacturing	Warehouse/transportation

Companies implementing Quality Function Deployment (QFD) may even include their customer(s) as a technical interface. In order for the *design process* to be *regularly reviewed*, "Design Review" meetings must be scheduled. These "Design Review" meetings should be formally documented and transmitted (copied) to the appropriate organizations (listed above). Possible text for this procedure could include:

The Project Manager will schedule design reviews at appropriate phases of the design process. Attendees must be sent notification at least one week prior to the meeting date so that alternates can be arranged when necessary.

This procedure may also contain a sample "Notification" form. Though not specifically required, I strongly suggest that a formal agenda be developed for each meeting. Evidence of these reviews is typically in the form of meeting minutes with various supporting documentation relating to the design itself. Meeting minutes normally indicate the status of the design and indicate action items delegated to the various team members along with anticipated commitment (due) dates.

This clause is best described as a requirement for the company to establish an infrastructure supporting the design process.

Q U A L I T Y   M A N U A L

4.4 Design Input

Design-input requirements relating to each product, including applicable statutory and regulatory requirements, will be identified, documented, and their selection reviewed by ABC Company for adequacy. Incomplete, ambiguous, or conflicting requirements will be resolved with those responsible for imposing these requirements. Design input will take into consideration the results of any contract-review activities.

Procedure

Design input typically begins with a product proposal that, once accepted, becomes the basis for design input. Aside from all other design inputs, the product must also meet all applicable laws, regulations, and codes. These must be identified, documented, and their selection reviewed for adequacy.

A product proposal is often in the form of a "Product Brief" describing the product and containing desired requirements such as the following:

- Performance requirements (e.g., functional specifications, environmental usage conditions, reliability)

- Sensory characteristics (e.g., style, color, taste, smell, texture)

- Installation configuration or fit (e.g., size, metric, compatibility)

- Applicable standards and statutory regulations

- Packaging

- Quality assurance and verification

In many industries* carrying out research and development activities, a detailed and specific definition of design input requirements may not be possible in the early stages of a product. Critical characteristics of some materials may be impossible to specify until the product is created or has demonstrated its performance in the desired application. In such instances, formal process development frequently begins only after the successful testing of prototypes, produced in relatively small quantities, has created a market for the product.

In this situation, you could describe the separate "Research and Development" process, describing *how* and *when* it is linked to the more formal design processes.

The following sample is common wording from a Design Input procedure.

Each ABC Company "Product/Design Proposal" (Product Brief) must include the following minimum "design input":

- *General product description*

- *Desired design/performance specifications (including any options)*

- *Applicable statutory and regulatory requirements*

- *Product certification requirements (BABT, CSA, TUV, PTB, UL, CE, etc.)*

- *Competitive analysis*

- *Contract requirements (if applicable)*

---

*This is most common in the chemical and process industries.

The Engineering Manager shall review and approve all proposed designs for completeness and adequacy prior to consideration for development.

This last sentence can be expanded to better define the word "adequacy" should you feel the need. The following is an example:

The Engineering Manager is responsible for the review/evaluation of (design input) drawings, schematics, and specifications with respect to their engineering adequacy. The review/evaluation shall include adequacy to standard engineering and design practices, compliance with applicable statutory and regulatory requirements, and adequacy with respect to design feasibility.

The design input review/evaluation shall also take into consideration the results of any contract-review activities.

An important consideration at this point should be performing a comparison with similar designs, with emphasis on failures. The new design should avoid duplicating previous problems.

A review of design input should also include a reexamination of the final accepted contract, taking these factors into consideration:

- Any additional design input that may have been detailed in the contract

- Any special provisions or customer approvals that may be required

- Any special licenses that may have been granted to use patented technology and/or software in the product as detailed in the contract

Upon completion, a "Design Input" documentation package should be compiled. In some way, it should be indicated that a "Design Input Review" has been performed by an authorized individual.

✍ Note

"EAC Guidelines on the Application of EN45012, The European Standard for Bodies Certificating Suppliers' Quality Systems" (2 December 1992) states under clause 7, *Certification personnel*:

EAC Interpretation
6. When assessing the design function under ISO 9001 appropriate regulatory requirements have to be complied with, whether they are specified by the customer or not. The assessor should be competent to assess whether or not the supplier's quality system meets this requirement (ISO 9001, clause 4.4.4 (c)).

This means that if you seek ISO 9000 registration, your auditor will probably be verifying your compliance with regulatory requirements.

> **Q U A L I T Y   M A N U A L**
>
> **4.5** Design Output
>
> Design output will be documented and expressed in terms that can be verified against design-input requirements and validated.
>
> Design output will:
>
> (a) meet the design-input requirements;
>
> (b) contain or make reference to acceptance criteria;
>
> (c) identify those characteristics of the design that are crucial to the safe and proper functioning of the product (e.g., operating, storage, handling, maintenance, and disposal requirements).
>
> Design-output documents will be reviewed before release.

Procedure

Design output is often expressed in the form of technical documents and data* such as these:

- Drawings or schematics**
- Software†
- Specifications (product, process, test/performance, material, etc.)
- Instructions (manuals, work instructions, etc.)
- Procedures (servicing, inspection and testing, disposal, etc.)

Characteristics of the design that are "crucial to the safe and proper functioning of the product (e.g., operating, storage, handling, maintenance, and disposal

---

*I suggest that "Design Output" technical documents and data be developed in accordance with industry recognized standards, conventions, and recommended practices (i.e., ANSI, ASME, AWS, IEEE, ISO, etc.).

**Drawings and schematics can exist in electronic CAD (computer-aided design) formats.

†I suggest referencing ISO 9000-3, "Quality Management and Quality Assurance Standards— Part 3: Guidelines for the application of ISO 9001 to the development, supply, and maintenance of software," for further guidance in defining your "Design Output" requirements.

requirements)" are typically identified in Specifications/Instructions/Procedures/Material Safety Data Sheets (MSDS).

Design output documentation and data relating to *specifications* should include, as applicable:

Product Specifications

- Permissible tolerances (product acceptance criteria)

- Aesthetic specifications (acceptance criteria)

- Storage requirements, shelf-life, and disposal requirements

- Packaging and handling requirements (including ESD considerations)

- Labeling requirements (warnings, identification, traceability, etc.)

- Material Safety Data Sheets (MSDS)

Process specifications

- Workmanship criteria (standards, codes, etc.)

- Personnel requirements (manpower and technical expertise requirements)

- Manufacturing flow (flow charts, block diagrams, etc.)

- Automation

- Environmental conditions

- Special process needs

- Capability to inspect and test (including special processes)

- Materials list/bill of materials—BOM (materials, components, subassemblies, etc.)

- Handling/packaging/safety requirements

Process specifications should include enough detail to allow suitable approval of processes. These final technical documents are then used by or for the following:

Purchasing	Installation
Production	Servicing/maintenance

Inspection and testing   Handling, storage, and packaging

Operation (user's manual)   Training (staff and users)

All of these considerations should be taken into account when defining the following:

- **What** form each of these documents will take

- **Who** is authorized or responsible for their review before release

- **How** evidence that a review has taken place is documented

Consideration should be given to the needs of the end user of these documents. Terminology that is confusing or difficult to understand should be avoided.

Q U A L I T Y   M A N U A L

4.6 Design Review

At appropriate stages of design, formal documented reviews of the design results will be planned and conducted. Participants at each design review will include representatives of all functions concerned with the design stage being reviewed, as well as other specialist personnel, as required. Records of such reviews will be maintained.

Procedure

Design reviews should be planned and conducted with a formal agenda typically established by the project manager. Your procedure should begin by addressing *who* is responsible for these reviews. For example:

> *Based on the product application and complexity, the Project Manager shall establish a time-phased design program with built-in design reviews and evaluation.*

Design reviews should be conducted through each phase of the design, concluding with a "Final Design Review." Approval of the final design review can also serve as the production release. Your procedure could also contain a set of standard topics for discussion at each meeting. You could even use this criteria in the form of a meeting checklist. For example, see Figure 4.4-2.

Design Review Meeting Agenda / Checklist

	Schedule (potential delays, problems, etc.)
	Cost (cost compared to projection, any cost issues with purchasing)
	Documentation status (drawings, schematics, test specifications, etc.)
	Design status/changes (electrical, mechanical, software, cosmetic)
	Regulatory requirements (as applicable)
	Validation (test specifications, procedures, results)

Figure 4.4-2:   Design Review Meeting Agenda/Checklist

Using this example, considerations for design review agendas could include the following:

Scheduling:

- Progress update (PERT, Gantt charts, timelines, etc.)

- Potential delays (subcontractor schedules, etc.)

- Completion/release date

Cost:

- Actual cost compared to cost goal

- Costed materials list (Bill of Materials—BOM)

- Any cost issues with purchasing

- Cost-reduction plans

Documentation Status (Design Output):

- Drawings/schematics

- Test specifications/inspection procedures

- Labeling readiness (brand logo—artwork, required labeling, etc.)

- User/service manual development

Design status/changes:

- Mechanical

- Electrical/electronic

- Software

- Cosmetic

- Compliance with regulatory requirements (as applicable)

Design validation status (test results):

- Mechanical

- Electrical/electronic

- Software

Design reviews can include several considerations not mentioned here—for example, comparison with similar designs to analyze previous quality problems and possible recurrence.

Each organization or function may have specific concerns to be addressed and should be involved to the extent and degree necessary. Depending upon the size and structure of your business, this could include the following:

Project management	Quality/reliability assurance
System engineering	Sales/marketing
Software engineering	Purchasing
Manufacturing engineering	Document control
Component engineering	Technical publications/training
Test engineering	Field service
Production/manufacturing	Warehouse/transportation

As mentioned previously under "Organizational and technical interfaces," a company implementing QFD may choose to involve their customer(s) in the design review process.

✍ Note

I suggest referencing MIL-STD-1521B, "Technical Reviews and Audits for Systems, Equipments, and Computer Software," for further guidance. Some tailoring will definitely be required, but it can serve as an excellent template in developing your own design review system.

QUALITY MANUAL

4.7 Design Verification

At appropriate stages of design, design verification will be performed to ensure that the design-stage output meets the design-stage input requirements. The design verification measures will be recorded.

In addition to conducting design reviews, design verification may include activities such as the following:

- Performing alternative calculations
- Comparing the new design with a similar proven design, if available
- Undertaking tests and demonstrations
- Reviewing the design-stage documents before release

Procedure

This requirement is easily converted to a procedure. After authority and responsibility are defined, the procedure should then address the various means used:

- Alternative calculations (to verify correctness of the original calculations and analysis)
- Comparison with a proven design, if available
- Testing and demonstrations (by model or prototype tests)
- Independent verification
- Design review

These "design verification measures" are typically recorded as part of the design reviews. Figure 4.4-3 is a sample design verification checklist derived from ISO 9000-2:1993, "Generic guidelines for the application of ISO 9001, ISO 9002, and ISO 9003."

ABC Company	C:\QUALITY\FORMS\DVC-494.DOC

Design Verification Checklist

Design/Project Number: _____

Y/N	Criteria
	Do designs satisfy all specified requirements for the product, process, or service?
	Are product design and processing capabilities compatible?
	Are safety considerations covered?
	Do designs meet functional and operational requirements, that is, performance and dependability objectives?
	Have appropriate materials and/or facilities been selected?
	Is there adequate compatibility of materials, components and/or service elements?
	Is the design satisfactory for all anticipated environmental and load conditions?
	Are components or service elements standardized, and do they provide for interchangeability, maintainability, and replacement?
	Are plans for implementing the design (e.g., purchasing, production, installation, inspection, and testing) technically feasible?
	Can the tolerance requirements consistently be met?
	Where computer software has been used in design computations, modeling, or analysis, has the software (and its configuration control) been properly validated, authorized, and verified?
	Have inputs to such software, and the outputs, been appropriately verified and documented?

Design verified by: _____   Date: _____/_____/_____

Figure 4.4-3: Sample Checklist for Design Verification
Derived from ISO 9000-2:1993

QUALITY MANUAL

4.8 Design Validation

Design validation will be performed to insure that product conforms to defined user needs and/or requirements. Design validation follows successful design verification and is normally performed under defined operating conditions.

Validation is typically performed on the final product, but may be necessary in earlier stages prior to product completion. Multiple validations may be performed if there are different intended uses.

Procedure

Many users have difficulty understanding the difference between *verification* and *validation*. In practice, these words can be defined as the process used to answer the following questions:

Verification = Does the design output match the design input requirements?

Validation = Does the design *function/operate/work* the way in which it is intended?

This requirement is also easily converted to a procedure. For example:

SOP 4.8 Design Validation

The Project Manager will establish a design validation program for evaluation and testing of each product, normally performed on the final product under defined operating conditions, to ensure that product conforms to defined user needs and/or requirements.

Multiple validations may be performed if there are different intended uses. In such a case, based on the product application and complexity, the Project Manager will establish a time-phased design validation program with built-in design evaluations and tests at significant design stages.

Design validation must follow successful design verification. However, preliminary evaluation and testing may be necessary in earlier stages.

Specific details will vary depending upon the organization of each company.

Validation of a design is typically performed through inspection and testing of prototype models and/or actual production samples. However, an increasing number of computer simulations are being used to validate designs. When software is used for this purpose, it is imperative that the program itself be validated.

Design validation can include analytical methods such as Failure Mode and Effect Analysis (FMEA), fault tree analysis, risk assessment, Design of Experiments (DOE), and/or simulations (field tests) on prototypes.

Your procedure should then address the various means used, such as the following:

- Inspections to verify that all product design features conform to defined user needs and/or requirements

- Performance tests to verify that all product design functions conform to defined user needs and/or requirements, such as operating, safety, storage, handling, and maintainability under defined storage and operational conditions (ref. ISO 9001, clause 4.4.5c)

Evidence of "Design Validation" would normally exist in the form of documented inspection and/or test results (either from in-house or independent external sources).

The results of design validation testing can initiate or influence immediate changes to these:

- Components/parts

- Raw materials

- Product composition or formulation

- Process control conditions/procedures

- Inspection/testing specifications and/or procedures

- Packaging and/or labeling

Responsible functions should be identified.

♀ *Equivalent Components or Parts*

Design validation typically involves minor changes affecting individual components or parts. This, in essence, is a functional evaluation of each component or part. The resulting "Parts List" is often called a "Bill of Materials" (BOM) and can be used as a basis for approving the supplier or subcontractor of those items.

Design validation is often extended to evaluate various equivalent components or parts for use in the event of shortages or excessive delivery delays once production has begun. The BOM will typically list these equivalent components, along with alternative sources for the purchasing department.

> **QUALITY MANUAL**
>
> **4.9** Design Changes
>
> All design changes and modifications will be identified, documented, reviewed, and approved by authorized personnel before their implementation.

Procedure

Design changes normally involve performance or reliability improvements, many of which are the result of customer or user feedback (including customer complaints). Other changes are made to remain in compliance with revised legal and regulatory requirements. In some cases, changes may be necessary to take advantage of improvements in the design of individual components, parts, or raw material used in the manufacture of the product.

In this procedure, be sure to give enough detail describing the following:

- **Who** may initiate design changes
- **How** design changes and modifications are identified
- **How** and **where** design changes and modifications are documented
- **Who** (by title) is responsible for review of design changes
- **How** review of design changes is documented
- **Who** (by title) is responsible for authorization of design changes
- **How** authorization of design changes is documented
- **How** design changes are controlled (issue and distribution)

Design changes may extend beyond the design itself to include these items:

- Process control conditions or procedures
- Testing procedures or specifications
- Packaging or labeling practices

Design change procedures should be consistent with "Document Control" procedures (clause 4.5).

Records

This portion of the standard either states or implies that several quality records are required. Allow me to explain. This section of ISO 9001 begins with:

4.4.1 General
The supplier shall establish and maintain documented procedures to control and verify the design of the product in order to ensure that the specified requirements are met.

Neither clause 4.4.6 nor clause 4.4.8 states a specific requirement for a quality record. Both, however, contain *specified requirements* in regard to the design process. In order to verify that these requirements were met, you must generate records.

ISO 9001, clause 4.4.8, "Design validation," is an excellent example of an implied requirement.

Design validation shall be performed to insure that product conforms to defined user needs and/or requirements.

How can this activity possibly be verified by your registrar unless it is recorded? The standard states in clause 4.4.9 that

All design changes and modifications shall be identified, documented, reviewed, and approved by authorized personnel before their realization.

This record generally exists as a change or modification to a drawing with the review and approval noted on the drawing itself. The only other associated quality record commonly generated would be an "Engineering Change Request" (ECR)/"Engineering Change Order" (ECO). Engineering Change Notices (ECNs) may also be generated to inform the production or servicing functions of the change(s).

A common approach toward meeting the record requirements for this section is to develop a Design Documentation Package. For example:

Design Documentation Package:

- *Project proposal (design input—"product brief"/contract)*

- *Design/project assignment*

- *Design review meeting schedule/announcements*

- *Design review agenda*

- *Design output (drawings, schematics, etc.)*

- *Design verification (may exist as a memo, letter, checklist, etc.)*
- *Design validation (inspection/test reports, etc.)*
- *Design review meeting minutes*

Design changes are most often documented separately after the initial design is in production. However, they can also be added to the package in order to maintain a complete history of the design.

☞ Guidance

For further guidance, refer to:

ISO 9000-2:1993, Quality Management and Quality Assurance Standards—Part 2: Generic guidelines for application of ISO 9001, ISO 9002, and ISO 9003
Section 4.4—"Design control"

ISO 9000-3:1991, Quality Management and Quality Assurance Standards—Part 3: Guidelines for the application of ISO 9001 to the development, supply, and maintenance of software

ISO 9004-1:1994, Quality Management and Quality System Elements—Part 1: Guidelines
Section 8—"Quality in specification and design"

ISO 9004-7, Quality Management and Quality System Elements—Part 7: Guidelines for configuration management (draft)

Federal Standards

FED. STD. NO. 595b, Colors

ASME (American Society of Mechanical Engineers)

A great deal of valuable data can be found in referencing ASME Standards and Codes. For example:

ANSI/ASME Y1.1, Abbreviations—for Use on Drawings and in Text

ASME Y10 Series, Letter Symbol Standards

ANSI/ASME Y14 Series, Drafting Standards

ANSI/ASME Y32 Series, Graphic Symbols Standards

IEEE (The Institute of Electrical and Electronics Engineers)

A great deal of equally valuable data can also be found in referencing IEEE Standards and Recommended Practices. For example:

IEEE 200-1975, IEEE Standard Reference Designations for Electrical and Electronic Parts and Equipment

IEEE 280-1985, IEEE Standard Letter Symbols for Quantities Used in Electrical Science and Electrical Engineering

IEEE 315-1975, IEEE Standard Graphic Symbols for Electrical and Electronics Diagrams

IEEE 945-1984, IEEE Recommended Practice for Preferred Metric Units for Use in Electrical and Electronics Science and Technology

Several ASME and IEEE Standards have been adopted jointly with ANSI.

Canadian Engineering Standards

CAN3-B78.1-M83, Technical Drawings—General Principles

CAN/CSA-B78.2-M91, Dimensioning and Tolerancing of Technical Drawings

B78.4-1979, Electrical and Electronics Diagrams
(Adopted ANSI Standards Y14.15-1966, Y14.15a-1971 & Y15b-1973 with CSA modifications)

American Welding Society (AWS)

Additional codes have been established by the American Welding Society (AWS). Some of these include:

ANSI/AWS D1.1-94, Structural Welding Code—Steel

ANSI/AWS D1.2-90, Structural Welding Code—Aluminum

AWS D1.3-89, Structural Welding Code—Sheet Steel

ANSI/AWS D1.4-92, Structural Welding Code—Reinforcing Steel

ANSI/AWS A2.4-93, Standards Symbols for Welding, Brazing, and Nondestructive Examination

All of the AWS codes listed above have also been adopted by the U.S. DoD.

Canadian Welding Standards

W47.1, Certification of Companies for Fusion Welding of Steel Structures

W47.2, Certification of Companies for Fusion Welding of Aluminum

CAN/CSA-W117.2-M87, Safety in Welding, Cutting, and Allied Processes

NFPA (National Fire Protection Association)

ANSI/NFPA 70, National Electrical Code

Canadian Electrical Code

C22.1, Part I—Safety Standard for Electrical Installation

C22.2, Part II—General Requirements

C22.3, Part III—Outside Wiring

AIAG Reference Manuals

Advanced Product Quality Planning and Control Plan

Potential Failure Mode and Effects Analysis (FMEA)

Other:

There are many industry or product-specific design standards and guidelines also available. In the electronics industry, for example:

IPC-D-249, Design Standard for Flexible Single- and Double-Sided Printed Boards

IPC-D-275*, Design Standard for Rigid Printed Boards and Rigid Printed Board Assemblies

IPC-DW-425A*, Design and End Product Requirements for Discrete Wiring Boards

Companies seeking product certification are often required to comply with:

CEI/IEC 1010-1 (1990), Safety Requirements for Electrical Equipment for Measurement, Control, and Laboratory Use.

Canadian Reliability Standards

CAN/CSA-Q632, Reliability and Maintainability Management Guidelines

CAN/CSA-Q633, Reliability, Availability, and Maintainability Design Guide for Electronic Products

CAN/CSA-Q634, Risk Analysis Requirements and Guidelines

Questions Your Registrar May Ask

Auditors typically use a "Concept to Production" approach toward design control. They should be able to verify that the design went through all of the steps required by ISO 9001. This is a rather large section, so I'll break down the questions by area.

* Approved for use by the U.S. Department of Defense.

4.4.2 Design and Development Planning

☑ Who is responsible for the development of plans for each design activity? Where is this defined (documented)?

☑ How are design phases and activities planned? What do design and development plans consist of?

☑ How do these plans define responsibility for their implementation?

☑ How do you determine that those individuals assigned responsibility are qualified and have adequate resources?

☑ How are design and development plans updated as the design evolves?

4.4.3 Organizational and Technical Interfaces

☑ How are organizational and technical interfaces between different groups that have input into the design process identified? Who makes this determination?

☑ How is the necessary information documented and transmitted to these different groups? How are reviews of this information documented?

4.4.4 Design Input

☑ How are design input requirements relating to the product (including applicable statutory and regulatory requirements) identified, documented, and their selection reviewed for adequacy?

☑ How are incomplete, ambiguous, or conflicting requirements resolved with those who imposed the requirements?

☑ Who is responsible for this review? How is acceptance indicated?

☑ Does design input take into consideration the results of any contract review activities? How?

☑ If design is started before all design-input requirements are defined, is there a system for tracking those requirements yet to be defined? Where is this system defined (documented)? Are deadlines established for defining these design-input requirements?

4.4.5 Design Output

☑ How is design output documented?

☑ How can one verify that the design output:

(a) meets the design input requirements?

(b) contains or references acceptance criteria?

(c) identifies those characteristics of the design that are crucial to the safe and proper functioning of the product (such as operating, storage, handling, maintenance, and disposal requirements)?

(d) includes a review of design output documents before release?

☑ Are design output acceptance criteria expressed in quantitative terms?

☑ Who is authorized to review and approve design output documents?

☑ Does the system allow release of draft-stage documents? How are these documents distinguished from those approved for production?

☑ Have all user and service manuals been reviewed and approved? Does the revision level of the design (including software revision—where applicable) match the revision levels discussed in the user and service manuals?

4.4.6 Design Review

☑ Are formal documented reviews of the design results planned (scheduled) and conducted?

☑ Has the scope of these design reviews been defined?

☑ Who is responsible for planning and conducting these reviews?

☑ How can we verify that design reviews included representatives of all functions concerned with the design stage being reviewed, as well as other specialist personnel, as required?

☑ Who is responsible for maintaining records of these reviews? Where is this responsibility defined (documented)? Where are these records of design reviews maintained?

4.4.7 Design Verification

☑ At what stages of the design is "design verification" performed to ensure that the design-stage output meets the design-stage input requirements?

☑ Which design-output documents must be verified, and what is the scope of the review?

☑ How is design verification accomplished?

☑ Who is responsible for performing design verification activities?

☑ Is computer software used for developing and/or verification of designs? If so, is the computer software validated?

☑ How are design verification measures and conclusions recorded (documented)?

4.4.8 Design Validation

☑ Who is responsible for performing design validation activities? Where is this responsibility defined (documented)?

☑ When are design validation activities performed? Where is this defined?

☑ Is the objective and scope of design validation activities defined?

☑ How are results of design validation documented?

☑ How is success or failure of design validation indicated?

4.4.9 Design Changes

☑ Who is authorized to identify the need for a design change? Where is this defined (documented)?

☑ How is the need for a design change documented and communicated to the design function?

☑ How are design changes and modifications identified and documented?

☑ Who is authorized to review and approve design changes before their realization? Has the scope of such reviews been defined?

☑ How is approval indicated?

4.5 Document and Data Control

At a Glance

9001	9002	9003
✓	✓	✓

You must do the following:

- Establish and maintain documented procedures to control all documents and data that relate to the requirements of ISO 9000, including, to the extent applicable, documents of external origin such as standards and customer drawings

- Ensure documents and data are reviewed and approved for adequacy by authorized personnel prior to issue

- Establish a readily available master list or equivalent document control procedure identifying the current revision status of documents to preclude the use of invalid and/or obsolete documents

- Ensure that the pertinent issues of appropriate documents are available at all locations where operations essential to the effective functioning of the quality system are performed

- Ensure that invalid and/or obsolete documents are promptly removed from all points of issue or use, or otherwise assured against unintended use

- Ensure that any obsolete documents retained for legal and/or knowledge preservation purposes are suitably identified

- Ensure that changes to documents and data are reviewed and approved by the same functions or organizations that performed the original review and approval, unless specifically designated otherwise. The designated functions or organizations must have access to pertinent background information upon which to base their review and approval.

QUALITY   MANUAL

5.0 DOCUMENT AND DATA CONTROL

5.1 General

ABC Company has established and maintains documented procedures to control all documents and data that relate to this quality system, including, to the extent applicable, documents of external origin such as standards and customer drawings. Documents and data can be in the form of any type of media, such as hard copy or electronic media.

Quality Manual

Don't state that your procedures "control all documents and data that relate to the requirements of ISO 9000." Your procedures should relate to *your* quality system, which in turn is in compliance with ISO 9000. In the sample quality manual, I have also incorporated note 15 from ISO 9001.

Paperless Quality Systems

Many companies are developing paperless quality systems. These can be much more efficient than a conventional paper system. The primary concerns of an ISO 9000 auditor will be these:

- Does the system have sufficient security measures in place to ensure that proper authorization and revision control are maintained?

- Do all employees have access (typically read-only) to the "on-line" quality manual?

These security access levels are typically maintained by a network or system administrator.

Procedure

Begin this procedure by defining which documents you intend to control. For example:

> *This procedure establishes and defines the methods and practices to control all documents and data that relate to the requirements of this Quality System, including, to the extent applicable, documents of external origin such as standards and customer drawings. All definitions*

and responsibilities not explained here are detailed in the ABC Company Quality Manual.

Controlled documents include, but are not limited to:

- *Quality manuals—internal only; all others upon request*

- *Company policies*

- *Standard operating procedure manuals*

- *Applicable quality standards (ISO 9001, ANSI/NCSL Z540-1, etc.)*

- *Applicable codes and regulations*

- *Quality plans*

- *Specifications (raw material, process, manufacturing, product and packaging)*

- *Accepted contracts/customer purchase orders*

- *Order entry procedures*

- *Production plans/schedules/work orders*

- *Approved subcontractor/vendor list*

- *Purchasing manuals and procedures*

- *Work instructions (including drawings/schematics)*

- *Test instructions*

- *Operation sheets*

- *Maintenance procedures and instructions*

- *Inspection checklists (forms)*

- *Inspection procedures and instructions*

- *Alignment/calibration procedures and data sheets (forms)*

- *Laboratory test methods*

- *Internal audit schedules*

- *Job qualification requirements (job descriptions)*

- *Training manuals and procedures*

- *Service bulletins, procedures, and instructions*

- *Sampling plans*

> *Uncontrolled copies of the ABC Company Quality Manual are permitted to be distributed to customers. However, controlled copies are available upon request. The ABC Company Standard Operating Procedure Manual is confidential and proprietary for use by ABC Company employees only.*

The "but not limited to" statement allows you to continue to operate under this procedure without revision as you add other controlled documents (which may be discontinued at a later date) in your system. This "open-ended control" ensures that specific documents will be controlled, which meets the requirements of ISO 9000. However, it also allows you the flexibility to control other documents as needed. For example, you may obtain a contract that requires additional document control specific to that contract or customer. This control could be stipulated in a "quality plan" rather than in your procedure.

Documents of External Origin

Documents of external origin must also be controlled as appropriate. The level of detail contained in your procedure should include *who* is responsible for maintaining current revisions, *which* external documents are to be controlled, *how* control is to be maintained (subscription services, customer contacts, periodic checks, etc.), and *where* each document will reside in the organization.

External documents can include, but are not limited to, the following:

- Quality standards/specifications

- Technical standards/specifications

- Customer drawings/schematics

- Inspection/test procedures

- Calibration procedures/laboratory test methods

- Material Safety Data Sheets (MSDS)

- Reference charts/conversion charts

As customers supply drawings, schematics, specifications, procedures, inspection/test methods, etc., your procedures must establish a means of ensuring that only the most current revisions are used. This type of procedure normally involves establishing a "Contract Administrator" who interfaces with each customer who has special concerns.

It is not uncommon for companies to require current Material Safety Data Sheets (MSDS) relating to the manufacturing process. The concern here is that the latest revision be available. While safety is not specifically addressed in this part of the standard, if it is contained in your procedures (through related laws or regulations), it is subject to interpretation as a part of your quality system.

Quality standards (such as ISO 9001) must also be controlled to the extent that you have a copy of the most current revision. Most registrars take on the responsibility of notifying their clients when a revision of ISO 9000 is issued. Industry and military standards are often updated through the use of subscription services.

External Document Revision Levels

Most ISO 9000 auditors require you to state the actual revision level of any external documents used (such as quality standards or military standards) in your procedures. A few do not. These few expect you always to use the most current revision of every document regardless of the revision level. This would often require that the company utilize a document-update subscription service. In many cases, this makes sense, but there are several instances where it does not. For example, if a commercial company were utilizing a military standard for welding, there could be little or no added value in their subscribing to an "update" service.

Not stating a revision level automatically requires you to use the most current revision. Stating the actual revision level used links you to a specific document, regardless of any updates. I suggest stating the actual revision level used.

Many contracts address this issue by stating:

> *The revision level of external documents in effect at the time of contract acceptance will (or may) remain the controlling document.*

It is generally not a contract requirement to update products or procedures as revisions to referenced documents occur, because there is an unknown impact on cost and delivery.

Reference Charts

Posted reference charts, conversion charts, etc., should be controlled because they become a part of the work instruction at some point in the process. Most auditors consider externally sourced reference charts, conversion charts, etc., acceptable provided that they clearly indicate their source (i.e., source responsible for the chart contents, usually a manufacturer of industry-related items).

In contrast, however, internally generated reference charts, conversion charts, etc., should contain authorization, revision, and issue control because they could contain errors in transferring information. These same charts may eventually require updating and, therefore, issue and revision control.

QUALITY MANUAL

5.2 Document and Data Approval and Issue

Documents and data will be reviewed and approved for adequacy by authorized personnel prior to issue. A master list or equivalent document-control procedure identifying the current revision status of documents will be established and will be readily available to preclude the use of invalid and/or obsolete documents.

This control shall ensure that:

(a) the pertinent issues of appropriate documents are available at all locations where operations essential to the effective functioning of the quality system are performed;

(b) invalid and/or obsolete documents are promptly removed from all points of issue or use, or otherwise assured against unintended use;

(c) any obsolete documents retained for legal and/or knowledge-preservation purposes are suitably identified.

Quality Manual

I suggest that you paraphrase this wording closely from the standard. While much greater detail could be defined here, this should be contained in your procedure manual.

Procedure

Begin this procedure by describing the following:

- **Which** documents require review and approval

- **Who** is authorized to "review and approve" documents (by job title)

- **How** review and approval is indicated

In paperless systems, approval can be indicated by a separate form, or security access.

The Master List

Because procedure manuals typically consist of many different individual procedures, a master list is usually found as a part of the contents page. A master revision level for the manual is then stated along with the most current revision level for each individual procedure (see Figure 4.5-1, Contents/Master List).

ABC Company	STANDARD OPERATING PROCEDURES			
Computer File:	C:\QUALITY\SOP-02.DOC	**Revision:**	2.0	
Quality Mgr.:	*Jane Doe*	**Date:**	5-DEC-94	
Section:	0.2	**Page:**	1 OF 1	
Title:	CONTENTS/REVISIONS			

Procedure	Title	Revision	Date
0.1	Introduction	1.0	3-OCT-94
0.2	Contents / Revisions	2.0	5-DEC-94
0.3	Description of Changes	2.0	5-DEC-94
1.0	Management Responsibility	1.0	3-OCT-94
2.0	Quality System	1.0	3-OCT-94
3.0	Contract Review	1.1	10-OCT-94
4.0	Design Control	2.0	5-DEC-94
5.0	Document and Data Control	1.3	24-OCT-94
6.0	Purchasing	1.2	17-OCT-94
7.0	Control of Customer-Supplied Product	1.1	10-OCT-94
8.0	Product Identification and Traceability	1.0	3-OCT-94
9.0	Process Control	2.0	5-DEC-94
10.0	Inspection and Testing	1.2	17-OCT-94
11.0	Control of Inspection, Measuring, and Test Equipment	1.7	14-NOV-94
12.0	Inspection and Test Status	1.1	10-OCT-94
13.0	Control of Nonconforming Product	1.0	3-OCT-94
14.0	Corrective and Preventive Action	1.0	3-OCT-94
15.0	Handling, Storage, Packaging, Preservation, and Delivery	1.0	3-OCT-94
16.0	Control of Quality Records	1.3	24-OCT-94
17.0	Internal Quality Audits	1.1	10-OCT-94
18.0	Training	1.2	17-OCT-94
19.0	Servicing	1.1	10-OCT-94
20.0	Statistical Techniques	1.0	3-OCT-94

CONFIDENTIAL & PROPRIETARY—FOR ABC COMPANY EMPLOYEES USE ONLY

Figure 4.5-1: Contents/Master List

A "master list or equivalent" should include, but is not limited to, the following:

- Quality manual
- Procedures (including all applicable forms)
- Work instructions
- Drawings/schematics

Additional documents may require control, depending upon your specific application.

Forms

When a procedure references a form, that form becomes subject to the same document control as the procedure. If the form itself is revised or updated, a revision status should reflect that change.

Some possible examples of forms that may require revision control include, but is not limited to, the following:

- Quality bulletins
- Engineering change order (request)
- Purchase requisition forms
- Purchase order forms
- Corrective action request forms

Only after a form has been completed does it becomes a "record."

Many companies identify forms by their location on the network computer instead of an unrelated form number. For example:

C:\QUALITY\FORMS\CAR-494.DOC

The last numbers of the specific file name indicate the date of the last revision (month/year). Another approach is to use the related procedure number as the prefix for the form number. Either method allows the master file to be located quickly.

Forms that are *not* a part of the formal quality system (forms used for "work sheets," personal notes or phone logs, etc.) do not necessarily require revision control.

Electronic Form Formats

If your company is reducing paper, you may prefer to define the *format* of documents rather than create actual forms. Obviously if your company is all on e-mail, it would be handy to send quality bulletins out on a group distribution. If you've standardized software packages, you could even send quality bulletins as attached files. If you choose this approach, be sure to define your form formats in your procedures.

Distribution Control of Quality/Procedure Manuals

The most common means of document control of manuals is to require a "receipt acknowledgment" to be completed (usually signed) and returned. This acknowledgment is then kept on file or in a database, creating a distribution list so that the recipients can be notified of changes and updates. This usually works best if you are issuing a large number of manuals to many people. In smaller operations, it is common to see a distribution list in the procedure itself. This distribution list should be by job title rather than by name.

The Paperless Master List

A master list can easily be maintained on computer. Again, the primary concern here would be defined security access or control.

Distribution Control

The standard requires that document control ensure that:

> *(a) the pertinent issues of appropriate documents are available at all locations where operations essential to the effective functioning of the quality system are performed.*

This is commonly referred to as "distribution" or "issue" control. This is often addressed for paperless systems through defined security levels for various user access capabilities (read only or read/print only).

◇ *Uncontrolled Copies of Quality Manuals*

Some auditors will issue "findings" when identifying *any* uncontrolled copies of quality manuals throughout the facility. Distribution of uncontrolled quality manuals is not specifically addressed in the standard; therefore, this is an arguable point. Many companies offer uncontrolled copies of their quality manual to customers and potential customers as a marketing tool communicating their commitment to quality. All employees must have access to a controlled copy of the manual, but may also wish to have additional uncontrolled copies (*not* a very good idea). In this instance, be sure that you can differentiate between the two types.

Identification of Controlled Quality/Procedure Manuals

The most common means of identifying controlled manuals is to number them. This number is usually on the "receipt acknowledgment" so that when it is returned you have a complete record.

Where the distribution list is placed in the procedure itself, in smaller operations, the manuals may simply be labeled for the appropriate individual's job title (such as "Operations Manager") or even the appropriate area (such as "Sales Dept.").

Color-Coding Documents

Controlled documents must be identified—and somebody, somewhere, always comes up with the bright idea of color-coding the paper. For example, uncontrolled documents are printed on white paper; controlled quality manuals are printed on "sunburst yellow" paper; controlled procedures are always printed on "hot pink" paper; etc. *Please* don't do this! People have already thought of it and tried it on a variety of different-colored papers. Most of the time the print tends to fade around the edges far worse than on normal white paper and becomes more difficult to read. Mostly it's just plain irritating. It is not uncommon for a registrar to return manuals printed on colored paper, asking for them on plain white paper.

If I can't talk you out of this approach, at least use soft colors. Light blue or off-white tend to be the least offensive. The primary concept behind this idea is to make controlled documents more easily identifiable. As an alternative approach, why not use plain white paper with different-colored preprinted borders (headers and footers). This is generally much more effective in achieving the same desired effect. Another approach is to use color-coded binders. While we're on the subject, why not throw in some color-coded tabs?

Color-Stamping Controlled Documents

Another common approach to identifying controlled documents is to stamp them with a colored stamp—usually red, green, or blue, any color but black. This way, if the controlled document is photocopied, the control stamp will be reproduced as black. Procedures then state that any document in which the control stamp is black is to be considered "uncontrolled."

This usually works right up until someone decides to acquire a photocopier with color capability (these copiers are becoming more popular as their price goes down). If Murphy's law applies, this will happen without the Quality element being informed and will be observed by the ISO 9000 auditor during the first surveillance visit, thus casting doubt on the effectiveness of document control and possibly (probably) resulting in a noncompliance.

If your quality documentation resides on a computer network with read/ print access only and you are using this approach for hard copies, be aware that the same consequences apply when a color printer is acquired.

☺ *Use of Permanent Impression Seals on Documents*

If we expand our concept of document control to areas outside manufacturing, you will see that many educational institutions, notaries public, etc., use a unique means of document control. They use a permanent impression seal that cannot be altered without being destroyed. I am not necessarily suggesting that you use this method for controlling your documents, but I do suggest that you explore different possibilities as appropriate.

♡ *Sheet Protectors*

Companies that require procedure manuals or standard work instructions to be placed in the factory or production area or in any dirty environment often use clear polypropylene sheet protectors for each individual page (the kind that won't lift the print). This will protect the individual sheets, preventing them from tearing or getting dirty. Many companies also laminate some work instructions and small drawings or schematics for the same purpose.

◈ *Machine Operating Instructions*

Some auditors will issue "findings" for lack of document control over machine operating instructions or maintenance manuals. This line of thinking would require that every computer running Microsoft Windows have a controlled copy of the Windows manual readily available! The debate concerns whether the work procedure is enough or must be supported with the machine's operating instructions. This is not specifically addressed in the standard. Thus, it is an arguable point.

Once an employee is trained in using Windows, should he or she have a controlled copy of the manual on hand for reference? Or should all such manuals be defined in the quality system as "uncontrolled reference manuals"? You decide. This becomes a more interesting point of discussion when the workers are illiterate, or when the manual is printed in a foreign language.

▦ *Using Microsoft Windows Cardfile for Distribution Control*

Many companies who are making the transition from handwritten cardfile systems to Windows-based computer systems overlook the built-in cardfile program that is included in Windows itself. The cardfile program can easily be used as a means of compiling a "Master List" and/or a distribution control listing. Depending on the number of documents to be controlled, the cardfile program alone can generally meet the needs of most small companies. A larger company may need to use a database program such as Microsoft Access.

⌐ *Control of Invalid and/or Obsolete Documents*

There are many instances in which retention of invalid and/or obsolete documents is necessary. A primary example is in the area of servicing. A company may need to maintain outdated documents (service manuals, drawings, schematics, etc.) in order to service older equipment.

The standard requires that:

(b) invalid and/or obsolete documents are promptly removed from all points of issue or use, or otherwise assured against unintended use;

(c) any obsolete documents retained for legal and/or knowledge-preservation purposes are suitably identified.

Obsolete documents must be either removed or identified. They are typically available throughout service departments that need access to them. In this case, the identification is simply by revision level (they are not *really* obsolete for discontinued products).

I have observed some products that had evolved over time such that a Rev. D manual was the most current for the design up to a specified serial number, even though the latest revision of the manual was much higher.

The following is suggested wording to consider before developing your procedure:

Invalid and/or Obsolete Documents:
Invalid and/or obsolete documents shall be promptly removed from all points of issue or use and disposed, or otherwise assured against unintended use. Any obsolete documents retained for legal and/or knowledge-preservation purposes shall be suitably identified. Continued maintenance of some obsolete documents may be required by specific customer contract or other business needs. When maintenance of obsolete documents is determined necessary by the local Quality Representative, or National Quality Manager, such documents will be removed from use and clearly marked in red ink as "OBSOLETE" to prevent inadvertent use.

Maintenance of "obsolete" documents will continue for such period of time as required by specific customer contract or, in the absence of such a contract, a maximum of two (2) years. Should business needs dictate, this time limit may be extended by the National Quality Manager in

accordance with ABC Company record retention policies and proce-
dures (Reference ABC Company Procedure 16, "Quality Records").

Notice that the example empowers employees other than the Quality Manager to make these determinations. This example is geared toward a large company with several satellite offices, but it can easily be tailored for a small business.

👍 Control of "Draft" Documents

As documents are being prepared and reviewed, there are often several "draft" copies being distributed for review and comment. This is also true of drawings and schematics. These documents should be clearly identified as such. These documents may be stamped (e.g., "DRAFT" and/or "NOT FOR PRODUCTION PURPOSES") or designated by some other means. Several methods may be used, depending upon each company's individual needs.

Q U A L I T Y   M A N U A L

5.3 Document and Data Changes

Changes to documents and data will be reviewed and approved by the same functions/organizations that performed the original review and approval, unless specifically designated otherwise. The designated functions/organizations will have access to pertinent background information upon which to base their review and approval.

Where practicable, the nature of the change shall be identified in the document or the appropriate attachments.

📖 Quality Manual

I suggest that you paraphrase this text closely from the standard. If you define responsible parties for documents in this level of documentation and later change it in your procedure, you tend to run the risk of creating contradictions.

📑 Procedure

While a member of executive management normally reviews and approves the quality manual, the quality manager typically reviews and approves the procedure manual. These are documents that should be somewhat stable. Companies often use a DCR (Document Change Request)/DCO (Document Change

Order) form to identify the need for, and justify, changes to the documented quality system. A similar ECR (Engineering Change Request)/ECO (Engineering Change Order) form is used to change drawings and/or schematics. A single form can often serve both purposes (see the example in Figure 4.5-2: Document/Engineering Change Request Form).

Work instructions and quality plans, however, often need much more flexibility. When a change in a contract results in a change to a work instruction, this change is often reviewed and approved on the spot by a department supervisor or work leader. When time is of the essence, these revisions are made in pen (handwritten) at the production area (the night shift shouldn't be forced to stop work because no one is empowered to make minor documentation changes). This is another area where employees can be empowered. This authority should be defined in your procedure manual. For example:

> *Changes to documents and data shall be reviewed and approved by the same functions/organizations that performed the original review and approval, unless specifically designated otherwise. Department Supervisors and Work Leaders are empowered to review and approve changes to work instructions and quality plans as circumstances dictate.*

💣 *Document Obliteration*

A common pitfall is changing documents or records through *obliteration* (this is also addressed in clause 4.16, "Control of Quality Records"). When changing a document or record by pen revision, use a single line to cross through the old text, then write the new text above or below it, as follows:

The quick ~~braun~~ fox jumps over the ~~lasy~~ dog.

Changes should only be made by authorized personnel. When making pen revisions, this can be indicated by initialing and dating all changes. Never make changes that obliterate or make the old text unreadable (such as using white-out or completely covering the old text with ink).

◇ *Pen Revisions in Black Ink Only*

Some auditors will issue "findings" when observing pen revisions in any color other than black. Clearly this is not a requirement contained in the ISO 9000 series. It is therefore an arguable point.

This practice has been promoted by a previous generation of auditors based on early "photocopy" machine technology. When photocopiers were first introduced, some operated on principles that involved using a blue light source

ABC Company
Document Change Request

Number #_____

(This section is to be filled out by the person requesting the document/engineering change.)

Name:_____ Date: ___/___/___

Dept.: _____ Phone: ( ) _____

Document/Drawing Number:	Document Drawing Revision/Date:

Document/Drawing Title:

Nature of Change: (Identify page number/section and include proposed rewrite, if possible)

_____
_____
_____
_____
_____
_____
_____
_____
_____

Reason for Recommendation:

_____
_____
_____
_____
_____
_____
_____
_____
_____

Disposition: (To be completed by Quality Manager)

☐ Approved   ☐ Rejected   ☐ More information required

Authorized By: _____ Date: ___/___/___

C:\QUALITY\FORMS\DCR-894.DOC

Figure 4.5-2: Sample "Document/Engineering Change Request" Form

to read the image. This blue light caused anything blue on the source document to be reproduced very lightly or not at all. Thus, authorizing signatures in blue ink might not appear on the photocopied document!

Many auditors do not fully understand why they have been trained to look for this. Explain this point to them, and perhaps even demonstrate that your photocopy machines will transfer blue ink images from source documents. The alternative, of course, is to just use black ink pens.

Software Revision

I know of at least one company that, prior to registration, had begun backing up their CNC machine software. One of their machines lost its program prior to a major run of a piece. No problem, thought the company. They loaded the back-up software and ran the order. After delivering the order, they realized that there had been a major revision to the software which was not included on the backed-up version. The cost of this one mistake would have paid for the company's registration.

🗁 *Records*

Many of the records relating to "Document and Data Control" may themselves be considered "Controlled Documents" as well. These records may include the following:

- Master lists (or equivalent)

- Distribution lists (or equivalent)

- Receipt acknowledgments (if used)

- Completed DCR/DCO/DCN forms (as applicable)

- Completed ECR/ECO/ECN forms (as applicable)

☞ *Guidance*

For further guidance, refer to:

> ISO 9000-2:1993, Quality Management and Quality Assurance Standards—Part 2: Generic guidelines for application of ISO 9001, ISO 9002, and ISO 9003
> Section 4.5—"Document control"

> ISO 9004-2:1991, Quality Management and Quality System Elements—Part 2: Guidelines for services
> Section 5.4.3—"Quality documentation and records"

ISO 5807:1985, Information processing—Documentation symbols and conventions for data, program and system flowcharts, program network charts, and system resources charts

⌣ *Questions Your Registrar May Ask*

This clause is rather vague. Thus, many of the following questions may very well not apply. I have included them here to provide insight for you in developing this procedure.

4.5.1 *General*

☑ Have all controlled documents, including forms, been defined? (e.g., QA manual, procedures, forms, quality plans, work instructions, manufacturing travelers, training manuals, service manuals, etc.)

☑ Who is responsible for document and data control? Where is this responsibility defined (documented)?

☑ How are documents controlled? Where is this defined?

☑ How is electronic (computer) data controlled? Where is this defined?

☑ How are documents of external origin, such as standards and customer drawings, identified and controlled?

☑ Who is responsible for the identification and control of documents from external sources, such as standards and customer drawings?

4.5.2 *Document and Data Approval and Issue*

☑ Who is authorized for the review and approval of documents? Where is this defined?

☑ Does the procedure for document review and approval also address sources of reference data (i.e., industry or military standards, national or international standards, statutory regulations) (if applicable)?

☑ How is review and approval of documents indicated (including electronic data/computer documents)? Where is this defined?

☑ Is a master list or equivalent document control established identifying the current revision status of documents and data? Who is responsible for it? How is it maintained?

☑ Are those documents essential to the effective functioning of the quality system defined and distributed to all appropriate locations? Where are these documents defined? Does this include documents issued to subcontractors (if applicable)?

☑ Who is responsible for ensuring that pertinent issues of appropriate documents are available at all locations where operations essential to the effective functioning of the quality system are performed? How is this accomplished?

☑ Are pertinent issues of appropriate documents also available to temporary employees?

☑ Does the system allow release of draft-stage documents? How are these documents distinguished from those approved for production?

☑ Who is responsible for ensuring that invalid and/or obsolete documents are promptly removed from all points of issue or use, or otherwise protected from unintended use? How is this accomplished?

☑ Who is responsible for ensuring that any obsolete documents retained for legal and/or knowledge preservation purposes are suitably identified? How is this accomplished?

4.5.3 Document and Data Changes

☑ Who is authorized to make changes (including handwritten or "pen" revisions) to controlled documents? How are these changes communicated to the document owners?

☑ How is the ability to change computer data controlled (if applicable)? Where is this defined?

☑ How does the document control system ensure that changes to documents and data are reviewed and approved by the same functions or organizations that performed the original review and approval, unless specifically designated otherwise?

☑ How does the document control system ensure that designated functions or organizations have access to pertinent background information upon which to base their review and approval?

☑ Where practicable, is the nature of the change(s) identified in the document or appropriate attachments?

☑ What approach does the company use to control product that is in production when document changes (revisions) are issued? Where is this approach defined?

4.6 Purchasing

At a Glance

You must do the following:

9001	9002	9003
✓	✓	✗

- Establish and maintain documented procedures to ensure that purchased product conforms to specified requirements

- Evaluate and select subcontractors on the basis of their ability to meet subcontract requirements, including quality-system and any quality-assurance requirements

- Define the type and extent of control you exercise over subcontractors

- Establish and maintain quality records of acceptable subcontractors

- Ensure that purchasing documents contain data clearly describing the product ordered

- Ensure that if you verify purchased product at a subcontractor's premises, the verification arrangements and the method of product release are specified in the purchasing documents

- Ensure that when specified in a contract, your customer or the customer's representative is afforded the right to verify at your subcontractor's premises, and your premises, that subcontracted product conforms to specified requirements

QUALITY MANUAL

6.0 PURCHASING

6.1 General

ABC Company has established and maintains documented procedures to ensure that purchased product ("hardware," "software," "processed material," "service," or a combination thereof) conforms to specified requirements.

Quality Manual

I have used the generic definition of product in the example because one never really knows what one will be purchasing in the future. This prevents you from painting yourself into the proverbial corner.

Procedure

In medium to large companies, it's common for these purchasing requirements to be documented in a separate procedure manual maintained by the purchasing department. This procedure manual generally contains additional accounting and financial guidelines (Good Accounting Practices) and information addressing items such as timesheets and expense reports. This manual is then controlled and distributed to the appropriate personnel.

Smaller companies generally find it easier to keep everything in one "Standard Operating Procedure" (SOP) manual.

> QUALITY MANUAL
>
> **6.2** Evaluation of Subcontractors
>
> ABC Company will:
>
> (a) evaluate and select subcontractors on the basis of their ability to meet subcontract requirements including quality system and any specific quality assurance requirements;
>
> (b) define the type and extent of control exercised by the supplier over subcontractors. This will be dependent upon the type of product, the impact of subcontracted product on the quality of final product, and, where applicable, on the quality audit reports and/or quality records of the previously demonstrated capability and performance of subcontractors;
>
> (c) establish and maintain quality records of acceptable subcontractors.

Quality Manual

I suggest paraphrasing the standard throughout this section. Wording should closely resemble text from the standard to avoid distorting the intent. You may choose to amplify your policy to include other aspects of supplier quality.

Price Tag Alone

Here is another area where W. Edwards Deming's philosophies apply. The fourth of his fourteen points can be addressed here.

> • *End the practice of awarding business on price tag alone.*

Purchasing departments customarily operate on orders to seek the lowest-priced vendor. Frequently, this leads to low quality. Deming insists that companies should seek the best quality and work to achieve it with a single supplier for any one item in a long-term relationship.

Procedure

First let us define "subcontractor." Most auditors are interpreting this to be any outside party providing goods and/or services. The primary purpose of 4.6.2a is to establish that a supplier (you) cannot select subcontractors (your suppliers) on the basis of cost alone. Quality *must* be a consideration. For many companies, this is a particularly challenging requirement to meet, especially if they are just now developing their first formal quality system. This is primarily because of a lack of experience and knowledge of the different approaches available.

Many companies have tried the old "grandfathering" approach with no formal basis. This won't work with a good auditor. Subcontractors or suppliers may be selected by any number of acceptable criteria. Let's begin by listing some of the many acceptable approaches:

Suppliers to manufacturers:

- Suppliers registered to an ISO 9000 series quality standard

- Products certified under a recognized private-sector or government program

- Site assessment by a qualified auditor

- Examination of supplier's verification data (e.g., laboratory or test reports, certificate of analysis, process control charts)

- Product qualification (first article inspection, evaluation of sample products)

- Historical performance with an ongoing monitoring or sampling program (previously demonstrated capability and performance must be documented)

- Sole source supplier (typically because of proprietary knowledge or a unique capability not available elsewhere)

Suppliers for repair or service centers:

- Suppliers registered to an ISO 9000 series quality standard

- Site assessment by a qualified auditor

- Suppliers approved for use by specific customer (for that specific customer only)

- Original Equipment Manufacturer (O.E.M.) supplied components or parts

- Distributors authorized by the O.E.M. to supply components or parts

- Suppliers to the O.E.M. (providing O.E.M. components)

- Sole source supplier (including obsolete or discontinued items)

Subcontractors for repair:

- Service centers registered to an ISO 9000 series quality standard

- Site assessment by a qualified auditor

- The O.E.M.

- Service centers authorized by the O.E.M.

- Service centers approved for use by specific customer (for that specific customer only)

Subcontractors for calibration/testing/servicing:

- National Standards Laboratories (NIST in the U.S., INMS in Canada, CENAM in Mexico)

- National Standards Laboratories of other countries (may not meet government requirements or standards—verify acceptance prior to use)

- State Weights and Measures Laboratories participating in the "State Standards Program" administered by NIST (Reference NIST Special Publication 791)

- Laboratories accredited by a recognized body or organization

- Laboratories registered to an ISO 9000 series quality standard

- Site assessment by a qualified auditor

- Service centers approved for use by specific customer (for that specific customer only)

Labor: Consultants and Temporary Employees:

- Consultants and temporary agencies registered to an ISO 9000 series quality standard

- Site assessment by a qualified auditor

- Resumes, training, degrees, certificates, etc.

- Consultants and/or temporary labor provided, specified, or approved for use by specific customer (for that specific customer only)

- Accredited educational institutions (colleges, technical schools, etc.)

Of course, you will also need to have (obtain) objective evidence supporting the basis for selection of each subcontractor or supplier.

Now, let's examine some of the selection criteria mentioned individually.

Suppliers Registered to an ISO 9000 Series Quality Standard

This is the whole reason for the ISO 9000 registration process: to reduce both the number of audits your company hosts by customers and the number it is compelled to conduct. Take advantage of your suppliers' being registered by recognizing and accepting *their* registration. Many companies complete the registration process only to find they are still being audited by their customers. In most instances, this is because their customer's quality system has not yet been revised to recognize and accept the registration of their suppliers. Usually this is an oversight.

Because there are a number of "non-accredited" registrars, registrars accredited by unrecognized agencies, and registrars operating under questionable MOUs with other registrars, I suggest defining *what* you consider an acceptable registration. For example:

> • *Suppliers registered to the ISO 9000 series quality standard by an NACCB, RvC, or ANSI/RAB accredited registrar.*

Of course, you have to determine who an acceptable accreditation body is. If you don't really feel comfortable in doing this, play it safe. For U.S. companies, I suggest using the sentence below "as-is."

> • *Suppliers registered to the ISO 9000 series quality standard by an IAAR (Independent Association of Accredited Registrars) member.*

That will cover the *vast* majority of reputable registrars operating in the U.S. and Canada.

Mexican companies may wish to consider only those registrars accredited by the "Dirección General de Normas" (DGN), because registration certificates from registrars not accredited under Mexico's National Accreditation and Certification System will not be accepted for regulatory and procurement purposes.

You must also consider a company's scope of registration. A company defines what areas and to what extent registration is to cover in its "scope of activities." A company can register specific locations or even specific product lines while excluding others. Ensure that the product lines or services in which you are interested are included in their scope. This is normally listed along with the ISO 9000 standard to which a company is registered. In most cases, you can simply ask the company to provide you a photocopy of their registration certificate as evidence of their compliance to ISO 9000.

A listing of all companies registered in the United States and Canada can be found in the "ISO 9000 Registered Company Directory" compiled by *Quality Systems Update* and distributed by:

CEEM Information Services
P.O. Box 200
Fairfax Station, VA 22039-0200
Tel: (703) 250-5900
         1-800-745-5565
Fax: (703) 250-5313

Dun & Bradstreet
ISO 9000 Services
899 Eaton Ave.
Bethlehem, PA 18025
Tel: 1-800-476-2446
Fax: (610) 882-7008

Dun and Bradstreet can supply specific company information, including confirmation of a company's ISO 9000 registration, effective date, the specific standard and scope of activities to which the certificate applies, and contact information. Upon request, Dun and Bradstreet can compile a state- or industry-specific list of ISO 9000–registered companies. A complete list of U.S. and Canadian ISO 9000 companies is also available by subscription. Any business can call between 8:30 A.M. and 5:00 P.M. Eastern Time to request this information, which will be delivered by mail or faxed within the hour.

A listing of all companies registered by an NACCB-accredited registrar is published in "The DTI QA Register" on sale from:

Her Majesty's Stationery Office
HMSO Publications Centre
P.O. Box 276
London SW8 5DT
Telephone number when called from the U.S.: 011-44-71-873-9090
(This is an international phone call to the U.K.)
Fax: 011-44-71-873-8200 (Credit card orders accepted.)

♡ Other Forms of "Certification" (NAPM, NADCAP, NUPIC, Etc.)

The National Association of Purchasing Management (NAPM) Rail Industry Group Quality System Standard Sub-committee (QSSS) has adopted the Association of American Railroads Specification for Quality Assurance (M-1003, Chapter 2) as the basis for evaluating suppliers. The program, initiated in 1989, is the result of a joint effort by the committee members representing major railroads in the United States and Canada, as well as representatives of suppliers to the rail industry. Audits are performed by auditors accredited by the Association of American Railroads, ASQC, or the Canadian Standards Association—Quality Management Institute.

This evaluation is designed to determine whether suppliers' quality processes are controlled and in compliance with M-1003. Suppliers must then be reaudited every three years to maintain approval status. Once a supplier has been evaluated and recognized, it will be added to the NAPM (National Association of Purchasing Management) Rail Industry Group QSSS's list of quality suppliers. This status might then be accepted by other railroads within the Rail Industry Group.

The National Aerospace and Defense Contractors Accreditation Program (NADCAP) is a third-party accreditation program administered by the Society of Automotive Engineers' (SAE) Performance Review Institute (PRI). It was founded on July 1, 1990. The program primarily focuses on nondestructive testing laboratories, but also includes materials testing laboratories, distributors, and heat-treating suppliers.

For a complete listing of companies accredited by NADCAP, reference the NADCAP Qualified Manufacturers List, available from:

Performance Review Institute   Tel: (412) 772-1616
163 Thornhill Road   800-352-7293
Warrendale, PA 15086-7527   Fax: (412) 772-1699

Similar programs are operated by the Nuclear Utilities Procurement Inspection Council (NUPIC) for the nuclear power industry. These certification programs are all very similar to ISO 9000 registration. The primary difference is that they are focused toward specific industries. All could be considered an acceptable basis for supplier selection if you include them under your quality system. If you have concerns surrounding this point, you should discuss them with your registrar in advance of selection.

For more information, refer to the *Directory of Private Sector Product Certification Programs—NIST SP 774* (see Appendix B for ordering information).

Site Assessment by a Qualified Auditor

This, too, is fairly straightforward, but it can be very time-consuming and expensive to maintain. If you choose this basis for some of your suppliers, be sure to create a formal audit system and qualify your auditors.

When developing your "Site Audit" system, reference the ISO 10011 series, "Guidelines for Auditing Quality Systems." It consists of only three documents and offers excellent advice on the format of a basic audit system. Several organizations are now offering formal training to the ISO 10011 series standards.

Another source for guidance is U.S. Military Handbook H 50, "Evaluation of a Contractor's Quality Program." Although this handbook was written to evaluate contractors for compliance with MIL-Q-9858A, you will find the handbook largely applicable to an ISO 9000 system. Many of the terms and expressions are exactly the same.

If auditing your calibration subcontractors, reference NCSL RP-2, "Evaluation of Measurement Control Systems and Calibration Laboratories." It even contains a basic audit checklist as an attachment. If you are imposing MIL-STD-45662A, "Calibration System Requirements" (currently being replaced by ANSI/NCSL Z540-1) on your calibration subcontractors, reference MIL-HDBK-52B, "Evaluation of Contractor's Calibration System." It also contains a checklist, found in its appendix. If you are imposing AQAP-6 (Allied Quality Assurance Publication—6, "NATO Measurement and Calibration Requirements for Industry,") on your calibration subcontractors, reference AQAP-7, "Guide for the Evaluation of a Contractor's Measurement and Calibration System for Compliance with AQAP-6." While AQAP-7 does not contain a checklist, it does list "significant questions" after each section, which could be used in creating a checklist.

A new U.S. national quality standard for calibration systems was released in 1994, titled ANSI/NCSL Z540-1, "General Requirements for Calibration Laboratories and Measuring and Test Equipment." This standard is in harmony with ISO standards (ISO 9000 and ISO Guide 25) and serves as the basis for the "U.S. Calibration Laboratory Accreditation Program." ANSI/NCSL Z540-1 has been adopted by the U.S. DoD and is expected eventually to replace MIL-STD-45662A (all branches of the DoD were represented on the committee that developed ANSI/NCSL Z540-1).

External Auditors

Several quality consulting companies also offer auditing services. Don't paint yourself into a corner by thinking only of your internal people. When establishing the qualification requirements for auditors, allow yourself to use external contracted auditors to perform site audits. This can be a great help if you fall behind schedule in maintaining your subcontractors or suppliers on your "Approved Vendor List" (AVL). In many instances, if the subcontractor has already audited a particular company, you may be able to obtain the audit report at a reduced cost. Remember to define your criteria for selecting and using external auditors.

Examination of Supplier's Verification Data

This can include, but is not limited to, the following:

- Laboratory reports
- Inspection/test reports
- Statistical reports
- Certificates of Analysis (C of A)
- Material Test Reports (MTRs)
- Process control charts

In order to enjoy the benefits of little or no receiving inspection, a company must establish strong partnerships with its subcontractors and suppliers. Developing criteria for, and accepting, your supplier's verification data is a significant step toward this goal. The long-term benefits can be well worth the effort.

☹ *Certificates of Compliance/Conformance*

Many subcontractors offer a "Certificate of Compliance/Conformance" (C of C). These certificates are rarely of any value. They generally state that the subcontractor "certifies" that the product meets the requirements of your purchase order. These certificates are often preprinted and very nonspecific. Although there are exceptions to every rule, *most* C of C's contain so little information that they are considered worthless.

A certificate of compliance is intended to be provided with chemicals or items (lots or batches) that *cannot be fully inspected upon completion*. A certificate of compliance (conformance) *must* state compliance with an industry-recognized standard or other criteria. Great care should be taken in determining whether you will recognize a C of C and what minimum criteria must be present.

✈ *The Fastener Act*

While a certificate of conformance can be an accepted means of approving a supplier, the most valid are supplied by an independent source. A certificate of conformance issued internally by the supplier must be viewed with skepticism. To emphasize this point, let me describe what has happened in the fastener (screws, bolts, etc.) industry.

Approximately 80% of the fasteners consumed in the U.S. are imported from China, Indonesia, Japan, Malaysia, or Taiwan, and more than half of those do not conform to their stated specifications, including stainless steel that rusts and locknuts that loosen. To date, more than $26 million in fines have been levied for false certification of fasteners.

According to an industry representative, who prefers to remain anonymous, ". . . There is a tremendous base of good standards available, but too many companies buy on price alone. A manufacturer should order fasteners for their specific application and at least ask the supplier for their source and chemistry. If the supplier cannot provide it, buy elsewhere." Many suppliers reportedly have two quality groups: a better quality for companies that watch what they are buying and ask questions, and a poorer quality for everyone else.

Falsification of certificates of conformance was so widespread that the problem eventually led to Congress passing the "Fastener Quality Act of 1990" (Public Law 101-592). This law requires the following:

- Certain fasteners sold in commerce must conform to the specifications in which they are represented to be manufactured

- NVLAP must provide for accreditation of laboratories engaged in fastener testing

- Standardized methods for inspection, testing, and certification of fasteners must be used in critical applications

While the "Fastener Act" will help mitigate problems in that industry, there are many other industries where the same basic problem exists.

Product Qualification

Product qualification is normally accomplished through one of the following methods:

- First article inspection (a sample of the supplier's "first run" submitted for your approval before continuing with production)

- Engineering evaluation of individual components, materials, parts, and subassemblies

First article inspection and/or an engineering evaluation would indicate that the supplier is *capable* of providing an acceptable product. However, it does not ensure that the level of quality remains constant. Approving that supplier on a provisional basis would allow you to monitor that supplier's performance until you are satisfied that the quality is consistent.

First Article Inspection: As the term implies, first article inspection is simply an early inspection of products provided by a subcontractor. This is a very minimal and inconsistent means of approving a subcontractor. It is not uncommon for companies providing product for "first article inspection" to manufacture "marginal" product that is held. Good product is then submitted to the customer for "first article inspection." Once accepted, the marginal product is shipped to the customer.

Engineering Evaluation: It is common for manufacturers who have engineering and design elements on staff to select and approve suppliers on the basis of "product qualification." This method is similar to the "first article" inspection, but is generally more thorough. These products are typically standard catalog items in which one or more are purchased and technically evaluated (qualified) for acceptability. Engineering staff normally acquire the manufacturer's published specifications and test the component or assembly to verify that the information is correct.

"Product qualification" can be documented in the form of individual tests or, if tested in a prototype of the final design, as the parts list itself (Bill of Materials—BOM). Your quality system should define which method is used. It generally pays to also test alternative equivalent (substitute) components for those items considered "critical" so that production will not have to wait on unexpected delays from suppliers should they occur.

◇ Published Specifications

At this point, I'm typically asked why a company should go to the expense of verifying a manufacturer's published specification. After all, doesn't anyone trust one another anymore? First, trust is something that should be earned; second, misinformation is not always intentional.

A few years ago, I was involved in evaluating a device in which the manufacturer's manual stated one specification and their marketing advertisements stated another. The advertised specification was much "tighter" than the manual stated. After testing more than twenty units, we found that less than half met the manual's stated specification, and none met the advertised specification.

Upon further research, we learned that the manufacturer was assembling these units on the same assembly line as an identical, but much less accurate, unit. The less accurate units were being mixed with the more accurate units before final marking and shipping. In addition, misinformation had been given to their marketing division, resulting in erroneous advertising literature. They lacked a formal, effective quality system.

▤ Logbooks and Notebooks

Engineers love to keep logbooks or notebooks of their activities. Although this is quite handy for the individual, it may be difficult for others to understand and usually lacks consistency within the organization. A simple solution is to create a "Product Qualification" form for documenting such evaluations. With a little creativity, you can standardize a form that will ensure evaluations are more consistent and complete.

If you choose to continue to use logbooks or notebooks, they may be considered as either documents or quality records requiring the appropriate level of control (i.e., distribution control, revision control).

● Catalog Items and Distributors

In many instances, Engineering may approve a product that is a standard catalog item, but the O.E.M. only supplies large orders. The only cost-effective way of purchasing the item is through a distributor. The problem is that the distributor is an unapproved vendor. To address this issue, one company added the following paragraph to its quality system:

> *For standard catalog types of items, development engineering selects the part manufacturer. The buyer has the latitude to purchase from various distributors providing the part manufacturer is on the Approved Vendor list.*

On the surface, this seems like a reasonable approach. However, it makes far too many assumptions. Will the company continue to purchase items when things like these occur?

- Parts arrive damaged in shipment from improper packaging

- The wrong catalog item is sent by mistake

- A similar but unqualified item is substituted without advance notice

- Electrostatic discharge–sensitive (ESDS) components arrive repackaged in the wrong type of packaging (thus being damaged either through the distributor's handling or by your receiving personnel opening and improperly handling the components because the proper markings were then missing)

As you can easily see, these examples could be just the beginning of your problems. Distributors handling product must be approved and monitored just like any other supplier.

Historical Performance

As mentioned earlier, many companies have tried the old "grandfathering" approach with no formal basis. "Grandfathering" subcontractors or suppliers is perfectly acceptable, provided you have historical evidence to support their selection. A good auditor will ask to see this historical evidence, which generally exists in the form of inspection records or supplier performance monitoring.

Most companies selecting subcontractors on the basis of historical performance incorporate the data collected into an ongoing "Supplier Rating System," where each supplier's performance is constantly monitored, reviewed, and evaluated.

Many companies will gather limited information (review of a subcontractor's or supplier's quality manual, for example) about a potential subcontractor or supplier, then approve them on a provisional basis until enough historical performance data has been gathered for proper evaluation and formal approval.

Provisional Approval of Subcontractors

In some cases, you may need to use a subcontractor before you can arrange a site audit. In other instances, it may cost too much to arrange a site audit. In either case, you may wish to approve a supplier on a provisional basis until a more comprehensive evaluation can be conducted. For example, you may need to purchase a larger quantity of product from a supplier to determine that the quality is consistent. Provisional approval is often based on the successful completion of a questionnaire.

The following criteria may also be considered. However, these points provide no evidence whatsoever that a supplier can perform satisfactorily. They should not be used alone, even as a basis for provisional approval:

- Reputation (industry leaders, consultants, etc.)
- Past experiences (undocumented)
- Recommendations from staff (unsubstantiated)

When subcontractors are approved on a provisional basis, that condition should be thoroughly described in your procedure. Be sure to address what actions must be taken for a supplier to become a fully approved subcontractor and how long the provisional status is valid. Also include this status on your ASL (Approved Supplier List) for those suppliers, when applicable.

Sole Source Suppliers

In many instances, there are items that simply are not available from more than one source. Reasons for this include the following:

- Patents
- New technology
- Obsolete technology
- Discontinued production

Approving suppliers who are the sole source is completely acceptable, but your auditor may ask how you know that a supplier *is* the sole source. Be prepared to back up this claim. This *justification* will serve as your documented basis for selection of that supplier.

O.E.M. Components or Services

Repair and service organizations maintaining equipment have little choice in approving their Original Equipment Manufacturers (O.E.M.) for components and parts. In many instances, an equipment manufacturer will not sell replacement components and parts directly to the user (or will have excessive minimum order quantities).

In this situation, the user (you) may be forced to approve

- Distributors authorized by the O.E.M. to supply components or parts

- Suppliers to the O.E.M. (providing O.E.M. components or parts)

These suppliers are similar, in many respects, to a sole source supplier. For more technically sophisticated equipment, which you are unable to repair or service, you may be forced to approve

- The O.E.M.

- Service centers authorized by the O.E.M.

Some O.E.M.s establish excessive minimum order quantities or prices as a marketing strategy, essentially forcing the users to send their equipment to the O.E.M. for repair and servicing.

Customer-Approved Suppliers

The customer is always right, even when wrong. Customer approval of subcontractors or suppliers is recognized as a legitimate basis for selecting a supplier for that customer's work *only*. Be sure to obtain a letter, or document the conversation(s), where approval was given for each supplier.

National Standards Laboratories

Referencing ISO 9001, clause 4.11, we see that inspection, measuring, and test equipment is normally calibrated "against certified equipment having a known valid relationship to internationally or nationally recognized standards."

This statement automatically "approves" your own national standards laboratory and the national standards laboratories of countries that have mutual recognition agreements with your country.

Most companies can easily have their calibration needs met by a commercial calibration laboratory (reference the NCSL "Directory of Standards Laboratories"). However, if your company has high-end or state-of-the-art instrumentation or special calibration requirements, you may need the services of your national standards laboratory.

NIST (U.S.A.)

The National Institute of Standards and Technology (NIST) is responsible for primary standards of physical measurements used in the U.S. as formally established by Congress. NIST Special Publication 250, "NIST Calibration

Services Users Guide," provides detailed descriptions of the currently available NIST calibration services, special-test services, and measurement assurance programs. For information, phone (301) 975-2002.

A companion document to SP 250 is NIST Special Publication 260, "NIST Standard Reference Materials Catalog." This document describes more than 1100 Standard Reference Materials (SRMs) certified by NIST for use in industrial quality control, materials testing, environmental testing, and clinical testing applications. A copy of SP 260 may be obtained by calling (301) 975-6776.

NRC-INMS (Canada)

In Canada, the National Research Council's Institute for National Measurement Standards (INMS) is responsible for primary standards of physical measurements as formally established by acts such as the Weights and Measures Act and the National Research Council Act. In 1990, Canada signed bilateral agreements with the U.S. National Institute of Standards and Technology (NIST) and Britain's National Physical Laboratory, affirming the equivalence of each other's national measurement standards. A similar agreement has been signed with the Commonwealth Scientific and Industrial Research Organization of Australia.

CENAM (Mexico)

The Centro Nacional de Metrologia (CENAM) is responsible for the National Reference Standards used in Mexico. CENAM was created as the head of a National Measurement System, giving coherence to the various accredited laboratories that offer metrological services to industry in the areas of calibration and testing. Furthermore, CENAM maintains direct collaboration with other related federal government entities, in addition to a reciprocal interchange of information between the official metrological agencies of other industrialized countries.

The organizational structure of CENAM consists of a General Administration that oversees five specific areas:

- Mechanical Metrology
- Electrical Metrology
- Reference Material Metrology
- Physics Metrology
- Technical Services

The area of Reference Material Metrology also offers "Certification of Technical Training" in addition to "Certification of Reference Materials" (CRMs).

NORAMET (NAFTA)

While the national standards laboratories of the U.S. and Canada have had longstanding relations, until recently this has not included Mexico. In 1994, the North American Collaboration on Calibration Standards and Services (NORAMET) was formed to develop closer collaboration among the NAFTA countries, to coordinate research in the development of new and improved measurement standards and services, to optimize the use of resources and services, to encourage the sharing of facilities, and to improve measurement services and their accessibility.

👍 Calibration and Testing Laboratory Accreditation

Many companies have asked why calibration subcontractors cannot be selected (approved) based on "previously demonstrated capability and performance." As we read in the standard, selection of subcontractors must consider "the impact of subcontracted product (service) on the quality of final product." Calibration is a very technical service in which companies subcontract virtually an entire element of the standard (clause 4.11). This service cannot be verified through a review of calibration and testing certificates alone. To address this need, several accreditation programs have been developed.

A2LA (The American Association for Laboratory Accreditation) is a non-profit, membership society administering a laboratory accreditation system for both testing and calibration laboratories. A2LA has a Memo of Understanding (MOU) with the U.S. Navy Naval Shipyard Laboratory Accreditation Program (NSLAP), and international mutual recognition agreements with HOKLAS (Hong Kong), NATA (Australia), and TELARC (New Zealand).

NVLAP (National Voluntary Laboratory Accreditation Program) is a program administered by NIST and headquartered in Gaithersburg, MD. The program was established in 1976 to accredit laboratories found competent to perform specific tests or types of tests. NVLAP has already accredited more than 1100 testing laboratories. In 1993, the program was expanded to include calibration laboratories.

State Weights and Measures Laboratories have the option of participating in the "State Standards Program," administered by the NIST Office of Weights and Measures. This certification program allows participating state laboratories to be viewed as an extension of NIST.

If you are conducting business internationally and have operations abroad, you may wish to also take advantage of those countries' laboratory accreditation programs.

Canada: The Calibration Laboratory Assessment Service (CLAS) was established by the National Research Council (NRC) in August 1988 to organize, in cooperation with the Standards Council of Canada (SCC), the Canadian Calibration Network (CCN). To become a member of the CCN, a calibration laboratory must be technically assessed by the NRC to criteria that are based on ISO Guide 25, then accredited by the SCC.

Mexico: The Service for Certification of Calibration Laboratories (SECLAC—Servicio de Certificacion de Laboratorios de Calibración) was established by the Centro Nacional de Metrologia (CENAM) in April 1994 to organize, in cooperation with the Director General de Normalizacion (DGN), the Mexican National Calibration System (SNC—Sistema Nacional de Calibración). To become a member of the SNC, a calibration laboratory must be technically assessed by the CENAM, then successfully undergo a quality audit by the DGN. The SECLAC Program is primarily based on the criteria of ISO Guide 25 and is essentially patterned after the Canadian CLAS Program.

North American Calibration Cooperation (NACC): On April 29, 1994, the U.S., Canada, and Mexico signed the North American Calibration Cooperation (NACC) Agreement. This agreement will eventually ensure mutual recognition of calibration laboratory accreditation programs among the three countries.

For a complete listing of calibration and testing laboratories accredited by A2LA, reference:

	Available from:
Directory	American Association for Laboratory Accreditation 656 Quince Orchard Road Gaithersburg, MD 20878
	Tel: (301) 670-1377 Fax:(301) 869-1495

For a complete listing of calibration and testing laboratories accredited by NVLAP, reference:

	Available from:
NIST Special Publication 810 *National Voluntary Laboratory Accreditation Program Directory*	Laboratory Accreditation Program National Institute of Standards and Technology Bldg. 411, Rm. A162 Gaithersburg, MD 20899
Listing also available on the NVLAP BBS (301) 948-2058	Tel: (301) 975-4016 Fax:(301) 926-2884

For a complete listing of laboratories participating in the "State Standards Program," reference:

Available from:

NIST Special Publication 791
*State Weights and Measures
Laboratories: State Standards
Program Description and
Directory*

The Office of Weights and
Measures
National Institute of Standards
and Technology
Bldg. 101, Rm. A617
Gaithersburg, MD 20899

Tel: (301) 975-4014
Fax: (301) 926-0647

For a complete listing of accredited calibration and testing laboratories in Canada, reference:

Available from:

Directory of Accredited
Calibration and Testing
Laboratories (CAN-P-1550)

Note: If purchasing this directory from the U.S., you will
need to pay for it in Canadian
dollars. The most economical
way to do this is to obtain an
International Money Order
from the U.S. Post Office (Cost:
$0.75 each).

Standards Council of Canada
1200-45 O'Connor
Ottawa, Ontario Canada
K1P 6N7

Tel: (613) 238-3222
       800-267-8220 (In Canada only)
Fax: (613) 995-4564

An official listing of Accredited Calibration Laboratories is published in an official gazette that is available from:

Director del Area de Metrologia
Dirección General de Normas (DGN)
Puente de Tecamachalco No. 6
Col. Lomas de Tecamachalco
Secc. Fuentes de Tecamachalco
Naucalpan, Edo. de Mex. C.P. 53950
Tel: 011-52-57-29-94-81
Fax: 011-52-55-89-93-43

✎ **Note**

A few poorly trained ISO 9000 auditors will accept past historical performance as a basis for selection of calibration subcontractors. This is generally the result of a breakdown in communication between the registrar's home office in Europe and their auditors working in North America. Most European countries have national calibration laboratory accreditation programs. In the U.K., for example, the National Physical Laboratory (NPL: equivalent to NIST in the U.S.) is complemented by the National Measurement Accreditation Service (NAMAS), which assesses, accredits, and monitors calibration and testing laboratories. Because the vast majority of calibration laboratories in the U.K. are accredited by NAMAS, a government agency, selection of calibration subcontractors is not viewed as a serious concern to ISO 9000 registrars. Their auditors simply verify that the calibration subcontractor is NAMAS-accredited and look no further. Therefore, a U.K.-based registrar, unaware that a similar program was not yet fully developed in the U.S., may take the position that selection criteria for calibration subcontractors was noncritical. As these misunderstandings surface, I think that you will find most legitimate registrars taking the position described earlier. This is a problem that will eventually solve itself.

Other Purchasing Considerations

After a supplier has met your minimum requirements, there may be other factors to consider. For example:

- **Price.** That's right. A subcontractor (supplier) must first be qualified "on the basis of their ability to meet subcontract requirements including quality system and any specific quality-assurance requirements" before consideration can be given to price. Poor quality at a great price does not equal value.

- **Manufacturing production capability.** Can the subcontractor supply the quantities you need by the date you require?

- **Personnel.** Are the subcontractor's labor relations stable, or are they subject to strikes or work stoppages that would interrupt supply?

- **Geographic/political considerations.** Is the subcontractor located in an area prone to natural disaster or political upheaval? Do communication or language barriers exist? Are delivery schedules followed?

- **Financial.** Is the subcontractor financially stable?

- **Safety.** A "Workers Compensation Modification Rate" of 1 point or less is a typical requirement (also called an EMR—Experience Modification Rate). This is an indication of a company's safety record. The lower the point rate, the better their safety record. This translates into lower insurance rates (which eventually are passed on to the customer) and less likelihood of liability claims. For obvious reasons, most companies prefer to do business with subcontractors (partners) who have effective safety programs. Recognizing that small divisions of larger companies may have a higher EMR due to other locations, a copy of that particular division's OSHA 200 log may be taken into consideration.

- **Litigation concerns.** Does the subcontractor have a history of being sued by other customers?

This list is far too short to address every company's needs, but you get the general idea.

 Office Supplies and Other Support Services

Be sure not to say something like "all purchased products or services will be obtained from approved suppliers or subcontractors." You generally wouldn't want to control whoever you purchase office supplies from. Right? Or how about the copier service company, the night-time cleaning service, the lawn service that maintains the plant grounds? Section 4.6.2b clearly defines the focus of subcontractor evaluation and selection to be on ". . . *quality of final product (service). . . .*" This is another excellent example of why you should try to paraphrase the text contained in ISO 9000 with as little tailoring as possible.

 Who Approves Subcontractors?

This seems like an obvious question. However, it is often not addressed in a company's procedures. Normally this is the responsibility of the purchasing department, but some manufacturing companies have given this responsibility to the engineering department, because they are evaluating and determining the suitability of specific components and subassemblies. Other companies rely on the quality department for this function. In several instances this responsibility is shared.

 Approved Suppliers List (ASL)

The standard requires that you:

> *(c) establish and maintain quality records of acceptable subcontractors.*

These records can be difficult to manage when trying to determine "which" subcontractors or suppliers are approved for use. The method of choice for quickly communicating this information to the purchaser is an "Approved Suppliers List" (ASL) (a.k.a., Approved Vendor List—AVL).

Although an ASL is clearly not a requirement of the standard, they are common. An ISO 9000 auditor will be attempting to verify the following:

- That the ASL is approved and maintained under document control

- That the ASL correctly reflects the approval of subcontractors based on *quality records*

An ASL can also exist in the form of a computer data base. In this case, you should have defined security levels, allowing access to change or update the system only to those individuals responsible for approving subcontractors or suppliers. Purchasing agents who do not have this authority should have "read only" access.

Revision and Issue Control of an ASL

If using a paper system, be sure to remember and address both revision control (you should be adding and deleting suppliers) and issue control of your "Approved Suppliers List." (Make sure those individuals who actually approve purchasing have the most current version.) This is a common oversight.

Disapproval and Removal of Subcontractors from the ASL

When defining "the type and extent of control exercised" over your subcontractors, remember to include a basis for disqualification and removal from your ASL. Be specific, but don't limit yourself by establishing strict criteria for immediate removal. For example:

> *Suppliers who exceed 15% rejection levels will be notified of unsatisfactory performance and reviewed by quality or purchasing management.*

Establish "feedback" mechanisms for notifying substandard suppliers of specific concerns. Of course, the type of action for removal will depend in part on the method initially used for approving and monitoring each individual subcontractor. For example, you must address ISO 9000–registered subcontractors who lose their registration and subcontractors who fail a site audit.

Freight Carriers and Haulers

Many assessors have interpreted the standard such that they believe it is a requirement to assess freight carriers and haulers and include them on your approved subcontractors list. I agree that this is a good idea, but it is not a specified requirement unless *contractually specified*. This interpretation is based on the fact that delivery is specifically addressed as a separate topic. Reference Section 4.15.6 for a detailed discussion.

◇ *Suppliers Who "Drop-Ship" on Your Behalf*

This has been a topic of great debate. Some registrars require registration of suppliers who make drop shipments on behalf of the registered company; others do not. Clearly this is not required by the standard. Again, the standard states:

> *The supplier shall evaluate and select subcontractors on the basis of their ability to meet subcontract requirements including quality system and any specific quality-assurance requirements*

and

> *define the type and extent of control exercised by the supplier over subcontractors.*

Whether the subcontractor has an ISO 9000–compliant quality system or not doesn't matter. If they are meeting the requirements that you have outlined and you can show that they are meeting those requirements, then you are in compliance with ISO 9000.

While you could make registration of subcontractors a requirement under your quality system, ISO 9000 itself does not require *any* of your subcontractors or suppliers to be registered.

All of this having been said, you can easily see that this is an area that could be abused. Your ISO 9000 auditor will be attempting to determine whether you have met both the requirements and the *intent* of ISO 9000 when selecting all subcontractors, including those who drop-ship directly to your customer. If this is a concern, you would be well advised to discuss this with potential registrars in advance.

QUALITY MANUAL

6.3 Purchasing Data

Purchasing documents shall contain data clearly describing the product ordered, including, where applicable:

(a) the type, class, grade, or other precise identification;

(b) the title or other positive identification, and applicable issues of specifications, drawings, process requirements, inspection instructions, and other relevant technical data, including requirements for approval or qualification of product, procedures, process equipment, and personnel;

(c) the title, number, and issue of the quality-system standard to be supplied.

ABC Company will review and approve purchasing documents for adequacy of the specified requirements prior to release.

Quality Manual

This clause is very clear and straightforward until the last sentence: "review and approve purchasing documents." In a small company, it is not uncommon to see one person both request and order parts. Therefore, no real check and balance exists. Many registrars expect to see one person act as the "requester" and another actually review and approve the order. In fact, most large companies have preprinted purchase order forms with a "Requested by" and "Approved by" field. The standard itself is not clear in stating that a person cannot review and approve his or her own purchase order. However, this is definitely a point that should be discussed and resolved with your registrar in advance.

A similar area in question would be where the "requester" was a computer. "Manufacturing Resource Planning" software packages (MRP Systems) generating purchasing requests based on projected work and existing orders are now commonplace. This should also be addressed in advance.

Procedure

In this procedure, be sure to give enough detail describing how to complete a purchase request or purchase order as is necessary. Many companies require additional approvals based on the dollar value of the order. And remember the following:

> *There are basically two types of purchasing requirements; those that are documented and those that are forgotten.*

External Purchasing Groups

Many large companies utilize purchasing groups external to their immediate operation. By external, I mean that they are not under the same quality system. In some instances, they may actually be a subcontractor. In any event, the best way to address such an external purchasing group is as if it were a subcontractor.

Paperless Purchasing Systems

Since many auditors are uncomfortable with "paperless" systems, you should discuss this with potential registrars in advance of your selection. Make sure that the registrar you choose is familiar with these types of systems and accepts their use. You may be surprised at some of the answers you get.

EDI (Electronic Data Interchange)

If you use EDI (Electronic Data Interchange), be sure to include it in your SOP. Review and approval can be indicated by the use of security levels incorporated into your computer system. Don't rewrite the software manual. Just reference it in your procedure and give a brief overview of what the system does, along with basic instructions for human interaction that are unique to your operation.

Computerized Forecasting

Some production systems (MRPs) review existing inventory and place orders based on production planning. Be sure to describe how your system functions in your SOP. Again, don't rewrite the software manual. Just reference it in your procedure and give a brief overview of what the system does, along with basic instructions for human interaction that are unique to your operation.

You may choose to state in your procedure that production planning, personnel entering orders, are actually the requesters. Further, you may choose to state that contract review and approval also serves a dual function in approving purchases. Of course, if this is all automated, you must also ensure that only approved suppliers are used.

> **QUALITY MANUAL**
>
> **6.4** Verification of Purchased Product
>
> **6.4.1** Verification at Subcontractor's Premises
>
> Where ABC Company proposes to verify purchased product at the subcontractor's premises, ABC Company will specify verification arrangements and the method of product release in the purchasing documents.

Quality Manual

Where this section of the standard refers to the *supplier*, that is your company or organization.

Procedure

The most simple and direct means of dealing with this requirement is to add a statement to your standard company terms and conditions of purchase, normally printed in very small type on the reverse of a purchase order. I suggest the following:

> *Inspection*
> *The ABC Company, or a representative of ABC Company, shall be afforded the right to verify at the source that the purchased product or service conforms to the specified requirements. Any audit, inspection, or test made on the premises of the Seller, or its supplier, shall be without additional charge. The Seller shall provide all reasonable facilities and assistance for the safety and convenience of the auditors/inspectors in the performance of their duties. All audits, inspections, and tests on the premises of the Seller or its supplier shall be performed in such a manner as not to unduly delay work. Such verification shall not be used by the Seller as evidence of effective control of quality. Verification by the ABC Company shall not absolve the Seller of the responsibility to provide acceptable product, nor shall it preclude subsequent rejection by the ABC Company.*

This is fairly common wording, but I further suggest you get input (or concurrence) from your company lawyer. If a problem were to develop, you would certainly want your lawyer both comfortable and confident with your position. This statement is sometimes called a "Right of Access" clause.

> **Q U A L I T Y   M A N U A L**
>
> **6.4.2** Customer Verification of Subcontracted Product
>
> Where specified in the contract, ABC Company's customer or the customer's representative shall be afforded the right to verify at the subcontractor's premises and ABC Company's premises that subcontracted product conforms to specified requirements. Such verification shall not be used by ABC Company as evidence of effective control of quality by the subcontractor.
>
> Verification by the customer shall not absolve the ABC Company of the responsibility to provide acceptable product, nor shall it preclude subsequent rejection by the customer.

📖 Quality Manual

To address this requirement in your quality manual, I suggest paraphrasing this clause, placing your company name everywhere it states "the supplier."

📄 Procedure

Whew! Good thing we just added that blanket statement about verification on the back of all your purchase order forms. If we hadn't, then you would have to go through each and every individual contract every time you subcontracted work (or set up some bureaucratic system to oversee subcontracted work). The wording in the previous section required your supplier to allow access to you *or* your representative. In this case, your representative could be your customer. In any case, you're set now!

📁 Records

- Approved subcontractors/suppliers list (optional)

- Basis for subcontractor selection (evidence of ISO 9000 certification/registration, site audit report, historical performance data, engineering evaluation/product qualification reports, etc.)

- Purchase orders (you will need to be able to show objective evidence that purchase orders are being reviewed and approved)

☞ *Guidance*

For further guidance, refer to:

ISO 9000-2:1993, Quality Management and Quality Assurance Standards—
Part 2: Generic guidelines for application of ISO 9001, ISO 9002, and ISO 9003
Section 4.6—"Purchasing"

ISO 9004-1:1994, Quality Management and Quality System Elements—
Part 1: Guidelines
Section 9—"Quality in purchasing"

ISO 10011-1:1990, Guidelines for Auditing Quality Systems—
Part 1: Auditing

ISO 10011-2:1991, Guidelines for Auditing Quality Systems—
Part 2: Qualification criteria for auditors

ISO 10011-3:1991, Guidelines for Auditing Quality Systems—
Part 3: Managing audit programs

The following books have all been prepared by the ASQC Vendor–Vendee Technical Committee:

How to Conduct a Supplier Survey

Procurement Quality Control—A Handbook of Recommended Practices, ISBN 0-87389-003-5

How to Establish Effective Quality Control for the Small Supplier, ISBN 0-87389-006-X

৶ *Questions Your Registrar May Ask*

4.6.1 General

☑ How does your purchasing system work? Where is this documented? (usually asked of someone actually working in the purchasing department)

4.6.2 Evaluation of Subcontractors

☑ Are subcontractors evaluated and selected on the basis of their ability to meet subcontract requirements (including the quality system and any specific quality-assurance requirements)?

☑ Where is the type and extent of control exercised by the company over sub-contractors defined (documented)? Is this dependent upon the type of product and the impact of subcontracted product on the quality of the final product?

☑ Are the evaluation/selection criteria applied to subcontractors of critical and/or custom products different from those applied to subcontractors of standard catalog items (distributors)?

☑ Are the evaluation/selection criteria applied to subcontractors of products/raw materials different from those applied to subcontractors of services (e.g., calibration or testing services)?

☑ Are calibration services subcontracted? What evaluation methods are applied to assure capability of the subcontractor to meet the requirements of clause 4.11 (particularly 4.11.2,f)?

☑ If grandfathering is used as a means of subcontractor/supplier selection, what is the basis for such grandfathering? Where is this defined?

☑ Do you use a "Vendor Rating System"? If so, where is this system defined?

☑ How does a subcontractor become disqualified? Where is this defined?

☑ May I see the qualification records for the auditor who visited this subcontractor? (if applicable)

☑ Are quality records maintained for each acceptable subcontractor?

☑ Do you use an "Approved Suppliers List"? Who supplies your "Approved Suppliers List" to you? How do you know this one is the most current revision? Who is responsible for its upkeep?

4.6.3 Purchasing Data

☑ How is a part or service initially requested? How can one identify who the requester is?

☑ How do you ensure that purchasing documents contain data clearly describing the product or service ordered? Does this include:

(a) the type, class, grade, or other precise identification?

(b) the title or other positive identification, and applicable issues of

• specifications?

• drawings?

- process requirements?

- inspection instructions?

- relevant technical data, including requirements for approval or qualification of product, procedures, process equipment, and personnel?

(c) the title, number, and issue of the quality-system standard to be supplied?

☑ Who reviews and approves a purchase order? How can one identify the individual who approved this one?

☑ Are review parameters defined? (Are verification requirements specified?)

☑ When complex requirements exist, are other departments included in the review and approval process?

☑ Do you issue documents (e.g., product specifications, drawings, workmanship standards) to subcontractors? If so, how are these documents controlled?

☑ Are substitutions allowed from your suppliers? Who approves or authorizes substitutions?

☑ If substitutions are allowed, what instructions are given to your supplier regarding who to contact for approval or authorization? How are they given?

☑ If calibration services are subcontracted, how are the requirements of section 4.11, as a minimum, invoked? (Is the quality-system standard to be applied specifically stated?)

4.6.4 Verification of Purchased Product

☑ Where applicable, how do you ensure that where you verify purchased product at a subcontractor's premises, the verification arrangements, and the method of product release are specified in the purchasing documents?

☑ When specified in a contract, how do you communicate to your subcontractor that your customer or the customer's representative is afforded the right to verify at the *subcontractor's* premises that subcontracted product conforms to specified requirements? Where is this procedure defined?

☑ How do you ensure that, when specified in a contract, your customer or the customer's representative is afforded the right to verify at *your* premises that subcontracted product conforms to specified requirements? Where is this procedure defined?

4.7 Control of Customer-Supplied Product

At a Glance

9001	9002	9003
✓	✓	✓

You must do the following:

- Establish and maintain documented procedures for the control of verification, storage, and maintenance of customer-supplied product provided for incorporation into the supplies or for related activities

- Record and report to the customer any such product that is lost, damaged, or is otherwise unsuitable for use

> **Q U A L I T Y   M A N U A L**
>
> **7.0** CONTROL OF CUSTOMER-SUPPLIED PRODUCT
>
> ABC Company has established and maintains documented procedures for the control of verification, storage, and maintenance of customer-supplied product provided for incorporation into the supplies or for related activities. Any such product that is lost, damaged, or is otherwise unsuitable for use will be recorded and reported to the customer. Verification by ABC Company does not absolve the customer of the responsibility to provide acceptable product.

📖 *Quality Manual*

Customer-supplied product should be interpreted as product (i.e., service, hardware, processed materials, software, or a combination thereof) owned by the customer and furnished to the supplier (you) for use in meeting the requirements of the contract (order). Only minimal tailoring is required, depending on how "customer-supplied product" is defined in your operation. Specific details should be contained in your procedure manual.

This Clause Does Not Apply

Many companies immediately jump to the conclusion that this clause does not apply to them because of their specific type of business. One would be surprised at how often an ISO 9000 auditor finds instances in which it does. This is typically due to an oversight on the part of the company. Play it safe on this one. Even if you don't think this clause applies, I suggest that you include the section in your quality manual, worded like the following example:

> *7.0 Control of Customer-Supplied Product*
> *ABC company does not normally accept customer-supplied product. However, should this situation develop, ABC Company will establish and maintain documented procedures for the control of verification, storage, and maintenance of customer-supplied product provided for incorporation into the supplies or for related activities. Any such product that is lost, damaged, or is otherwise unsuitable for use will be recorded and reported to the customer. Verification by ABC Company does not absolve the customer of the responsibility to provide acceptable product.*

Now you're covered. If the situation arises, you need only develop a procedure.

📑 *Procedure*

Customers may provide all manner of product for incorporation into your stock. While the details concerning each customer may be contained in that customer's contract, ISO 9000 establishes minimum criteria that must be met. You should also recognize that a customer will quite often provide specialized instructions. The following statement is a good beginning for this procedure:

> *Customer-supplied product will be received and verified by inspection personnel in the same manner as other like or similar purchased product. The customer will be responsible for providing any specialized acceptance criteria for receiving inspection and/or special instructions for handling, storage, and maintenance.*

"Customer-supplied product provided for incorporation into the supplies" should also include the following:

- Customer-owned buffer stock and/or

- Consignment stock

Interpret this clause as it relates to your specific business with your quality system tailored likewise. In so doing, "customer-supplied product" could exist as the following:

- Hardware (subcomponents or subassemblies)

- Consumables (batteries, lamps, packaging materials, containers, etc.)

- Artwork (stencils, templates, etc.)

- Labels or tags

- Raw material

- Processed material (chemicals, additives, blend components, etc.)

- Equipment (fixtures, jigs, patterns, etc.)

- Instrumentation

- Software (inspection and test verification programs, ROM chips, etc.)

- Services (calibration, inspection, testing, training, transportation, etc.)

- Personnel (technical specialists, advisors, contract labor, etc.)

- Vehicles

- Buildings or facilities

. . . all of which should be addressed in your documented quality system to the appropriate degree. The last few items listed may at first appear to be stretching the point, but these are examples of customer-supplied product* "for related activities."

Let's discuss some practical examples of customer-supplied product "for related activities." In some instances, a customer may supply personnel to a supplier for engineering, testing, training, or support purposes. The customer-supplied personnel would then perform these supporting functions, which are essential to the supplier in meeting contract requirements. To address such situations, a company may choose to add the following text to their procedure:

> *Any instances where personnel provided by the customer, who do not meet with agreed performance criteria, shall be recorded and reported to the customer.*

Continuing with this example, a customer may provide specialized equipment or instrumentation in situations where, because of the level of technical sophistication, proprietary controls, specialized nature, limited availability, unique application, or circumstance, such equipment is not otherwise available. Specialized equipment or instrumentation may be provided for inspection, measuring, and test purposes or manufacturing or production utilization. Your procedure can address customer-supplied equipment or instrumentation as follows:

> *Any instances where equipment or instrumentation provided by the customer does not meet with agreed performance criteria shall be recorded and reported to the customer.*

Such equipment or instrumentation may require periodic maintenance and/or calibration. This should also be addressed where required.

Maintenance, Repair, and/or Calibration Services

An organization providing maintenance, repair and/or calibration services would not ordinarily consider the instruments in which the service is to be performed as "customer-supplied product." This is their primary process and would be more appropriately addressed in the applicable "Process Control" procedures. Such an organization may, however, consider "accessories" provided by their customer as being "customer-supplied product."

---

*Remember that the definition of product may include service, hardware, processed material, software, or a combination thereof.

How are these accessories tracked to ensure that they are returned to the proper customer? Accessories may include, but are not limited to, the following:

- Test leads

- Power cords

- Instrument cases

- Calibration/repair/servicing procedure manuals

Destructive and Nondestructive Testing (NDT) Services

An organization performing destructive testing would not ordinarily consider the product (sample) as being "customer-supplied" in terms of the standard. However, an organization supplying either nondestructive testing or analysis may consider the sample as being "customer-supplied product" because the customer may wish to have the sample returned or retained for a specified period of time.

Testing laboratories may also consider customer-supplied product to include reusable containers and test methods (procedures).

Customer-Supplied Product That Is "Damaged or Otherwise Unsuitable for Use"

ISO 9000 requires "any such product that is lost, damaged, or is otherwise unsuitable for use" to be recorded and reported to the customer. This can include the following:

Corrosion	Decay	Pilferage
Contamination	Deterioration	Spoilage

See Section 4.15 for more details.

In this procedure, be sure to give enough detail relating to the *who, what, when,* and *where*:

- **Who** is authorized or responsible for receiving customer-supplied product

- **Who** is authorized or responsible for *verifying* (inspecting) customer-supplied product

- **Who** is authorized or responsible for the *maintenance* of customer-supplied product

- **When** and how often maintenance of customer-supplied product will be performed

- **Who** is authorized or responsible for *recording* instances of such product that is lost, damaged, or is otherwise unsuitable for use
- **When** and **where** instances of such product that is lost, damaged, or is otherwise unsuitable for use will be recorded
- **Who** is authorized or responsible for *reporting* to the customer any such product that is lost, damaged, or is otherwise unsuitable for use
- **When** and **how** customer-supplied product that is lost, damaged, or is otherwise unsuitable for use will be reported to the customer

Be sure to specify *who* by job title, not by name.

Records

This clause of the standard requires:

- Records generated to report to the customer any "customer-supplied product" that is lost, damaged, or is otherwise unsuitable for use
- Records generated to demonstrate "verification, storage, and maintenance of customer-supplied product provided for incorporation into the supplies or for related activities."

☞ Guidance

For further guidance, reference:
ISO 9000-2:1993, Quality Management and Quality Assurance Standards—Part 2: Generic guidelines for application of ISO 9001, ISO 9002, and ISO 9003
Section 4.7—"Purchaser supplied product"

᧞ Questions Your Registrar May Ask

It is difficult to translate this section into a standard series of questions because of the wide variety of possibilities. The sample questions given here are based on the assumption that the customer-supplied product is hardware intended to be incorporated into a final product.

☑ Is customer-supplied product examined upon receipt to check for

- Correct quantity?
- Correct identity?
- Any transit damage?

How are discrepancies reported to the customer?

☑ How is customer-supplied product identified to differentiate it from other product? Where is this defined (documented)?

☑ How is customer-supplied product stored? How are special storage and maintenance requirements communicated from the customer to those responsible for its storage and maintenance?

☑ Who is responsible for the storage and maintenance of customer-supplied product? Where is this authority defined?

☑ Is customer-supplied product periodically inspected to

- Detect signs of deterioration?

- Verify that proper storage conditions are being maintained?

- Identify product that has exceeded its storage time limitations (expiration date)?

☑ If customer-supplied product is lost, damaged, or otherwise unsuitable for use, how is each instance recorded and reported to the customer? Where is this documented?

☑ Who is responsible for reporting customer-supplied product that is lost, damaged, or otherwise unsuitable for use to the customer?

4.8 Product Identification and Traceability

At a Glance

You must do the following:

9001	9002	9003
✓	✓	L

- (Where appropriate) establish and maintain documented procedures for identifying the product by suitable means from receipt and during all stages of production, delivery, and installation

- (Where and to the extent required) establish and maintain documented procedures for unique identification of individual product or batches (traceability). This identification must be recorded

QUALITY MANUAL

8.0 PRODUCT IDENTIFICATION AND TRACEABILITY

Where appropriate, ABC Company will establish and maintain documented procedures for identifying the product by suitable means from receipt and during all stages of production, delivery, and installation.

Where and to the extent that traceability is a specified requirement, ABC Company will establish and maintain documented procedures for unique identification of individual product or batches. This identification will be recorded.

Quality Manual

While the "product identification" portion of this clause can easily be paraphrased to suit a manufacturer or service provider when a product is involved, it clearly is not applicable when no tangible product exists. If that is the case, don't just ignore the clause. State in your quality manual that it doesn't apply. In some cases, you may feel it appropriate to state why it doesn't apply.

In a service (repair, maintenance, calibration, testing, etc.) organization, this clause could be expanded to address certificate or report numbers and tracking of customer-owned items throughout the service process.

Procedure

Product identification may be indicated by using the following methods:

- Bar coding

- Tags

- Labels

- Stamping

- Markings

- Imprinting (permanent impression)

- Model numbers

- Product numbers

- Color coding (color is typically added to gasoline to identify different grades)

The standard requires product identification "from receipt and during all stages of production, delivery, and installation." This includes raw material, components, and subassemblies, not just the finished product.

The method(s) that you use for product identification should be clearly documented and, where applicable, should define how the addition of any options is identified. The product identification itself is often used to satisfy certain traceability requirements.

When traceability is required for services, the emphasis is typically placed on identifying the individual(s) who performed the service and the equipment, instruments, and reference materials used (i.e., calibration and/or test services).

☺ *Label Control Programs*

In the food and drug industries, labels are often preprinted indicating the product, batch or lot number, and expiration date. This necessitates a formal "Label Control Program" that ensures that the information found on each label is absolutely correct. Labels are received and stored in a secured, limited-access area until use. After each batch or lot is completed, all unused labels should be destroyed to avoid any possibility of mislabeling.

☺ *Bar Codes*

If you are using bar-coding, be aware that several different formats and types exist. These are identified in the American Identification Manufacturers (AIM) Uniform Symbol Specifications (USS). Some of the more popular bar codes include the following:

UPC-A	Code 39	EAN-8
UPC-E	Code 49	EAN-12
Code 16K	Code 93	PostNet
Interleaved 2 of 5	Code 128	Codeabar

It is well worth the effort to understand and document which type you are using. For more information on bar codes, I suggest referencing:

The Bar Code Book
Reading, Printing, and Specification of Bar Code Symbols
By Roger C. Palmer

ISBN 0-1911261-05-2 (Paperbound)
ISBN 0-1911261-06-0 (Hardcover)

Helmers Publishing, Inc.
174 Concord Street
Peterborough, New Hampshire 03458

👣 *Traceability*

ISO 9000 addresses traceability only when it is *a specified requirement*. Although it appears to be implied that this requirement will typically be stated in a contract, it could be specified in various codes, regulations, or laws. Traceability can be a requirement for a product (hardware), processed material, software, or even a service. Traceability is often a requirement for food and drugs (U.S. FDA requirement found in 21 CFR 820). The primary purpose of traceability is to allow for corrective action in the event that nonconforming product is erroneously released.

This can include, but is not limited to, the following:

- Recall or notification of product contamination

- Hardware or software upgrades

- Recall for repair(s), rework, blending, or reprocessing

Some common means of maintaining traceability include, but are not limited to, these:

- Batch numbers

- Date codes

- Lot numbers

- Serial numbers

Serial numbers can be utilized to identify the product (model number), design revision level, traceability, and any options. For example:

580B-03-132943-234

Key:

580B = Model number (580) with revision level (B)

03 = Option code (if applicable)

132943 = The *132*nd day of 19*94*, *3*rd shift

234 = The 234th item produced on that date/shift

A great deal of creativity can be applied in meeting this requirement.

◈ *Identification of Indirectly Related Products*

Some ISO 9000 auditors interpret this clause to include products or supplies indirectly used in the manufacturing or servicing process (cleaners, coolants, lubricants, packaging, preservatives, etc.). Because most of these products are considered to be hazardous substances, they are already required to be labeled by related government codes, laws, or regulations (EPA/OSHA). Therefore, this topic generally becomes a moot point. However, if identification of these substances is not addressed by other requirements, it should be considered a good quality practice.

Records

There are no specific records required under this clause, as it relates to "product identification." This is usually placed on the product in some manner and leaves the facility with that product. However, records would be required as they relate to traceability when that is a specified requirement. While the standard does not require any specific records, product traceability data could include, but is not limited to,

- Batch or lot numbers of raw materials
- Certificates of Analysis or Material Test Reports for component parts and raw material used in manufacturing the product
- Production and laboratory data generated during manufacture
- Inspection and test results
- Product disposition records

Guidance

For further guidance, reference:

ISO 9000-2:1993, Quality Management and Quality Assurance Standards—Part 2: Generic guidelines for application of ISO 9001, ISO 9002, and ISO 9003
Section 4.8—"Product identification and traceability"

ISO 9004-1:1994, Quality Management and Quality System Elements—Part 1: Guidelines
Section 11.2—"Material control, traceability, and identification"

Questions Your Registrar May Ask

Depending upon your application, many of the following questions may not apply. I have included them here to provide insight for you in developing this procedure.

☑ How is product identified? Where is this defined (documented)?

☑ Are part, lot, or batch numbers used? If so, how are they controlled? How is consistency maintained?

☑ Does the method used for component part identification reflect the appropriate revision level (where applicable)?

☑ Who is responsible for assigning part, lot, or batch numbers?

☑ How is product identification and traceability maintained from receipt and during all stages of production, delivery, and installation?

☑ If an in-process component part was found that had been misplaced between operations, could it be identified by someone who was unfamiliar with the part? How? Does this approach or method also identify the revision level under which the part was manufactured?

☑ Where and, to the extent that traceability is a specified requirement, how is the need for traceability communicated to the production function? Can you show me an example of how this works?

☑ How and where is traceability recorded? May I see an example of this?

4.9 Process Control

At a Glance

9001	9002	9003
✓	✓	✗

You must do the following:

- Identify and plan the production, installation, and servicing processes that directly affect quality

- Ensure that these processes are carried out under controlled conditions

QUALITY MANUAL

9.0 PROCESS CONTROL

ABC Company will identify and plan the production, installation, and servicing processes that directly affect quality and will ensure that these processes are carried out under controlled conditions. Controlled conditions will include the following:

(a) documented procedures defining the manner of production, installation, and servicing, where the absence of such procedures could adversely affect quality;

(b) use of suitable production, installation, and servicing equipment, and a suitable working environment;

(c) compliance with reference standards/codes, quality plans, and/or documented procedures;

(d) monitoring and control of suitable process parameters and product characteristics;

(e) the approval of processes and equipment, as appropriate;

(f) criteria for workmanship, which shall be stipulated in the clearest practical manner (e.g., written standards, representative samples, or illustrations);

(g) suitable maintenance of equipment to ensure continuing process capability.

Where the results of processes cannot be fully verified by subsequent inspection and testing of the product and where, for example, processing deficiencies may become apparent only after the product is in use, the processes will be carried out by qualified operators and/or will require continuous monitoring and control of process parameters to ensure that the specified requirements are met.

The requirements for any qualification of process operations, including associated equipment and personnel, will be specified. Such processes requiring prequalification of their process capability are frequently referred to as special processes.

Records will be maintained for qualified processes, equipment, and personnel, as appropriate.

📖 *Quality Manual*

For manufacturers, I suggest paraphrasing as much of this original text as possible in your quality manual with details contained in your procedure manual. Very little tailoring should be required. I suggest addressing special processes, as applicable, by paraphrasing the associated notes into your quality manual (Ref. ISO 9001/2, clause 4.9, Note 16).

For the service industry, a great deal of tailoring may be required, particularly when no actual product is involved. In this case, I would still suggest paraphrasing the standard to the greatest extent possible.

📄 *Procedure*

Today it is quite common to see production planning performed either through, or in conjunction with, a computer MRP (Manufacturing Resource Planning) program. If you use such a system, the details surrounding *how* it meets the requirements of ISO 9000 should be addressed in your procedure. This should include *how* data is *input* into the system and *who* reviews and approves the production plans, along with any other interactions necessary to work with the program.

Production planning should address the following:

* Specific or unique customer orders

* Standard or Catalog Items for stock or inventory

Process control must be carried out under controlled conditions. Each of these stated conditions must be addressed. Let's discuss these individually.

(a) Documented Procedures

The intent of developing "documented procedures" is to add consistency to the process. It is very common for companies to miss this point. Auditors often verify compliance with this requirement by interviewing employees, simply asking them to describe the process or job function they are performing. The auditor makes a mental flow chart and then verifies that the procedure reflects these steps.

Procedures can be documented using a variety of methods. For example:

* Written procedures

* Flow charts

* Illustrations (pictograms, storyboards, animation or cartoons, etc.)

Pictograms are generally considered acceptable for procedures. For example, the instructions for emergency evacuation from an airplane are typically depicted in pictograms. Written procedures are often supported by photographs, illustrations, and/or representative samples.

As discussed earlier, the level of detail contained in each procedure or work instruction will vary for each company, depending upon the complexity of the processes and the level of detail contained in the training program.

 ### Tribal Knowledge

When developing these procedures, try to approach them from the standpoint of training a new employee. A common pitfall is to leave out too much detail because it is "common knowledge" (a.k.a. tribal knowledge) or "common sense." Often it is not. Sometimes an auditor will ask an employee to explain a work process as if training him to perform that job.

 ### Schematics, Drawings, and Flow Charts

Some companies have created their own individual schematic and drawing practices. This is particularly inefficient and often creates difficulty in the contract review process. Specific engineering standards for schematics and drawings have been established by ANSI, ASME, AWS, IEEE, ISO, etc. (reference Section 4.4, Guidance).

Companies often use flow charts with no explanation of what the various symbols mean. I suggest referencing "ISO 5807:1985, Information processing—Documentation symbols and conventions for data, program and system flowcharts, program network charts, and system resources charts."

There are two basic types of process flow charts:

- **Top-down flow charts** depict only the major steps in a process or project. These flow charts may reference several predefined processes or procedures that are subject to change. This allows the user to stay focused on the big picture. Top-down flow charts usually lack the detail needed to stand alone as a procedure.

- **Detailed flow charts,** as the name implies, depict much greater detail with very specific information about every step of the process. Detailed flow charts often uncover waste and inefficiency in a process that would never be apparent in a top-down flow chart.

Both top-down and detailed flow charts can be expanded into a "Deployment Flow Chart." This can be an excellent addition to any procedure.

☺ *Use of International Symbols*

As companies become more culturally diverse, the national language cannot be taken for granted as being the first language of many employees. I strongly encourage the use of international symbols wherever possible. Remember that mathematical symbols are universal. Instead of posting "less than 12" on a machine control setting, post "<12." Your employees should be able to understand the "less than" symbol (assuming they have had basic math in their native country).

♀ *Dedicated Work Instructions*

GE in Minneapolis, MN, has developed a practice of "dedicating" work instructions to those areas where they are routinely used. For example, electronic or mechanical assembly areas have clear Plexiglas or plastic desktop protectors over their workbenches. Work instructions are placed under these clear protectors so that they are always available and directly in front of the employee for immediate reference. In some instances, these work instructions are simply posted on the wall over a workbench.

GE Test Equipment Management Services in Syracuse, NY, has some measurement standards that are unique to specific calibrations. They have posted the calibration procedures over those measurement standards that must be used to perform the calibration. In some instances, the calibration procedure is chained or tied in some way to the measurement standard (much as public telephone books are chained near the telephone).

Many companies keep manuals and other related documentation readily available on or near the machine or area where a regular work function is performed. The common theme here is speed and simplicity, with immediate access to commonly used work instructions.

💣 *Home Office Management System*

Do you have employees who work out of their homes? The number of companies that do is on the rise, and these employees are not exempt from this clause. Whether employees work out of their homes full-time or part-time, you should have documented procedures addressing *how* they perform their work activities. The home office is simply an extension of the company.

(b) Suitable Equipment and Working Environment

The word "suitable" is very difficult to audit. Therefore, it is your responsibility to define what is "suitable" in your procedures. This can include the following:

- The capability and environmental limitations of production, installation, and servicing equipment (reference equipment specifications and usage instructions)

- Safety considerations (reference OSHA requirements in the U.S.)

(c) Reference Standards and Codes, Quality Plans, and/or Procedures

Most registered Lead Auditors have not been trained to assess compliance with specific reference standards or codes, and I don't foresee ISO 9000 registrars training their auditors in this area in the future. It remains the responsibility of the company to be in compliance with any applicable reference standards or codes. This determination will normally be made by the engineering department.

Procedures (SOPs) or work instructions may either describe the detailed steps necessary to ensure compliance, or simply reference them. Remember that reference standards or codes are subject to revision. As such they should be considered "documents of external origin" that must be controlled (ref. clause 4.5.1).

Quality plans and/or documented procedures (work instructions) should be readily available to those employees performing the related job functions.

(d) Monitoring and Control of Process

Process control and monitoring instruments are common in manufacturing. Again, it is your responsibility to define what is "suitable" in your procedures regarding *which* process parameters or product characteristics are to be monitored or controlled. I suggest that you include in your procedure the following text:

> *Monitoring and control of suitable process parameters and product characteristics during production, installation, and servicing shall include, as a minimum, those characteristics of the design that are crucial to the safe and proper functioning of the product.*

This defines a minimum expectation, while allowing you the flexibility to monitor additional *process parameters and product characteristics* as necessary.

(e) Approval of Processes and Equipment

This requirement is rather straightforward. Your procedure should detail, as appropriate:

- **Which** processes and equipment require approval

- **When** processes and equipment must be approved (e.g., prior to use)

- **Who** is authorized to approve processes and equipment

- **How** approval of processes and equipment is indicated

(f) Criteria for Workmanship

I encourage you to use industry-recognized workmanship standards wherever practicable. If no standard exists, or if existing standards are inadequate, then I encourage you to approach the appropriate organization(s) and work toward developing new standards.

While written standards are suitable for most applications, sometimes a representative sample conveys instructions better. Representative samples should be clearly and uniquely identified with some record of approval. Illustrations and photographs are also an excellent means of communicating work instructions. I've observed some companies' procedures where a photograph had been approved (separately) and included (taped) in a work procedure.

☝ Referencing Workmanship Standards

When referencing workmanship standards in your procedures, always include the revision level, particularly for those from external sources. I realize that many DoD auditors will tell you not to do this, but their intent is for you to always use the most recent and current version of a workmanship standard. If you do not include the revision level, you must provide evidence that you do, in fact, have the most recent and current version of that standard.

This can be accomplished by subscribing to a service that will notify you of any changes in these standards. Such services can be quite expensive and contribute little value toward the quality of the final product. This should only be of concern to manufacturers serving the DoD or regulated industries. If you specify a revision level, you have eliminated the need for such a subscription service while satisfying the requirements of ISO 9000.

(g) Suitable Maintenance of Equipment

Let's first attempt to define "suitable" maintenance as it appears in the standard. One's first reaction may be to interpret this as a requirement for a preventive maintenance system. This is not necessarily the case. Because of their nature, many processes may not require a formal preventive maintenance system. A company should research the recommendations made by the manufacturer of each item of production, installation, and servicing equipment and, taking into consideration their application or usage, determine whether there is a need for such a system. Particular attention should be given to equipment characteristics that contribute to key, or critical, product characteristics.

Obviously, as tool wear occurs, variability will be seen in the finished product and you will see process drift. For most manufacturers, this requirement will be most easily met by formalizing and documenting a preventive maintenance system.

When a formal, planned maintenance system is required, it should

- Identify which equipment is included in the system

- Schedule maintenance as necessary (may be based on manufacturer's recommendations)

- Identify the maintenance to be performed (e.g., manufacturer's service manual)

- Record maintenance actions taken (e.g., lubrication, changed filters, worn parts replaced)

Maintenance of equipment can be recorded in logs (notebooks), computer databases, etc. This will provide evidence of past compliance while scheduling future planned maintenance activities.

Equipment is often tagged, indicating when the last maintenance was performed, as well as when the next maintenance is scheduled (see Figure 4.9-1).

☹ *Reactive Maintenance Policy*

While the wording of subclause (g) is vague, I seriously doubt that any legitimate auditor or registrar would accept a policy of "We fix it when it breaks"; at least not without some valid justification. This is clearly reactive and would not meet the intent or spirit of ISO 9000. Although this subclause does not use the term "preventive maintenance," I suspect it will be referenced as such by companies and ISO 9000 auditors alike.

Figure 4.9-1: Preventive Maintenance Label

😞 *Maintenance/Calibration Schedules*

Some companies have confused "maintenance" with "calibration." The two are quite different. Maintenance addresses the continuing proper operation of equipment in all respects, including its ability to produce accurate measurement results (proper calibration). Calibration should be viewed as a totally different, but additional, function. An employee who is trained and capable of performing routine maintenance is not always qualified to calibrate the same equipment.

👍 *Prequalification of Processes (Special Processes)*

The results of some processes cannot be fully verified by subsequent inspection and testing of the product. Processing deficiencies may become apparent only after the product is in use. These processes must be carried out by qualified operators and/or require continuous monitoring and control of process parameters to ensure that the specified requirements are met.

These processes are often referred to as "special processes." Examples of such processes commonly include, but are not limited to,

- Welding
- Brazing
- Soldering

Requirements for any qualification of process operation, including associated equipment and personnel, must be specified. Several industry standards exist addressing this topic. See "Guidance" for more details.

⚒ *Quality Systems Requirements*

Compliance with QS-9000, section I, clause 4.9, entails meeting several additional requirements:

4.9.1, Process Monitoring and Operator Instructions

4.9.2, Preliminary Process Capability Requirements

4.9.3, Ongoing Process Performance Requirements

4.9.4, Modified Preliminary or Ongoing Capability Requirements

4.9.5, Verification of Job Set-ups

4.9.6, Process Changes

4.9.7, Appearance Items

Clearly, QS-9000 far exceeds the requirements of ISO 9001 in this area.

Records

Determining which subclauses of this section require records can be somewhat confusing. Actually, a great deal of flexibility is contained in this clause. Most of the requirements are directed to, or can be addressed in, documented procedures and/or work instructions alone. The following list details the various options for each subclause:

(a) Procedures

(b) Procedures and/or work instructions (compliance may be supported by records)

(c) **Records** (implies inspection)

(d) Procedures, work instructions, and **records**

(e) Procedures, work instructions, and/or records

(f) Procedures and/or work instructions (compliance may be supported by records)

(g) Procedures, work instructions (service manuals), and **records**

Oddly, this clause of the standard contains a note that is followed by more requirements. After note 16, the standard states:

> *Records shall be maintained for qualified processes, equipment, and personnel, as appropriate (See 4.16).*

This is clearly intended to be a requirement because it uses the word *shall*.

Guidance

For further guidance, refer to:

ISO 9000-2:1993, Quality Management and Quality Assurance Standards—Part 2: Generic guidelines for application of ISO 9001, ISO 9002, and ISO 9003
Section 4.9—"Process control"

ISO 9004-1:1994, Quality Management and Quality System Elements—Part 1: Guidelines
Section 11—"Control of processes"

Industry Standards

There are many industry- and product-specific procedures or guidelines available. In the electronics industry, for example:

> ANSI/IPC-R-700C, Suggested Guidelines for Modification, Rework, and Repair of Printed Boards and Assemblies

> ANSI/IPC-CM-770C, Component Mounting Guidelines for Printed Boards

Another source for guidance in this area is the American Production and Inventory Control Society (APICS). See Appendix A.

Guidance on welding and allied processes can be found in:

> ISO Handbook 19—Welding

Handbook 19 is a compilation of more than 68 ISO standards, most of which were developed by ISO Technical Committee 44, Welding and Allied Processes. It also includes standards relating to gas cylinders, developed by ISO/TC 58, Gas Cylinders, seven standards dealing with personal eye-protection devices established by ISO/TC 94, Personal Safety—Protective Clothing and Equipment, and two standards from ISO/TC 164, Mechanical Testing of Metals.

The American Welding Society (AWS) has established standards for qualifying both your processes and personnel in:

> AWS B2.1-84, Standard for Welding Procedure and Performance Qualification

> ANSI/AWS B2.2-91, Standard for Brazing Procedure and Performance Qualification

ISO Handbook 19 and AWS standards are both available from the American Welding Society. See Appendix A.

> Section IX of the ASME Boiler and Pressure Vessel Code—"Qualification Standard for Welding and Brazing Procedures, Welders, Brazers, and Welding and Brazing Operators"

Questions Your Registrar May Ask

Since this clause contains a great deal of flexibility, many of the following questions may not apply. This checklist assumes that compliance with several of the requirements contained in the subclauses will have already been verified in your document review. I have developed these questions to provide you with insight for developing your procedures.

4.9 Process Control

☑ Who is responsible for identifying and planning production, installation, and servicing processes that directly affect quality? Where is this defined (documented)?

☑ How are production, installation, and servicing processes planned (e.g., flow charts, production plans, production schedules)? How do you ensure that these processes are carried out under controlled conditions?

☑ How is production of standard or catalog items for stock or inventory differentiated from specific or unique customer orders (if applicable)?

☑ Are all production, installation, and servicing processes that directly affect quality adequately documented?

☑ How and where is "suitable" production, installation, and servicing equipment defined? Who is authorized to make this determination?

☑ How do you define a "suitable working environment"? Where is this documented?

☑ How can compliance with reference standards or codes, quality plans, and/or documented procedures (work instructions) be verified?

☑ What product characteristics (attributes or variables) are you monitoring or controlling? What parameters of the process are you required to control?

☑ Which processes and equipment, if any, require approval? Who is authorized to issue that approval? How is it indicated?

☑ How are criteria for workmanship stipulated?

☑ Who is responsible for the maintenance of equipment, to ensure continuing process capability?

☑ How is suitable maintenance of equipment, to ensure continuing process capability, accomplished? What records are available to verify this?

☑ Do any processes require prequalification (special processes)?

☑ Are procedures established for qualifying special process operations, including associated equipment and personnel?

☑ Are records maintained for qualified (special) processes, equipment, and personnel, as appropriate? Who is responsible for maintaining these records?

4.10 Inspection and Testing

At a Glance

9001	9002	9003
✓	✓	∟*

You must do the following:

- Establish and maintain documented procedures for inspection and testing activities in order to verify that the specified requirements for the product are met

- Address inspection and testing, and the records to be established, in the documented quality plan or documented procedures

- Ensure that incoming product is not used or processed until it has been inspected or otherwise verified as conforming to specified requirements

- Record and positively identify incoming product, when released for urgent production purposes prior to verification, in order to permit immediate recall and replacement in the event of nonconformity to specified requirements

- Address "in-process" inspecting and testing activities

- Carry out all final inspection and testing in accordance with the quality plan and/or documented procedures to complete the evidence of conformance of the finished product to the specified requirements

- Establish and maintain records that provide evidence that the product has been inspected and/or tested; these records must show clearly whether the product has passed or failed the inspections and/or tests according to defined acceptance criteria

- Identify the inspection authority responsible for the release of product in records

*Although this clause is included in ISO 9003, it is limited to "Final" inspection activities only.

QUALITY MANUAL

10.0 INSPECTION AND TESTING

10.1 General

ABC Company has established and maintains documented procedures for inspection and testing activities in order to verify that the specified requirements for the product are met. The required inspection and testing, and the records to be established, are documented in the quality plan or documented procedures.

Quality Manual

I suggest paraphrasing the standard throughout this section. Wording should closely resemble text from the standard to avoid distorting the intent. Some minimal tailoring may be required, but specifics should be left in your procedure(s). Even if you never plan to apply ISO 9001/2, clause 4.10.2.3, you should allow yourself this option. Release of product under positive recall is strongly discouraged, but can help you out of a bind when practiced sparingly and responsibly.

Procedure

Receiving, in-process, and final inspection or testing activities can all be addressed in one procedure under different headings. Each area should define the following:

- **Who** is authorized to perform inspection or testing activities
- **What** product characteristics are to be inspected or tested
- **When** inspection or testing activities will be performed
- **Where** each inspection or testing activity will be performed (e.g., "hold points" and/or "quarantine" areas)
- **How** acceptance or rejection is indicated

The specific details of inspection or testing activities can be documented in the quality plan, documented procedures, or a combination of both. It is common to see specific "Inspection/Test Instructions" or "Methods" describing *how* to perform each inspection or test activity. The standard also allows for the use of sampling plans in performing inspection or testing activities.

☹ *Terminology*

Your ISO 9000 auditors will be asking questions relating to Inspection and testing activities. They will be concerned with "inspectors." Some companies have decided that they don't like the word "inspector" and refer to them as "auditors." These are two entirely different functions.

When I say that I have a friend who is a pilot, what do you think he pilots? Most people immediately think of an airplane (except for some areas along the Mississippi where they also think of riverboat pilots). To call your inspectors "auditors" would be much like calling your truck driver a truck pilot. Sure, it works, but in the end you look rather silly and your auditor is confused. Please call your inspectors "inspectors." (I've also seen companies refer to the inspection process as an "appraisal.")

QUALITY MANUAL

10.2 Receiving Inspection and Testing

10.2.1 ABC Company will ensure that incoming product is not used or processed (except in the circumstances described in 10.2.3) until it has been inspected or otherwise verified as conforming to specified requirements. Verification of the specified requirements will be in accordance with the quality plan and/or documented procedures.

10.2.2 In determining the amount and nature of receiving inspection, consideration will be given to the amount of control exercised at the subcontractor's premises and the recorded evidence of conformance provided.

10.2.3 Where incoming product is released for urgent production purposes prior to verification, it will be positively identified and recorded in order to permit immediate recall and replacement in the event of nonconformity to specified requirements.

🗐 *Procedure*

"Receiving inspection" can take many different forms, the most basic of which is commonly called a "kick and count." This typically consists of comparing the packing list to the contents of each package; checking for damages, shortages, overages, and proper part number(s) accompanied by supporting documentation (e.g., certificates, test reports, control charts, etc.); then comparing this information to your purchase order.

Receiving Inspection procedures should address the following:

- Receipt of overages or shortages

- Receipt of partial shipments (with or without back orders)

- Receipt of substitute product(s)

- Receipt of damaged goods (product)

- Receipt of incorrect product or other discrepancies

In most instances, discrepancies would need to be reported to the purchasing element. Procedures should also specify corrective action plans to follow in the event of a noncompliance. These considerations are common to almost every industry. Receiving inspections and tests can vary to the extreme depending upon the type and criticality of the product, the history of the supplier, etc.

There are other means of verifying conformance. As the standard states:

> *The supplier shall ensure that incoming product is not used or processed until it has been inspected or <u>otherwise verified</u> as conforming to specified requirements.*

This allows you to rely on your supplier's inspection activities, provided that you have verification that their inspection is adequate. This could be tied back to your initial basis for supplier or subcontractor selection. For example:

- Suppliers or subcontractors registered to an ISO 9000 series quality standard

- Site assessment by a qualified auditor

- Examination of supplier's verification data (e.g., Laboratory Reports, Certificate of Analysis, Process Control Charts)

- Past history of performance with statistical evidence of quality (e.g., Deming's *kp* Rule)

Any of these criteria could be used to justify the elimination of "Receiving Inspection" for a supplier. In any event, you would need to have some documented basis for accepting product without an incoming inspection. If you have paraphrased the text from ISO 9000, no more is needed in your quality manual, but detail would be required in your procedure. The following is an example of allowing such for those suppliers or subcontractors who are ISO 9000–certified:

> *Suppliers/subcontractors who are ISO 9000–certified by an accredited registrar may deliver product or materials directly to inventory or to the assembly area. The purchase order for such product or materials shall indicate "NO RECEIVING INSPECTION REQUIRED."*

The first sentence defines the conditions under which receiving inspection is to be bypassed. The second sentence defines *how* you will specify when this applies. The statement being printed on the purchase order also communicates this instruction to your receiving (inspection) department.

Although this example focuses on an external supplier, this circumstance is much more common between different divisions of the same company. The bottom line here is that you must define *when* and *where* receiving inspection is to be bypassed, if at all.

☰ *Deming's* kp *Rule*

Dr. W. Edwards Deming advocated an all-or-none approach toward receiving inspection. While this may sound incredible at first, it is based on history of a supplier's performance and statistical evidence of quality. The plan is derived mathematically with emphasis on the total cost, or value added, to the total process. If you use this approach, it should be thoroughly described in your procedures. (Reference *Quality, Productivity, and Competitive Position* by Dr. Deming, pp. 267–311, for more detailed information.)

♀ *Use of Accredited Testing Laboratories*

Many companies have elected to use independent external testing laboratories to perform some of their inspection and testing. (See Section 4.6 for more detail on accredited testing laboratories.) In some instances, the use of "accredited" testing laboratories is required by the customer (ref. QS-9000, clause 4.10.2).

☜ *Damaged Goods*

Your receiving inspection procedure should also address product damaged in transit. This procedure should include the *who, what, when, where,* and *how* relating to the following:

- Refusing a shipment
- Identification and segregation of nonconforming product
- Notification of shipper
- Filing a claim with the shipper, etc.

A great deal of guidance is available on this topic.

✎ *Note*

For U.S. companies, the American Trucking Association's "National Motor Freight Classification 100-T" contains a representative sample of a "Standard Form for Presentation of Loss and Damage Claim" with instructions as to its use. (Ref. Section 4.15 for more information.)

For Canadian companies, the Canadian Trucking Association's "National Freight Claims Manual" contains detailed instructions and forms:

The Canadian Trucking Association   Tel: (613) 236-9426
130 Albert Street, Suite 300   Fax:(613) 563-2701
Ottawa, Ontario Canada
K1P 5G4

Receiving Inspection of Services

This clause is often interpreted as applying to raw material and products only, but it can in fact apply to services or servicing as well. In these instances, you simply want to ensure that the service you received was the one that you requested. When you subcontract calibration or testing services, for example, you will typically receive a certificate and/or report. These documents reflect both the activity and the results. Your receiving inspection of calibration services should verify that the calibration report or certificate you received states compliance with the calibration system quality standard(s) or requirements that you specified, and that a correct calibration status label is on the instrument. If you requested calibration data, you should verify that you received it. If a limited calibration was provided, you want to verify proper "Limited Calibration" labeling of the instrument.

If you subcontract testing activities, you should verify that each test report (certificate of analysis, etc.) reflects all of the tests that you requested.

When you review these documents, you may often find that the subcontractor did not provide all of the information you requested. This can be due to a number of reasons, but you would not have identified the problem had you not performed a receiving inspection of the documentation.

With such a problem identified, the corrective action process should involve notifying the purchasing element to ensure that the requirements stated in the purchase order (or contract) were unambiguous and understood by the subcontractor. For example, a purchase order that simply states

Calibrate to Mfg. Specs.

is ambiguous. Such a simple statement would omit many requirements. This can most easily be addressed by invoking a quality standard. For example:

Calibrate to Mfg. Specs. in accordance with ISO 9002.

Although this is better, ISO 9002 is really a very minimal standard for calibration activities. You may choose to invoke a quality standard specifically developed for calibration laboratories. For example:

Calibrate to Mfg. Specs. in accordance with ANSI/NCSL Z540-1 or

> *Calibrate to Mfg. Specs. in accordance with ISO 10012.*

And for testing laboratories:

> *Perform stated tests using ASTM methods in accordance with ISO Guide 25.*

The more specific your request, the more likely you are to receive what you require. If in doubt, contact your calibration and/or testing subcontractor and ask how much detail they would like on your purchase orders. (They're usually frustrated by such minimal P.O. wording, too.)

Calibration and testing services directly relate to the quality of the product. Therefore, they must be included under this clause. However, there are other services you receive that may not relate to the product. While these other services may not be considered to require receiving inspection (under ISO 9000), the same quality concepts could apply as a requirement by your quality system.

Release under Positive Recall

ISO 9001/2, clause 4.10.2.3, states:

> *Where incoming product is released for urgent production purposes prior to verification, it shall be positively identified and recorded (see 4.16) in order to permit immediate recall and replacement in the event of nonconformity to specified requirements.*

This is commonly referred to as "release under positive recall" and carries a certain degree of risk that must be weighed whenever it is practiced.

Although I suggest leaving yourself this option, the release of incoming product subject to recall should be discouraged as a matter of good management practice. Items should only be released subject to recall if the following is true:

- An objective evaluation of quality and solution of any nonconformities can still be implemented

- Correction of nonconformities will not compromise the quality of adjacent, attached, or incorporated items

Your procedure should clearly define responsibilities and authority of personnel who may allow incoming product to be used without prior demonstration of conformance to specified requirements for quality. Your procedure should also define how such product will be positively identified and controlled in the event that subsequent inspections or tests identify nonconformities.

> **QUALITY MANUAL**
>
> **10.3** In-Process Inspection and Testing
>
> ABC Company will:
>
> (a) inspect and test the product as required by the quality plan and/or documented procedures;
>
> (b) hold product until the required inspection and tests have been completed or necessary reports have been received and verified, except when product is released under positive-recall procedures (see 10.2.3). Release under positive-recall procedures shall not preclude the activities outlined in 10.3a.

Procedure

In-process inspection and testing applies to all forms of products (including hardware, processed material, software, and services). It allows early recognition of nonconformities and timely disposition of product. Statistical control techniques are commonly used to identify trends for both product and process before nonconformities actually occur.

In-process inspection and testing activities must be clearly defined in your quality plan and/or documented procedures (as such, performing in-process inspection and testing is not a requirement unless specified in *your* quality plan and/or documented procedures). In-process inspection and testing may require that "hold points" be established. Unless carefully planned, hold points can create bottlenecks in the production process.

The location and frequency of in-process inspection and testing should depend upon the criticality of the characteristics and the ease of verification at the stage of production.

First Article Inspection

"First article" inspection is a common form of in-process inspection. First-article inspections are typically associated with process machinery that must be set up and adjusted until it is producing the proper result.

First-article inspection is typically used to approve items that are simple in design. They need only be "fit for purpose and function" with loose tolerances and minimal quality requirements. For example, a subcontractor may be producing simple parts for incorporation into a larger assembly that you manufacture. You would have the subcontractor ship a sample of his first run to you for approval before continuing with production. This method is most often used with small local subcontractors producing unique, simple, noncatalog items. Be sure to document such first-article inspections to show evidence of the activity.

👍 *Neighbor Inspection*

Many companies now have each worker, or process step, inspect the work performed by the previous worker, or process. This provides a much higher level of confidence than "self-inspection," while controlling the costs of inspection.

👁 *Machine Inspection*

In-process inspection and testing may be achieved by the use of machines. For example:

- Automatic analysis or inspection (e.g., material composition by on-line gas chromatographs and infrared scanners, machine vision)
- Instrument sensor readings (e.g., temperature, pH, weight)

Automated inspections are often quicker and more accurate. The use of machine inspection should be detailed in your quality plan and/or documented procedures.

👍 *"Burn-in" Tests*

In-process inspection may consist of "burn-in" functional testing (typically of electrical or electronic products). At various points in the manufacturing process, a product may be taken to a test bay and set to run a series of functional exercises for a specific period of time. At the end of each test or cycle, an inspector will check the product for proper operation (usually by observing that the product is continuing to cycle through its tests successfully) and indicate acceptance. After each product has completed its burn-in test, it is ready for any final processing that is necessary. Such burn-in testing should be described as a "step" in the quality plan and/or documented procedure.

✍ *Note*

Caution must be taken in developing such burn-in tests to ensure that the tests are not detrimental to the final product.

💡 *Do You Need a Certified Welding Inspector?*

Companies that rarely utilize special processes, such as welding, may have difficulty in locating qualified inspectors. In response to this need, the American Welding Society (AWS) has developed a program that can provide companies with a list of currently certified welding inspectors for any area. For more information, call the American Welding Society Q&C Department at 1-800-443-WELD, extension 273.

QUALITY MANUAL

10.4 Final Inspection and Testing

ABC Company will carry out all final inspection and testing in accordance with the quality plan and/or documented procedures to complete the evidence of conformance of the finished product to the specified requirements.

The quality plan and/or documented procedures for final inspection and testing will require that all specified inspection and tests, including those specified either on receipt of product or in-process, have been carried out and that the results meet specified requirements.

No product will be dispatched until all the activities specified in the quality plan and/or documented procedures have been satisfactorily completed and the associated data and documentation are available and authorized.

Procedure

The finished product (hardware, processed material, software or service) must receive some form of final inspection and testing. Unlike in-process inspection and testing, final inspection and testing is a requirement of the standard. You should define the extent and nature of final inspection and testing in your quality plan and/or documented procedures. Final inspection and testing activities must do the following:

- Verify conformance of the finished product to the specified requirements
- Ensure that all specified inspection and tests, including those specified either on receipt of product or in-process, have been carried out

This can be accomplished in a number of ways including, but not limited to, these:

- 100% inspection
- Lot sampling
- Process control

- Continuous sampling (in the case of product released via pipeline, consider the use of on-line analyzers)

Your procedure must define the following:

- Authority for release of final product

- What associated data or documentation shall indicate final acceptance

If final inspection is performed through process control, documentation should exist in the form of process control charts. These too must be authorized.

☑ Checklists

Many companies start using checklists only to find that they quickly become a useless bureaucratic formality. Although checklists are great for new inspectors, they should be used primarily as a training aid. After your inspectors are comfortable with their task, simply laminate a checklist and place it in the inspection area for reference as a memory aid. Remember, there are more ways to document inspection than a checklist. Complete and retain checklists only where there is "value added" to having this information.

◇ Self-Inspection

This is a hot topic of debate. Can someone inspect his or her own work? This particular practice is not fully addressed here. However, under ISO 9001/2, section 4.17, the standard states that internal audits must "be carried out by personnel independent of those having direct responsibility for the activity being audited." Because these are similar concepts, one can easily arrive at the conclusion that "self-inspection" does not meet the intent of the standard. Those who support the concept of self-inspection argue that ISO 9000 does not specifically forbid the practice and therefore feel that it should be acceptable. This position is further supported by the term "self-inspection" being defined in the current draft of ISO 8402 (implying that the practice is acceptable).

Supporters of self-inspection often state the difficulties that a small company with few employees might encounter if self-inspection was generally considered unacceptable. While the standard should be tailored to best suit the needs of the user, this is *not* a valid argument. It could be viewed as a lack of compliance with ISO 9001/2, clause 4.1.2.2, "Resources." If you use "self-inspection" techniques, I suggest that you check each registrar's position on this topic before making your selection.

I personally feel that the term "self-inspection" is an oxymoron (a contradiction similar to "dry water" or "clean dirt"). Proponents often cite examples where self-inspection works well in the manufacture of a very simple product where the process itself is in control. However, as the product and/or process becomes more complicated (or less stable), the effectiveness of self-inspection quickly deteriorates. I am not alone in this opinion. Several regulatory agencies require that inspection and testing be performed by someone other than the individual who performed the work. Although every company should have conscientious employees who ensure that their work is correct, self-inspection is no inspection. Many have confused the term "self-inspection" with the concept of employees simply monitoring and adjusting a process.

Q U A L I T Y   M A N U A L

10.5 Inspection and Test Records

ABC Company will establish and maintain records that provide evidence that the product has been inspected and/or tested. These records will show clearly whether the product has passed or failed the inspections and/or tests according to defined acceptance criteria. Where the product fails to pass any inspection and/or test, the procedures for control of nonconforming product will apply.

Records will identify the inspection authority responsible for the release of product.

Procedure

This procedure should describe *what* form of inspection and test records are to exist. These records must demonstrate that the stated requirements for quality have been fulfilled. Regulatory requirements and product liability concerns should also be taken into consideration.

Records

Inspection and test records can take many different forms. As a minimum, these records must do the following:

- Provide evidence that the product has been inspected and/or tested

- Show clearly whether the product has passed or failed the inspections and/or tests according to defined acceptance criteria (all specified inspection and tests, including those specified either on receipt of product, in-process, or final inspection)

- Complete the evidence of conformance of the finished product to the specified requirements

- Identify the inspection authority responsible for the release of product

Laboratory reports, certificates of analysis, process control charts, etc., received with the product (raw material) from subcontractors are also an element of these records.

Don't forget about ISO 9001/2, clause 4.10.2.3:

Where incoming product is released for urgent production purposes prior to verification, it shall be positively identified and <u>recorded</u> in order to permit immediate recall and replacement in the event of nonconformance to specified requirements.

☞ ## *Guidance*

For further guidance, refer to:

ISO 9000-2:1993, Quality Management and Quality Assurance Standards—Part 2: Generic guidelines for application of ISO 9001, ISO 9002, and ISO 9003
Section 4.10—"Inspection and testing"

ISO 9004-1:1994, Quality Management and Quality System Elements—Part 1: Guidelines
Section 12—"Product verification"

ANSI/ASQC E2-1984, Guide to Inspection Planning

ANSI/ASQC Q3-1988, Sampling Procedures and Tables for Inspection of Isolated Lots by Attributes

ANSI/ASQC S1-1987, An Attribute Skip-Lot Sampling Program (to be used *only* with ANSI/ASQC Z1.4-1981)

ANSI/ASQC Z1.4-1981, Sampling Procedures and Tables for Inspection by Attributes (compatible with MIL-STD-105)

ANSI/ASQC Z1.9-1980, Sampling Procedures and Tables for Inspection by Variables for Percent Nonconforming (corresponds with MIL-STD-414 and is interchangeable with ISO 3951:1989)

MIL-STD-105E, Sampling Procedures and Tables for Inspection by Attributes

MIL-STD-414, Sampling Procedures and Tables for Inspection by Variables for Percent Defective

MIL-STD-1235C, Single- and Multi-level Continuous Sampling Procedures and Tables for Inspection by Attributes, Functional Curves of the Continuous Sampling Plans

Special Processes

There are also specific inspection guides available for special processes. For example:

ANSI/AWS B1.10-86, Guide for Nondestructive Inspection of Welds (Adopted by U.S. DoD)

ANSI/AWS B1.11-88, Guide for Visual Inspection of Welds

MIL-STD-1890A (AT), Inspection of Welded Joints

Industry-Specific

There are many industry- or product-specific inspection standards and guidelines available. In the electronics industry, for example:

ANSI/IPC-A-600D, Acceptability of Printed Boards

ANSI/IPC-A-610A, Acceptability of Printed Board Assemblies

ANSI/IPC-S-804A, Solderability Test Methods for Printed Wiring Boards

FED-STD-228, Methods of Testing Insulated Cable and Wire

Fed. Test Method Std. No. 141—Paint, Varnish, Lacquer, and Related Materials; Methods of Inspection, Sampling, and Testing

IFI-125, Test Procedure for the Locking Ability Performance of Chemical Coated Lock Screws

IFI-137, Inspection and Quality Assurance for General-Purpose Blind Rivets

Safety:

IEEE 510:1983, Recommended Practices for Safety in High-Voltage and High Power Testing

Canadian Standards (Special Processes)

W178.1, Certification of Welding Inspection Organizations

W178.2, Certification of Welding Inspectors

☌ *Questions Your Registrar May Ask*

Additional questions regarding inspection and testing may be asked depending upon your approach toward compliance with this section.

4.10.1 General

☑ Are all inspection and testing activities defined in quality plans and/or documented procedures?

☑ Are all drawings and specifications used by Inspectors the same revision level as those from which the products were manufactured? How is that control maintained?

☑ Is calibrated inspection, measuring, and test equipment used in performing all inspections and tests? How is that indicated?

☑ How is the required inspection, measuring, and test equipment identified to be used?

☑ Are any representative samples referenced for inspection and testing purposes? How are they identified and controlled?

☑ Are the qualifications for all persons performing inspection and testing activities defined (documented)? Where?

☑ Are all inspection and testing personnel properly trained? How is that documented?

4.10.2 Receiving Inspection and Testing

☑ Who is authorized to perform receiving inspection and testing activities? Where is this defined (documented)?

☑ Which products require receiving inspection or testing? Where is this defined?

☑ How do you know what receiving inspection or testing activities are required (e.g., 100%, random, statistical sampling techniques, Deming's *kp* rule)?

☑ What does receiving inspection or testing consist of (e.g., checklists, statistical sampling tables)? Where is this defined?

☑ How are purchasing requirements communicated to those individuals performing receiving inspection and testing for verification? How are special handling requirements (e.g., for hazardous material or perishable product) communicated to receiving personnel? Where is this defined?

☑ How are amendments to purchase orders communicated to the appropriate inspectors? Are "open" purchase orders kept current? How?

☑ Where specified as the control method, do suppliers submit statistical data as required?

☑ How do procedures ensure that incoming product is not used or processed until it has been inspected or otherwise verified as conforming to specified requirements (are "Receivers" compared to P.O.s)?

☑ How is product that is received "incomplete" (e.g., partial shipments, missing C of A, missing MTR) handled?

☑ How are "damaged" goods handled? Where is this defined?

☑ Can you show me an example of a product that has passed inspection? Can you show me an example of a product has failed inspection? How do you document these results?

☑ Do receiving inspection and test procedures address how to feed back information to Purchasing regarding the poor quality performance of a subcontractor?

☑ Are you allowed to release incoming product, for urgent production purposes, prior to verification? If yes, then what procedures do you follow?

☑ Who is authorized to release incoming product, for urgent production purposes, prior to verification? How is positive identification maintained?

4.10.3 In-Process Inspection and Testing

☑ Who is authorized to perform in-process inspection and testing activities? Where is this defined (documented)?

☑ Which products require in-process inspection and testing? Where is this defined?

☑ How do you know what the required in-process inspection and tests are? Where is this defined?

☑ What does receiving inspection and testing consist of (e.g., checklists, statistical techniques)? Where is this defined?

☑ How do you know when all of the required in-process inspection and tests have been completed or necessary reports have been received and verified?

☑ Can product be released prior to all of the required in-process inspection and tests being completed or necessary reports being received and verified?

4.10.4 Final Inspection and Testing

☑ Who is authorized to perform final inspection and testing activities? Where is this defined (documented)?

☑ How do you know what the required final inspection and tests are? Where is this defined?

☑ What does receiving inspection and testing consist of (e.g., checklists, statistical sampling tables, etc.)? Where is this defined?

☑ What happens to those items that fail to pass their final inspection? Where is this defined?

☑ How do you indicate that all of the required final inspection and test activities specified in the quality plan and/or documented procedures have been satisfactorily completed and the associated test data and documentation are available and authorized?

☑ Who is authorized to release finished product? When can product be released?

4.10.5 Inspection and Test Records

☑ How do you know that all of the specified (required) inspection and tests, including those specified either on receipt of product or in-process, have been carried out and that the results meet specified requirements?

☑ How are inspection and testing results documented or recorded?

☑ Do inspection and test records

- Show clearly whether the product has passed or failed the inspections and/or tests according to defined acceptance criteria?

- Identify the inspection authority responsible for the release of product?

4.11 Control of Inspection, Measuring, and Test Equipment

At a Glance

You must do the following:

9001	9002	9003
✓	✓	✓

- Establish and maintain documented procedures to control, calibrate, and maintain inspection, measuring, and test equipment (including test software)

- Ensure that measurement uncertainty is known and is consistent with the required measurement capability

- Ensure that test software or comparative references such as test hardware used as suitable forms of inspection are checked, to prove that they are capable of verifying the acceptability of product, prior to release for use during production, installation, or servicing, and are rechecked at prescribed intervals

- Ensure that where the availability of technical data pertaining to the measurement equipment is a specified requirement, such data is made available, when required by the customer or customer's representative, for verification that the measuring equipment is functionally adequate

- Establish a formal metrological confirmation (calibration) system for inspection, measuring, and test equipment.

QUALITY MANUAL

11.0 CONTROL OF INSPECTION, MEASURING, AND TEST EQUIPMENT

11.1 General

ABC Company has established and maintains documented procedures to control, calibrate, and maintain inspection, measuring, and test equipment and devices (including test software) used by ABC Company to demonstrate the conformance of product to the specified requirements. Inspection, measuring, and test equipment will be used in a manner that ensures that the measurement uncertainty is known and is consistent with the required measurement capability.

Where test software or comparative references such as test hardware are used as suitable forms of inspection, they will be checked to prove that they are capable of verifying the acceptability of product, prior to release for use during production, installation, or servicing, and will be rechecked at prescribed intervals. ABC Company will establish the extent and frequency of such checks and will maintain records as evidence of control.

Where the availability of technical data pertaining to the measurement equipment or device is a specified requirement, such data will be made available, when required by the customer or customer's representative, for verification that the measuring equipment or device is functionally adequate.

Quality Manual

I suggest paraphrasing text from the standard as closely as possible throughout this section. Some minimal tailoring may be required, but specifics should be left in your procedure(s). Particular attention should be given to the subclauses contained in ISO 9001/2/3, section 4.11.2. Excessive tailoring of such detailed subclauses can result in an auditor having greater difficulty in verifying your compliance. By following the original format and structure, you reduce this risk considerably.

For companies offering a service where no inspection, measuring, and test equipment is involved, other less tangible measuring techniques may be used (e.g., polling, questionnaires, surveys, etc.). It is the responsibility of the company to identify which, if any, of these less tangible measuring techniques are to be used.

Companies that operate "in-house" calibration laboratories and desire to exceed the minimal requirements of ISO 9000 should consider additional compliance with specific "Calibration Systems Requirements" standards such as ANSI/NCSL Z540-1 or ISO 10012-1. I suggest paraphrasing the text from these standards as closely as possible, and merging them with those of ISO 9000 in your quality manual. As with ISO 9000, some minimal tailoring may be required, but specifics should be left in your procedure(s).

Procedure

This section begins by requiring the user to establish a calibration system. While the standard itself may be referenced in developing such a system, Note 18, at the end of ISO 9001/2/3, clause 4.11.2, references ISO 10012-1 for guidance. That standard is primarily intended to be used by a fully functional calibration laboratory.

Recognizing the different needs of companies, ANSI/NCSL Z540-1 was developed in two parts. Part One is intended for the fully operational calibration laboratory, while a less comprehensive Part Two is specifically directed toward those companies that subcontract all of their calibration. This allows the user to avoid addressing those requirements that do not relate to their application.

Measurement Uncertainty

ISO 9000 requires that inspection, measuring, and test equipment be used in a manner that ensures that the measurement uncertainty is known and is consistent with the required measurement capability. This is often one of the least understood concepts contained in the standard.

For the most comprehensive study of measurement uncertainty available, refer to NCSL RP-12, "Determining and Reporting Measurement Uncertainties." For additional guidance on dimensional measurement uncertainty, refer to "Searching for Zero—A Guide for Calibration and Uncertainty Factors in Dimensional Metrology" (an AMTMA publication).

For more information on these organizations and obtaining both of these documents, refer to Appendix A.

Test Software and Hardware

Both test software and hardware must be checked to prove that they are capable of verifying the acceptability of product, prior to release for use during production, installation, or servicing, and must be rechecked at prescribed intervals.

Validation of test software normally consists of demonstrations verifying proper operation. Records documenting these validation activities should be maintained. After the initial validation, test software rarely requires any form of ongoing verification. Because software should not change over time, the most common way in which a program becomes corrupt is through contact with a computer virus. Scanning the software for computer viruses could be viewed as a form of verification. Another approach is to use the software to check a known "good" sample of product.

Validation of test hardware normally consists of demonstrations verifying proper functionality and operation. Test hardware (e.g., jigs, fixtures, templates, patterns) must be checked at prescribed intervals to ensure continued suitability. For example, a microprocessor-based instrument that digitally tests other microprocessor-based products must be checked (or verified) at prescribed intervals. A practical approach would be to periodically run a series of functional tests on the instrument to ensure it is continuing to operate properly. Jigs, fixtures, templates, and patterns would be checked for damage or excessive wear.

Availability of Technical Data

It is quite common for companies to require calibration data for high-precision instruments used in critical or safety-related inspections, tests, etc., to increase their level of confidence in the results. This is particularly true of regulated industries. To address this, the standard states:

> *Where the availability of technical data pertaining to the measurement equipment is a specified requirement, such data shall be made available, when required by the customer or customer's representative, for verification that the measuring equipment is functionally adequate.*

This means that calibration data can be stated as a requirement in a customer's contract, a regulation, or in your own quality system. (Although the term "technical data" could mean "specifications/accuracy," this is already required in ISO 9001/2/3, clause 4.11.2.)

Full "As Received" and "As Left" calibration data is normally only of value when you are monitoring your measuring and test equipment. Each instrument will have its own stability and drift rate characteristics. Instruments that are stable with low drift rates are typically assigned to critical process stages or high-production areas. Instruments that perform poorly may be assigned to noncritical areas where less accuracy is required. Calibration data is also used as a basis for calibration interval adjustment. If you are not routinely monitoring the performance of your equipment, full calibration data would have little or no added value.

¦Ⱦ *Quality Systems Requirements*

QS-9000, section 4.11.3, "Inspection, Measuring, and Test Equipment Records," requires records of calibration and verification activities on all gages, measuring, and test equipment, including employee-owned gages, to include "gage conditions and actual readings as received for calibration/verification."

If you state compliance with, or accept contracts that invoke QS-9000, you are automatically required to maintain "As Received" data on all inspection, measuring, and test equipment.

QUALITY MANUAL

11.2 Control Procedure

ABC Company will:

(a) determine the measurements to be made and the accuracy required, and select the appropriate inspection, measuring, and test equipment that is capable of the necessary accuracy and precision;

(b) identify all inspection, measuring, and test equipment that can affect product quality, and calibrate and adjust them at prescribed intervals, or prior to use, against certified equipment having a known valid relationship to internationally or nationally recognized standards. Where no such standards exist, the basis used for calibration will be documented;

(c) define the process employed for the calibration of inspection, measuring, and test equipment, including details of equipment type, unique identification, location, frequency of checks, check method, acceptance criteria, and the action to be taken when results are unsatisfactory;

(d) identify inspection, measuring, and test equipment with a suitable indicator or approved identification record to show the calibration status;

(e) maintain calibration records for inspection, measuring, and test equipment;

(f) assess and document the validity of previous inspection and test results when inspection, measuring, and test equipment is found to be out of calibration;

(g) ensure that the environmental conditions are suitable for the calibrations, inspections, measurements, and tests being carried out;

(h) ensure that the handling, preservation, and storage of inspection, measuring, and test equipment is such that the accuracy and fitness for use are maintained;

(i) safeguard inspection, measuring, and test facilities, including both test hardware and test software, from adjustments that would invalidate the calibration setting.

Procedure

All of the subclauses listed in the standard should be addressed in the same "Calibration System" manual for ease of use. How you develop this system depends primarily on whether you have personnel within the company calibrating and maintaining equipment or have this activity subcontracted. If calibration services are subcontracted, you are still responsible for ensuring that all of the requirements contained in this section are met.

Let's discuss each subclause contained in this section of the standard.

(a) Equipment Selection

This subclause requires you to

determine the measurements to be made and the accuracy required, and select the appropriate inspection, measuring, and test equipment that is capable of the necessary accuracy and precision

in relation to the *product*. This requirement is addressed when you create your "Quality Plan" selecting the appropriate inspection, measuring, and test equipment.

You must define each inspection and test point of the product, including acceptable tolerance limits and accuracy required. You should also determine an acceptable test accuracy ratio (TAR) to be maintained.

For example:

Step 7—Verify 5 V ±0.3 V at test point #12.

How accurate should the inspection or test equipment be that is used to verify this test point? If you specify a voltmeter that also has an accuracy of ±0.3 V, then you have a 1:1 test accuracy ratio.

However, you would generally want a higher ratio than 1:1. If your voltmeter is actually reading low by 0.15 V (still within its stated tolerance), and the test point reads +0.25 V (acceptable), it may really be +0.4 V (unacceptable).

ISO 10012-1 recommends that a 3:1 test accuracy ratio be maintained as a minimum. Following that advice, the example should use a voltmeter with an accuracy of ±0.1 V. In this case the voltmeter would have to be out-of-tolerance by 300% before a 1:1 test accuracy ratio is reached! The greater the test accuracy ratio, the higher your confidence level.

✍ Note

The guidance given in NCSL RP-3, "Calibration Procedures," can easily be applied to development of individual "Inspection and Test Procedures."

(b) Calibration Intervals and Traceability

This subclause requires you to

> identify all inspection, measuring, and test equipment including measurement devices that can affect product quality and calibrate and adjust them at prescribed intervals, or prior to use, against certified equipment having a known valid relationship to internationally or nationally recognized Standards. Where no such Standards exist, the basis used for calibration shall be documented.

Identification of all inspection, measuring, and test equipment used is normally accomplished by compiling a list or database. This database is then used to assure that calibrations are performed at prescribed intervals. When defining calibration intervals for inspection, measuring, and test equipment, you may consider the manufacturer's recommended interval or other industry guidelines. Be sure to describe your procedure for changing calibration intervals, as needed, on specific items.

▦ Calibration System Databases

While many calibration-system database management software packages are available, these can be expensive for a small company. In the past, small companies have relied on simple card-file systems to alert them to calibration due dates. I would like to point out that Microsoft Windows includes a cardfile application that can easily be used for this purpose. However, this approach is very limiting and can quickly be outgrown.

▢ "Calibration Due Date" Filing Systems

Filing records for each item of inspection, measuring, and test equipment by its "due date" is another technique used by small companies to ensure timely calibration. At the end of each month the individual responsible for the calibration system will pull those records filed as being due for calibration during the following month, and arrange for their calibration. Color coding of files may be used to enhance this system. Some companies with computer databases use this filing method as a failsafe to ensure that all calibrations are performed as required.

⌛ *Calibration Interval Adjustment*

Don't state in your quality manual or procedure(s) that

Recalibration intervals are specified in the calibration procedures

or

Instruments will be calibrated at intervals recommended by their manufacturer.

These statements paint you into another corner. The manufacturer's recommended calibration interval is great as a basis for initial establishment of an interval, but these are generally conservative. Allow yourself the freedom to lengthen or shorten calibration intervals based on individual instrument performance.

This just makes sense. If the instruments you have are stable, then why calibrate them every six months when you can lengthen that cycle to nine or twelve months? By the same token, if you have instruments that are constantly found out of tolerance, a more effective corrective action would be to shorten their calibration cycle until they remain in tolerance. Both of these practices can result in significant cost savings and are completely acceptable. In fact, they are quite common in the calibration industry.

✍ *Note*

For additional guidance refer to NCSL RP-1, "Establishment and Adjustment of Calibration Intervals."

💡 *Calibration Interval Extensions*

There are occasionally instances where inspection, measuring, and test equipment cannot be calibrated on or before its calibration due date, yet inspection or production needs require its continued use. The simple fact that an instrument is due for calibration does not necessarily mean that its results are no longer valid. Many companies allow "one-time" calibration interval or due date extensions for a specified, and limited, period of time. Procedures allowing this practice must detail

- **When** a calibration interval extension is allowed

- **How** calibration interval extensions are documented

- **What** is the maximum period of time allowed for a calibration interval extension

- **Who** is authorized to approve calibration interval extensions

- **How** approval of calibration interval extensions is indicated

- **What** is the basis for allowing each calibration interval extension

Calibration interval extensions are commonly based on the history of each instrument's performance and its known drift rate. Interval extensions are difficult to justify if you have not been requiring full calibration data (indicating drift rate).

 Calibration Subcontractors and Calibration Due Dates

Calibration subcontractors generally supply reports or certificates of calibration (or equivalent) with all inspection, measuring, and test equipment they calibrate. These reports or certificates indicate a calibration due date, which is normally on any "calibration status" labels they apply to the equipment as well.

These subcontractors typically have no way of knowing the calibration interval that you have established. Therefore, the due date indicated on the reports, certificates, or status labels is a "recommended" due date. The *actual* calibration due date is established and maintained by *you* in *your* calibration system. The "due date" on an externally supplied calibration report or certificate is thus easily explained as not applying. However, a subcontractor's status label remaining on the equipment could present a problem.

There are several ways to address this situation. Here are a couple of the more common solutions:

- Notify the calibration subcontractor of the calibration interval or due date established for each item of equipment they calibrate (so that their calibration report or certificate can reflect the proper due date).

Or,

- Upon receipt of each item of equipment, make a handwritten "pen" revision on the report or certificate and calibration status label to reflect the proper calibration due date. For example:

26 March 1995 RCR

Calibration Due: ~~26 Sept. 1995~~

Some companies subcontract *all* of their calibration requirements, including maintenance of the calibration system itself. This is completely consistent with the requirements of the standard, provided the calibration subcontractor provides services that meet all of the detailed requirements of this section of ISO 9000.

Calibration Traceability

Having a "known valid relationship to internationally or nationally recognized standards" is typically referred to as "traceability" in the calibration industry. This word was probably not used here to avoid confusion with "product traceability."

In regard to calibration traceability, I suggest you exactly follow the words of the standard. Be aware that your national standards laboratory may not be able to calibrate everything. You may have instruments that must be calibrated with traceability to one of these:

- Fundamental or natural physical constants

- National standards of other countries that may, or may not, be correlated with your national standards

- Ratio types of calibrations

- Comparison to consensus (industry) standards

A listing of national standards of other countries that are correlated with your national standards can usually be obtained by contacting your national standards laboratory. (See Figure 4.11-1 for the U.S.)

Since there is currently no U.S. National Standard for hardness (work is underway by NIST to develop such a national standard), it is common to have the manufacturer calibrate these items, typically in accordance with ASTM E-18, "Standard Methods of Test for Rockwell Hardness and Rockwell Superficial Hardness of Metallic Materials." Calibration traceability is usually to the manufacturer. In each of these instances, the basis of calibration traceability must be documented.

💣 NIST, Not NBS

Get the name right. Be sure *not* to say:

> . . . *all calibrations shall be traceable to the National Bureau of Standards.*

The U.S. "National Bureau of Standards" changed its name in 1988 to the "National Institute of Standards and Technology." This little mistake immediately sends the message to your auditor that you are *way behind the times* when it comes to calibration.

April 16, 1993

RECOGNITION OF EQUIVALENCY STANDARDS BETWEEN NATIONAL INSTITUTE OF STANDARDS AND TECHNOLOGY AND NATIONAL STANDARDS LABORATORIES OF OTHER COUNTRIES

AUSTRALIA

Length
Time
Electrical Potential
Electrical Resistance
Electrical Capacitance
Temperature
Luminous Intensity

FRANCE

Length
Mass
Time
Dc Electrical Potential
Electrical Resistance
Electrical Capacitance
Temperature
Luminous Intensity
Activity

ITALY

Length
Time
Voltage
Electrical Resistance
Electrical Capacitance
Temperature Scales
Luminous Intensity
Pressure

CANADA

Length
Mass
Time
Time Scale
Voltage
Electric Resistance
Capacitance
Temperature
Luminous Intensity

ISRAEL

Electrical Potential
Time

UNITED KINGDOM

Length
Time
Voltage
Electrical Resistance
Electrical Capacitance
Temperature

Figure 4.11-1: Recognition of Equivalency Standards between the NIST (U.S.) and National Standards Laboratories of Other Countries

◇ *Are Actual, Applicable NIST Test Numbers Required?*

This is a difficult question to answer because it is misleading. The real question is, "How can traceability be demonstrated?" While requiring the actual, applicable NIST test numbers to be on your calibration certificate or report is one means, there are others. These numbers can be meaningless if not substantiated by a site audit where traceability is verified. This can be achieved through assessing the subcontractor yourself or accepting the audit reports or certifications of others. For example:

Laboratories accredited by a recognized body, such as:

- The National Voluntary Laboratory Accreditation Program (NVLAP—U.S.)

- The American Association for Laboratory Accreditation (A2LA)

- The Calibration Laboratory Assessment Service (CLAS—Canada)

- The Service for Certification of Calibration Laboratories (SECLAC—Mexico)

State Weights and Measures Laboratories participating in the "State Standards Program" administered by NIST

Laboratories registered to an ISO 9000 series quality standard

Laboratories audited and accepted for use by industry groups such as NAPM, NADCAP, NUPIC, Bellcore

Site assessment by a government auditor

In this instance, you could accept a simple statement of traceability on the calibration certificate or report.

 ### Single Calibration Devices

In some instances, you may find inspection, measuring, and test equipment that requires a single initial calibration (verification) only. After the device is initially calibrated (verified), it will not change physically unless the device is contaminated, damaged, worn, or destroyed. These devices may be checked periodically for contamination, damage or wear, but they cannot be adjusted.

A common example of this is volumetric glassware. The manufacturer of these measuring devices should be able to provide a certificate stating that it had been checked in accordance with ASTM Standard E-542 and found to comply with a specified "Class" of tolerance as defined in ASTM Standard E-1272. The certificate should also include the serial number of the glassware and a statement of traceability (typically to NIST).

Other similar examples can include, but are not limited to, the following:

- Steel rulers (excluding some steel tape measures)

- Hydrometers (reference ASTM E-126)

- Wire-cloth sieves (reference ASTM E-11)

You should identify and address single calibration devices as appropriate throughout your calibration system.

It should also be noted that some inspection, measuring, and test equipment cannot realistically be calibrated because of its extreme variability. For example, cloth tape measures can easily be stretched to invalidate any meaningful calibration. Use of these devices should be clearly defined.

(c) Calibration System Description

Subclause (c) requires you to

> *define the process employed for the calibration of inspection, measuring, and test equipment including details of equipment type, unique identification, location, frequency of checks, check method, acceptance criteria, and the action to be taken when results are unsatisfactory.*

These requirements are typically addressed in the calibration system itself, with specific information regarding each item of inspection, measuring, and test equipment contained in a database or cardfile.

 ### Check Methods

For the purpose of this clause, "check methods" (work instructions) are actually specific "calibration procedures" or "test methods." In the U.S., the term "calibration procedure" includes "performance verification" procedures. The word *calibrate* implies that you always adjust, or optimize, an instrument. But in practice, a "performance verification" procedure is most often used where the performance of the instrument is verified. A report or certificate of calibration is then issued stating that the instrument was found to be operating within stated specifications (normally the instrument manufacturer's stated accuracy or tolerances) with a known uncertainty.

Some calibration subcontractors will optimize instruments after they pass a certain percentage of their tolerance, but this is by no means guaranteed. A true calibration procedure is generally only used when an instrument fails some portion of its "performance verification."

The term "check method" is most appropriate for the standard because it should also be interpreted as being applicable to "test hardware" discussed earlier. The "acceptance criteria and the action to be taken when results are unsatisfactory" would normally be contained in each specific instrument's "Calibration/Verification Procedure" or "Check Method."

 ### Manufacturer's Calibration Procedures

Here is a common pitfall *not* to place in your quality manual or procedure:

> *Each instrument will be calibrated according to its own calibration procedure as indicated by the manufacturer.*

Although this meets the requirement contained in ISO 9000, it is also an excellent example of painting yourself into a corner. Many calibration laboratories do not use the manufacturer's calibration procedure. Why? Because most manufacturers write very conservative calibration procedures that check each and every parameter, range, and function of the device.

Several calibration laboratories, including test equipment manufacturers, use abbreviated versions of these procedures. This practice is generally quite acceptable. In fact, many calibration laboratories utilize calibration procedures developed by the U.S. military and obtained through the Government and Industry Data Exchange Program (GIDEP).

But there are even more practical reasons why you should state this differently. For example, let's say you are using temperature monitors or controllers that have a range from 0 to 900 °F. Your application only utilizes them from 300 to 600 °F. If several of these temperature monitors or controllers were found to be out of tolerance, let's say in the 0 to 75 °F and 825 to 900 °F areas, and could not be adjusted or repaired, you would be forced to replace them. This condition is quite common in temperature monitors or controllers as they age and change characteristics.

However, if you allow yourself to utilize "Limited Calibration Devices," you could label them as such and continue to use them *or* develop a calibration procedure that only checked those items in the range they are operating. These practices are generally considered completely acceptable.

The only serious concern regarding the use of alternative calibration procedures is where the procedure may have been abbreviated to the point that it is virtually useless. Although this is rare, some of the less reputable calibration laboratories have been caught doing it (including manufacturers!). If alternative calibration procedures are used by a subcontractor, simply ask for copies of them. If the subcontractor refuses, which can be common, there are several other steps you can take, including a review of the calibration procedures during a site audit of the subcontractor. If you aren't allowed to review the calibration procedures used on your equipment, then you are probably not receiving the service you are paying for. In this situation, the only sensible action is to find another calibration subcontractor.

If you are developing your own calibration procedures, don't reinvent the wheel by writing a procedure describing their layout and structure. Refer to NCSL RP-3.

(d) Calibration and Test Status Labeling

This subclause requires that you

> *identify inspection, measuring, and test equipment with a suitable indicator or approved identification record to show the calibration status.*

| CALIBRATION |
| BY _____   DATE _____ |
| DUE _____   I.D. # _____ |

Figure 4.11-2: Calibration
Status Label

| VERIFICATION |
| BY _____   DATE _____ |
| DUE _____   I.D. # _____ |

Figure 4.11-3: Verification
Status Label

There are several ways in which you can meet this requirement. The most common way to address this requirement is to attach a label to each device (Figure 4.11-2) indicating the following:

- Calibration authority (calibration technician or calibration subcontractor)
- Calibration due date
- Calibration date (optional)
- Asset or serial number of the instrument (optional)

Test hardware can't really be given a calibration status label if it wasn't really calibrated. Right? In this instance, it's common to attach a "Verification Status" label (Figure 4.11-3) that indicates the following:

- Verification authority (verification technician or verification subcontractor)
- Verification due date
- Verification date (optional)
- Asset or serial number of the instrument (optional)

You may also have inspection, measuring, and test equipment that must be standardized or calibrated before each use. This is most common in the calibration or testing laboratory itself. In this case, the instrument would need to be labeled accordingly (Figure 4.11-4). Similarly, some instruments require standardization (calibration) at very regular intervals (daily, weekly, monthly, etc.). It is also typical for such instruments to be labeled with that interval and an actual record, or log, of when each standardization occurred (Figure 4.11-5).

**STANDARDIZE
BEFORE EACH USE**

Figure 4.11-4: "Standardize
before Each Use" Label

CALIBRATE WEEKLY

Figure 4.11-5: "Calibrate
Weekly" Label

The performance of these instruments is often charted in a graph as evidence of confidence in their stability and reliability.

Some instruments require correction values that must be known in order to properly perform a measurement. This is sometimes called a "special calibration." The correction values are typically supplied on a calibration report or certificate or data sheet, but in some cases are also included on the calibration status label for ease of use.

As mentioned earlier, you may have inspection, measuring, and test equipment that has been designated as a "limited calibration device." In this instance, the fact that the instrument does have limitations must be clearly evident on the labeling. Many "limited calibration" status labels look like any other, simply stating that the calibration is limited without indicating which range, function, or parameter. This raises a flag to auditors. They will typically check to see which functions are being used and which are limited. Quite often the limitation has been ignored.

A better approach is to use a larger, more comprehensive "Limited/Special Calibration" label or tag that offers more detail whenever possible (see Figure 4.11-6). Most of the better calibration subcontractors will provide these on your instrument when this is encountered. Many measuring devices must be calibrated, or standardized, using a certified reference material (CRM) or substance (e.g., chemicals, agricultural standards). These materials often have a shelf life and must also be labeled accordingly (see Figure 4.11-7: "Shelf Life" label).

Uncalibrated measuring equipment must also be identified. In many instances, you will have measuring equipment that is not used for inspection and test purposes. This instrumentation may be monitoring noncritical aspects of the process that do not affect the quality of the product. Uncalibrated measuring

LIMITED / SPECIAL CALIBRATION	
BY _____ DATE _____	
DUE _____ I.D. # _____	
Range / Function / Parameter / Value	Limitations / Corrections

Figure 4.11-6: "Limited/Special Calibration" Label

```
┌──────────────────────────┐
│  ████ SHELF LIFE ████     │
│  OF _____ AT _____ │
│  EXPIRES _____  │
└──────────────────────────┘
```

Figure 4.11-7: "Shelf Life" Label

```
┌──────────────────────────┐
│                          │
│   CALIBRATION NOT        │
│      REQUIRED            │
│                          │
└──────────────────────────┘
```

Figure 4.11-8: "Calibration Not Required" Label

equipment often raises a flag to auditors. Be prepared to justify *why* each instrument that is not calibrated continues to be used.

At this point you may be thinking "I thought everything had to be calibrated." While this is a good idea, it's not always practical. For clarification, let's look at clause 4.11.1 again:

> *The supplier shall establish and maintain documented procedures to control, calibrate, and maintain inspection, measuring, and test equipment (including test software)* **used by the supplier to demonstrate the conformance of product to the specified requirements.**

To help you differentiate, as a minimum, the following areas *must* all have calibrated equipment:

* Design validation

* All formal, documented inspection and test points (receiving, in-process, and final)

* All process controls or monitors and inspection, measuring, and test equipment gathering data for statistical evaluation

* All inspection, measuring, and test equipment used to calibrate or verify other inspection, measuring, and test equipment

Clearly, this clause is an integral portion of many other quality system elements. It should also be pointed out that the cost of calibration can be self-funded by reducing the amount of waste produced through inconsistencies introduced by neglected and "drifting" instruments or controllers.

✍ *Note*

A good source for standard "off-the-shelf" calibration and verification status labels:

Q-CEE'S Products Division   Customer Service: (800) 950-4922
The Mountain Corporation   (713) 686-0145
P.O. Box 924647
Houston, TX 77292-4647   Fax: (800) 285-7016

💣 *Lack of Calibration Status Indicators*

A few companies have taken the position that inspection, measuring, and test equipment that is not used for final inspection or test, or is in storage, will be identified through the lack of any status indicator. They argue that they simply have too many instruments to reasonably control. This is a poor argument. In fact, it could be viewed as a lack of compliance with clause 4.1.2.2, "Resources."

The standard clearly states:

The supplier shall identify inspection, measuring, and test equipment with a suitable indicator or approved identification record to show the calibration status.

The lack of a *suitable indicator or approved identification record* as a means of showing *the calibration status* does not, in any way, meet the intent of this requirement.

Bellcore "Quality System Generic Requirements," TA-NWT-001252 (a telecommunications industry–specific standard based on ISO 9001, similar to QS-9000), states:

Tools, gauges, test equipment, etc., that are inactive or do not require calibration, shall be so identified.

This should *not* be viewed as an additional requirement. It is simply a further clarification of the standard.

(e) Calibration Records

This subclause requires you to

maintain calibration records for inspection, measuring, and test equipment.

Several specific requirements for calibration records are mentioned throughout this section. You must require all calibration service subcontractors to supply reports or certificates of calibration (or equivalent) with all inspection, measuring, and test equipment that address all of the applicable requirements of the standard. (See "Records" and the end of this chapter for more detail.)

🚰 *Chemicals*

Chemicals used in inspection and testing activities are often supplied with a statement or "Certificate of Compliance/Conformance" (C of C). A common example is chemicals supplied with a statement of certification by the American Society of Chemists (ASC) on their label. While a C of C is generally considered worthless, there are exceptions to this (as discussed in Section 4.6). I consider this an example of an acceptable C of C.

(f) Impact Analysis

This subclause requires that you

> *assess and document the validity of previous inspection and test results when inspection, measuring, and test equipment is found to be out of calibration.*

This is typically called an "Impact Analysis" and is based on out-of-tolerance calibration data. The standard stops short of explaining what you are supposed to do with this data. Most commercial manufacturers use inspection, measuring, and test equipment that is far more accurate than is needed for its application (greater than 3:1 Test Accuracy Ratio—TAR). In this instance, there is often no adverse impact on the final product, and therefore no further action is required (other than to document this conclusion).

Most companies consider out-of-tolerance inspection, measuring, and test equipment to be a nonconformity that is documented on a "Corrective Action Request" form. Immediate corrective action is often simply to recalibrate the device and perform an impact analysis. Action taken to prevent recurrence can include shortening the calibration interval of the device, acquiring other inspection, measuring, and test equipment, or developing new methods of verification (inspection).

Manufacturers who are measuring critical tolerances that approach "state-of-the-art" limitations (or just the limitations of their inspection, measuring, and test equipment) are much more concerned with the impact of out-of-tolerance conditions. In many instances, because the nature of the product, traceability and the provision for customer notification, product recall may be a specified requirement (by either the contract or regulatory agencies).

ǀ⅄ Quality Systems Requirements

QS-9000, section 4.11.3, "Inspection, Measuring, and Test Equipment Records," requires "notification to customer if suspect material has been shipped."

⟨?⟩ Customer Notification/Product Recall

Subclause (f) definitely needs clarification in regards to customer notification and/or product recall. Some auditors believe that this subclause requires you to either notify the customer or recall product that has been improperly verified by out-of-tolerance inspection and test equipment. To do this, you would need reverse traceability of the product from the time of the first receiving inspection of raw material or subcomponents used in manufacturing the product through completion *and* forward traceability to the customer or end user. While the clause certainly implies product recall, if we remember clause 4.8, "Product identification and traceability," *traceability* is not a requirement unless *specified*. Therefore, "product recall" is not required unless specified.

Perhaps the next version of the standard should have a subclause following (f) with the following words:

> *The supplier shall:*
> *(f¹) notify the customer when inspection and test results are invalid and traceability is a specified requirement.*

While this clause would not specifically require a product recall, it would clarify the intent and add meaning to the purpose of traceability.

⟨?⟩ *"Significant Out-of-Tolerance" Conditions*

Although you can require ISO 10012-1 as a quality standard for calibration, if you subcontract calibration you will find that the majority of U.S. calibration laboratories are in transition from compliance with MIL-STD-45662A* to ANSI/NCSL Z540-1. Both of these standards require that "Out-of-Tolerance" data be recorded and reported to the user and are, therefore, generally considered to comply with the ISO 9000 series, section 4.11. However, there is one area for concern: "Significant Out-of-Tolerance" conditions.

Both MIL-STD-45662A and ANSI/NCSL Z540-1 allow a calibration laboratory to define "Significant Out-of-Tolerance" conditions. This allows the calibration laboratory to *forego* reporting an out-of-tolerance condition until it meets some specific value that they have established as being significant, typically at 200% of tolerance or greater. ISO 9000 does not recognize or allow this. In clause 4.11.2 f, it requires you to

> *assess and document the validity of previous inspection and test results when inspection, measuring, and test equipment is found to be out of calibration.*

But this is not the whole picture. MIL-STD-45662A requires that the calibration laboratory maintain a 4:1 test accuracy ratio (TAR) between the measurement standard used and the device being calibrated or state what ratio was maintained. Therefore, if a 4:1 test accuracy ratio was maintained, an instru-

---

*According to an NCSL survey dated Oct. 1990, the vast majority of calibration laboratories operating in the U.S. state compliance with MIL-STD-45662A.

ment may not be affected by an out-of-tolerance condition unless the measurement standard was found to be 400% out-of-tolerance. Theoretically, the impact of this out-of-tolerance condition may only result in a calibration test accuracy ratio reduced to 1:1.

The bottom line here is this: If a 4:1 or greater test accuracy ratio is maintained for *all points* tested and the calibration laboratory has defined a "Significant Out-of-Tolerance" condition to be *no greater* than 400% of the tolerance, then the *intent* of ISO 9000 is still being met by the MIL-STD-45662A–compliant system.

Although ANSI/NCSL Z540-1 does not contain a specific minimum test accuracy ratio requirement, a similar approach may be taken.

 ## Traceability of Subcontracted Calibration Services

Traceability is most certainly a requirement where calibration services are subcontracted. This applies to both subclauses (b) and (f). It is common in the metrology (calibration) industry for a record or log (typically on computer) to be maintained listing all instruments calibrated with each specific measurement standard. This allows for notification of the user if that measurement standard is later found to be out-of-tolerance (this is addressed in ISO 10012-1, MIL-STD-45662A & ANSI/NCSL Z540-1).

 ## Assigned Values for "Fixed" Devices

Some inspection, measuring, and test equipment cannot be adjusted (such as a standard capacitor, resistor, or inductor). Their values are fixed. As the instrument's characteristics change over time, its value must be periodically monitored and recorded. When *calibrated*, the results are typically reported as an "Assigned Value."

Because tolerances for these devices are normally stated in terms of drift during a stated period of time, an externally generated report or certificate of calibration would not ordinarily indicate whether the device was found in or out of tolerance. You would need to review past calibration results in order to make such a determination before you can comply with subclause f.

Carefully reading the literature accompanying "fixed"-value devices, you will occasionally find that the stated accuracy was only valid at the time of manufacture. This is particularly true of older devices. In this instance you must establish and assign the device an accuracy. I strongly encourage you to call upon expert, experienced advice before addressing this issue. This problem is most easily addressed when you are initially purchasing the device from the manufacturer (qualify your suppliers).

Retiring Inspection, Measuring, and Test Equipment

Nothing lasts forever. Eventually, you will replace various inspection, measuring, and test equipment. In order to fully meet the intent of this clause, you must ensure that equipment taken out of service was "in tolerance" at that time. This process is typically called "decertification." It usually involves calibrating or verifying the equipment just prior to taking it out of service to document that it was still within tolerance.

(g) Environmental Conditions

This subclause requires you to

ensure that the environmental conditions are suitable for the calibration, inspections, measurements, and tests being carried out.

The performance of many devices and instruments can easily be influenced by

Temperature	Vibration	Radiation
Humidity	Noise	Pressure

Gage blocks, for example, expand and contract with temperature. Measuring devices whose operation is based on natural physical constants may require correction data. For example, when using a mercury manometer to calibrate pressure indicators, one would need to make adjustments to the readings based on the temperature of the mercury. Specific operating requirements are generally contained in the user's manual for each instrument.

(h) Handling, Preservation, and Storage

This subclause requires that you

ensure that the handling, preservation, and storage of inspection, measuring, and test equipment is such that the accuracy and fitness for use is maintained.

The performance of high-accuracy instrumentation can easily be influenced by factors such as these:

- Environmental conditions (temperature, humidity, etc.)
- Shock (tossing equipment around, improperly padding for movement, etc.)
- EMF (electromagnetic fields)
- ESD (electrostatic discharge)

Other factors may also need to be considered, depending upon each instrument's intended use. Particular attention should be given to those instruments being moved, handled, and used extensively. Specific operating requirements are generally contained in the user manual for each instrument. Don't forget about inspection, measuring, and test equipment used by "Servicing," if applicable.

(i) Tamper-Resistant Seals

This subclause requires that you

> *safeguard inspection, measuring, and test facilities, including both test hardware and test software, from adjustments which would invalidate the calibration setting.*

This is generally interpreted as requiring the use of tamper-resistant seals on inspection, measuring, and test equipment. These seals, or other devices, restrict access to adjustments whose setting affects the calibration (reference ISO 10012-1, clause 4.12, "Sealing for integrity").

Your procedure must address their use, as well as the disposition of any equipment whose seal has been violated (broken). When developing this procedure, consider instances where you may need to remove a seal to access equipment for other purposes (such as changing a battery or lamp bulb). I suggest that you authorize the quality manager, or his or her designate (usually a quality representative), to access equipment and promptly reapply a new tamper-resistant seal. In the case of test software, this is normally accomplished by "write-protecting" or "pass-word encrypting" the test program.

 ## Records

Evidence of compliance with this section may be contained in databases and procedures, as well as records. For example, see Figure 4.11-9.

Guidance

For further guidance, refer to:

> ISO 9000-2:1993, Quality Management and Quality Assurance Standards—Part 2: Generic guidelines for application of ISO 9001, ISO 9002, and ISO 9003
> Section 4.11—"Inspection, measuring, and test equipment"

> ISO 9004-1:1994, Quality Management and Quality System Elements—Part 1: Guidelines
> Section 13—"Control of inspection, measuring, and test equipment"

Sub-clause	Requirement	Database/Procedure/Record
a	Accuracy Required	Inspection, measuring, and test procedures, drawings, schematics, etc.
	Selection (based on accuracy/precision)	Inspection, measuring, and test procedures/equipment manual
b	Identify all inspection, measuring, and test equipment	Card-file or database
	Calibration interval	Card-file or database
	Known valid relationship to internationally or nationally recognized standards—or other	Report or Certificate of Calibration (calibration traceability)
c	Calibration system	
	Equipment type	Card-file or database
	Unique identification	Card-file or database
	Location	Card-file or database
	Frequency of checks	Card-file or database
	Check method	Calibration procedure
	Acceptance criteria	Calibration procedure
	Actions to be taken	Calibration procedure
d	Suitable indicator of calibration status	Typically a calibration status label (Not typically viewed as a record but can be a calibration log or other record)
e	Maintain calibration records	Databases/procedures/records
f	Assessment of impact of out-of-tolerance condition	Corrective Action Request or equivalent with "record of use"
g	Environmental conditions	Chart recordings (if internal) Report or Certificate of Calibration (if external)
h	Handling, preservation, and storage	Equipment manual
i	Tamper-resistant sealing	Does not typically require a record

Figure 4.11-9: Calibration Records

ISO 10012-1:1992, Quality Assurance Requirements for Measuring Equipment—
Part 1: Metrological confirmation system for measuring equipment

ISO/IEC Guide 25:1990, General Requirements for the Competence of Calibration and Testing Laboratories

ISO Guide 31:1981, Contents of Certificates of Reference Materials

ISO Guide 33:1989, Uses of Certified Reference Materials

ANSI/NCSL Z540-1:1994, General Requirements for Calibration Laboratories and Measuring and Test Equipment

MIL-STD-45662A, Calibration Systems Requirements

MIL-HDBK-52B, Evaluation of Contractor's Calibration System

Selected NIST Publications

NIST Handbook 133, Uniform Laws and Regulations

NIST Handbook 143, State Weights and Measures Laboratories Program Handbook

NIST Handbook 145, Handbook for the Quality Assurance of Metrological Measurements

NIST Special Publication 791, State Weights and Measures Laboratories: State Standards Program Description and Directory

NIST Technical Note 1297, Guidelines for Evaluating and Expressing the Uncertainty of NIST Measurement Results (a complete copy is included in NCSL RP-12)

NCSL Recommended Practices

Some of the best guidance on developing a calibration quality system is available from the National Conference of Standards Laboratories (NCSL). For more information, refer to Appendix A. The NCSL offers a series of "Recommended Practices" addressing many of the aspects surrounding the operation of a calibration laboratory. They include the following:

RP-1 "Establishment and Adjustment of Calibration Intervals"

RP-2 "Evaluation of Measurement Control Systems and Calibration Laboratories"

RP-3 "Calibration Procedures"

RP-4   "Calibration Systems Specification"

RP-5   "Preparation of Specifications"

RP-6   "Medical Products and Pharmaceutical Industry Calibration Control System Guide"

RP-7   "Laboratory Design"

RP-8   "An individual Equipment Evaluation Guide"

RP-9   "Calibration Laboratory Capabilities Documentation Guidelines"

RP-10 "Establishment and Operation of an Electrical Utility Metrology Laboratory"

RP-11 "Reports and Certificates of Calibration"

RP-12 "Determining and Reporting Measurement Uncertainties"

Other Common Application-Specific Useful Documents

ASTM E 376, Practice for Measuring Coating Thickness by Magnetic Field or Eddy Current Test Methods

ASTM E 77, Standard Test Method for Inspection and Verification of Liquid-in-glass Thermometers

NBS Circular 600, Calibration of Liquid-in-glass Thermometers

NIST Technical Note 1265, International Temperature Scale of 1990 (ITS-90)

NIST Handbook 44, Specifications, Tolerances, and Other Technical Requirements for Weighing and Measuring Devices

NBS Monograph 133, Mass and Mass Values

MIL-STD-120, Gage Inspection

Books

Calibration: Philosophy in Practice, Fluke Corp., Everett, WA
ISBN 0-9638650-0-5 (hardcover—second edition)

Government and Industry Data Exchange Program (GIDEP)

To obtain access to GIDEP, contact:

GIDEP Operations Center	Tel: (909) 273-4677
P.O. Box 8000	Fax: (909) 273-5200
Corona, CA 91718-8000	BBS (909) 273-0200

North American National Standards Laboratories

Canada—NRC:

National Research Council	Tel: (613) 993-7666
Institute for National	
Measurement Standards	Fax: (613) 952-5113
Institute Program Office	
Building 36, Montreal Road	
Ottawa, Canada	
K1A 0R6	

Mexico—CENAM:

	Tel: (42) 15-37-83
Centro Nacional de Metrologia	(42) 16-33-09
Km. 4.5 Carretera a los Cués	(42) 16-65-76
Mpio. El Marqués	(42) 15-53-33
Querétaro C.P. 76900	(42) 15-53-34
	Fax: (42) 16-26-26
	(42) 15-37-34
	International, Dial: 011-52-number

USA—NIST:

National Institute of	
Standards and Technology	
Calibration Program	Tel: (301) 975-2002
Bldg. 411, Rm. A104	Fax: (301) 926-2884
Gaithersburg, MD 20899-0001	

Standard Reference	
Materials Program	Tel: (301) 975-6776
Building 202, Room 204	Fax: (301) 948-3730
Gaithersburg, MD 20899-0001	

National Voluntary Laboratory	
Accreditation Program (NVLAP)	Tel: (301) 975-4042
Building 411, Room A162	Fax: (301) 926-2884
Gaithersburg, MD 20899-0001	

Questions Your Registrar May Ask

Obviously, a company's calibration system can easily exceed the minimum requirements of ISO 9000. The questions in this area will remain focused on the requirements contained in ISO 9000.

4.11.1 General

☑ Who is responsible for maintaining and managing your calibration system? Where is this authority defined?

☑ Do the requirements of this calibration system extend to include inspection, measuring, and test equipment that is loaned, rented, borrowed, or provided by the customer? Where is this documented?

☑ How do you ensure that measurement uncertainty is known and is consistent with the required measurement capability?

☑ How do you ensure that test software or comparative references such as test hardware (e.g., jigs, fixtures, templates, patterns) used as suitable forms of inspection are checked to prove that they are capable of verifying the acceptability of product, prior to release for use during production, installation, or servicing, and are rechecked at prescribed intervals? Can you show me examples of this?

☑ How do you ensure that where the availability of technical data pertaining to the measurement equipment is a specified requirement, such data is made available, when required by the customer or customer's representative, for verification that the measuring equipment is functionally adequate?

4.11.2 Control Procedure

☑ Who is responsible for determining the measurements to be made and the accuracy required? How is this determined? Where is this documented?

☑ Who is responsible for selecting the appropriate inspection, measuring, and test equipment and ensuring that it is capable of the necessary accuracy and precision? Where is this documented?

☑ Who is responsible for identifying all inspection, measuring, and test equipment that can affect product quality? Does this include employee-owned equipment? Who ensures that this equipment is calibrated and adjusted at prescribed intervals, or prior to use?

☑ How is inspection, measuring, and test equipment that has exceeded its calibration due date identified and handled? Are temporary calibration interval extensions allowed? If so, where is this documented?

☑ Is all inspection, measuring, and test equipment calibrated against certified equipment having a known valid relationship to internationally or nationally recognized standards? Where no such standards exist, is the basis used for calibration documented? How can this be verified?

☑ Does your calibration system define the process employed for the calibration of inspection, measuring, and test equipment, including details of

- Equipment type?
- Unique identification?
- Location?
- Frequency of checks (calibration interval)?
- Check method (calibration procedure)?
- Acceptance criteria?
- Action to be taken when results are unsatisfactory?

Where is this defined (documented)?

☑ How does your calibration system identify inspection, measuring, and test equipment to show the calibration status? Does this include test software or comparative references such as test hardware?

☑ Does your calibration system allow for "Limited Calibration" or "Special Calibration" instruments? If so, how are they identified as such?

☑ What calibration records does your calibration system require you to maintain?

☑ What happens to the calibration records of equipment that is transferred to another division or business unit (where applicable)?

☑ What happens to the calibration records of equipment that is reclassified, retired, or taken out of service?

☑ How do you assess and document the validity of previous inspection and test results when inspection, measuring, and test equipment is found to be out of calibration? Where do you document this? What actions do you take?

☑ How do you ensure that the environmental conditions are suitable for the calibrations, inspections, measurements, and tests being carried out? Is there any documented evidence to support this?

☑ How do you ensure that the handling, preservation, and storage of inspection, measuring, and test equipment is such that the accuracy and fitness for use are maintained?

☑ How do you safeguard inspection, measuring, and test facilities, including both test hardware and test software, from adjustments that would invalidate the calibration setting? (Do you require the use of tamper-resistant seals? Do you "write-protect" or "password-encrypt" test software?)

4.12 Inspection and Test Status

At a Glance

9001	9002	9003
✓	✓	✓

You must do the following:

- Identify inspection and test status of product by suitable means that indicate conformance or nonconformance of product with regard to inspection and tests performed

- Maintain the identification of inspection and test status of product

- Define methods used to identify inspection and test status in quality plan(s) and/or documented procedures

- Ensure that only product that has passed the required inspections and tests [or released under an authorized concession] is dispatched, used, or installed

> QUALITY MANUAL
>
> **12.0** INSPECTION AND TEST STATUS
>
> The inspection and test status of product will be identified by suitable means, which indicate the conformance or nonconformance of product with regard to inspection and tests performed. The identification of inspection and test status will be maintained, as defined in the quality plan and/ or documented procedures, throughout production, installation, and servicing of the product to ensure that only product that has passed the required inspections and tests [or released under an authorized concession (see 13.2)] is dispatched, used, or installed.

Quality Manual

Although this clause can easily be paraphrased to suit a manufacturer or service provider when a product is involved, it can be confusing for a service company where no tangible product exists. Many service companies have been creative in applying this clause to supporting documentation (such as a report, certificate, or other document).

Procedure

Begin your procedure by defining *who* is authorized to change the inspection and test status of product. Since this procedure rarely requires a separate third-level work instruction, you should also describe *how* status is indicated.

Inspection and test status may be indicated by using the following:

- Markings
- Authorized (controlled) stamps
- Tags
- Labels
- Routing cards
- Inspection records (test results, Certificates of Analysis, etc.)
- Test software (automated systems, data loggers, computers, etc.)
- Physical location (marked areas, labeled shelves or carts, etc.)
- Coding
- Travelers
- Checklists

Bear in mind that other suitable means may also exist. If you are using physical location to indicate inspection status, clearly mark that area (painted lines on floor, signs, labeled cabinets/shelves, etc.). Several companies use moveable carts with magnetic label strips. These magnetic strips allow the status of the cart to be quickly changed as needed.

Status categories may include, but are not limited to, the following:

Not Yet Tested	Test in Progress
Awaiting Test Results	Nonconforming
Quarantine	Rejected
Passed	Hold
Failed	Accepted As-Is

Define and document how each status of product (e.g., purchased product, isolated intermediates, finished product, material in storage, in-process) will be identified, along with examples where applicable (e.g., tags, labels).

Allow the use of quick, efficient inspection status indicators. For example, if your product requires certain labels or tags (safety- or information-related) that are going to be put on the product anyway, apply them during the process at points where they can also indicate inspection and test status.

In the chemical and process industries, separate storage areas for quarantine of uninspected or nonconforming material, or hold/day tanks for material awaiting testing (test results), are often used. When material is not held, as in the case of a process feeding directly into a pipeline or further process, on-line controls that ensure conformance may also be used.

♀ *Inspection Status by Color-Coded Rubber Bands*

Many companies handle product in a dirty or oily environment that can make inspection and test status difficult to maintain. Some of these companies use different-colored rubber bands on the product to identify its status.

♀ *Inspection Status by Color-Coded Baskets*

Several companies use different-colored metal baskets both to identify status and to transport bulky molded parts. Although various colors mean that an item is to proceed to the next step in the process, red is typically reserved for nonconforming product, regardless of the stage in which the nonconformance was identified. In a similar approach, most often used by smaller companies, the baskets are not painted; instead, a different colored metal sign is hung on each basket to indicate its status. This approach is typically taken because a limited number of baskets are available.

♀ *Inspection Status by Color-Coded Areas*

Flexible Metal Hose Company, Tucker, GA, has painted lines on the floor with the meaning stenciled in the painted lines. For example, nonconforming areas are always indicated by a red painted line. This line has the word "Nonconforming" painted in yellow on the red line. This immediately defines the key for the color code. Yellow means "Awaiting Inspection," and green means "Complete."

❸ *Authorized Stamps*

Rather than indicate authorization by an initial or signature, some companies use "Authorized Stamps." These stamps can take on a number of different shapes and meanings. This includes "signature" stamps. If you are using different colors of ink in stamps, try to avoid using black. Once a document is photocopied, they will all be black. That is one way you can tell that the document is a duplicate. Consider using translucent ink. This allows you to read through the stamp, thus not altering or in any way damaging the original document or record.

Any stamps that are used in your quality system to indicate responsibility or authorization must be controlled. This is typically done through the use of a "Stamp Control Log" (refer to Figure 4.12-1 for example). This log normally contains an impression of each unique stamp and identifies the individual who holds that stamp. Of course, control also requires some responsibility on the part of the users. The following is an example of a procedure addressing stamp control:

> *Controlled stamps are not to be left unattended and must be stored in a secured location when not in use or in possession of the assigned user. The quality manager will maintain a secured (locked) area to store unused or unassigned stamps.*

This control ordinarily would not extend to a "Received By: _____" or "Received On _____/_____/_____" stamp. Of course, you must also address "lost" stamps and "misuse" of authorized stamps. Here is an example:

> ### *Lost Stamps*
> *Lost stamps must be reported to the quality manager within 24 hours after they are discovered missing. The quality manager shall note in the "Returned" section of the "Stamp Log" that the stamp was **LOST** and note the date. A new stamp will be issued to the individual who lost the stamp. The lost stamp will not be duplicated and replaced.*

> ### *Misuse of Stamps*
> *The quality manager will document the misuse of stamps in a nonconformance form and forward copies of the form to the district manager*

C:\QUALITY\FORMS\SCL-1094.DOC

ABC Company

Stamp Control Log

Page _____ of _____

Name: Signature:	Stamp Number	Stamp Imprint	Issue Date	Return Date

Figure 4.12-1: Sample "Stamp Control Log" Form

or supervisor. If stamps are being misused to purposefully "falsify" documentation and/or records, disciplinary action up to and including termination of employment may result.

 Records

There are no specific records requirements under this clause, because status indicators (tags, labels, etc.) are not normally retained. However, related records are addressed in ISO 9001/2/3, clause 4.10.5.

If you are using controlled stamps, your "Stamp Control Log," or equivalent, may be considered a record.

☞ Guidance

For further guidance, refer to:

ISO 9000-2:1993, Quality Management and Quality Assurance Standards— Part 2: Generic guidelines for application of ISO 9001, ISO 9002, and ISO 9003
Section 4.12—"Inspection and test status"

ISO 9004-1:1994, Quality Management and Quality System Elements— Part 1: Guidelines
Section 11.7—"Control of verification status"

ᕔ Questions Your Registrar May Ask

☑ Who is authorized to change or update (maintain) the identification of inspection and test status? (Remaining questions are usually directed at that person.)

☑ What inspection and test status categories are used? Where are they defined (documented)?

☑ How is inspection and test status identified throughout production, installation, and servicing of the product? Can you show me an example in process?

☑ Can you show me an example of how nonconforming product is identified?

☑ How do you ensure that only product that has passed the required inspections and tests [or released under an authorized concession] is dispatched, used, or installed?

☑ Where is this process defined in your quality plan and/or documented procedures?

4.13 Control of Nonconforming Product

At a Glance

You must do the following:

9001	9002	9003
✓	✓	✓

- Establish and maintain documented procedures to ensure that product which does not conform to specified requirements is prevented from unintended use or installation

- Provide for identification, documentation, evaluation, segregation (when practical), and disposition of nonconforming product, and for notification to the functions concerned

- Define (document) responsibility for review and authority for the disposition of nonconforming product

- Review and disposition nonconforming product in accordance with documented procedures

- (When required by contract) report the proposed use or repair of product that does not conform to specified requirements for concession to the customer or customer's representative. The description of nonconformity that has been accepted, and of repairs, must be recorded to denote the actual condition

- Reinspect repaired and/or reworked product in accordance with the quality plan and/or documented procedures

QUALITY MANUAL

13.0 CONTROL OF NONCONFORMING PRODUCT

13.1 General

ABC Company has established and maintains documented procedures to ensure that product that does not conform to specified requirements is prevented from unintended use or installation. This control will provide for identification, documentation, evaluation, segregation (when practical), and disposition of nonconforming product, and for notification to the functions concerned.

Quality Manual

Although this clause can easily be paraphrased to suit a manufacturer or service provider when a product is involved, it can be confusing for a service company where no tangible product exists. Most service companies can be creative in applying this clause to a by-product (such as a report, certificate, or other document), but it should also be interpreted as applying to any intermediate phase of the service being supplied.

Procedure

ISO 9000 defines product as:

> *The result of activities or processes; a product may include service, hardware, processed material, software, or a combination thereof and shall apply to the "intended product" offering only.*

From this definition, it is clear that any activity or process can produce nonconforming product. The word "product" can, therefore, be interpreted to include raw material, parts, components, subassemblies, services, etc. It has also been made clear that "by-products" (waste) of activities or processes are not considered nonconforming. If we refer to the guidance provided in ISO 9000-2, we see that this clause also includes "nonconforming product received by the supplier," whether from subcontractors or customer supplied.

Unfortunately, the ISO 9000 series provides only limited guidance on this topic. I suggest that you refer to MIL-STD-1520C, "Corrective Action and Disposition System for Nonconforming Material." While this military standard exceeds the requirements of ISO 9000, it provides an excellent template to reference in developing a system for control of nonconforming product. I will refer to MIL-STD-1520C throughout this chapter. Further guidance in the application of MIL-STD-1520C is provided in MIL-HDBK-350, "A Guide for MIL-STD-1520C Corrective Action and Disposition System for Nonconforming Material." The complete text from MIL-STD-1520C is contained in MIL-HDBK-350, so you only need to obtain the single document.

Your procedure should primarily focus on the second sentence of this clause:

> *Control shall provide for identification, documentation, evaluation, segregation (when practical), disposition of nonconforming product, and for notification to the functions concerned.*

I will address each requirement separately.

Identification

When nonconforming product (material) is found, it should be conspicuously identified and positively controlled. Methods of identifying nonconforming product can include, but are not limited to, the following:

- Physical identification (marking, tags, labels, etc.)

- Physical location (controlled areas such as cribs, cabinets, bonded areas, etc.)

- Identification on accompanying paperwork (travelers, work orders, etc.)

- Identification in electronic data systems

This procedure should describe the methods of identification used, with detail as to when and how they are used. Although nonconforming material is commonly placed in a designated (and clearly marked) "Nonconforming Material" (NCM) area for future disposition, there may be some products that are too large or heavy to be easily moved. In this case tagging is often the preferred alternative.

I suggest including the following wording, where appropriate, in your procedure:

> *Identification of nonconforming product shall be by marking, tagging, or other methods that will not adversely affect the end use of the product. If identification of each nonconforming product is not practical, the container, package, or segregated storage area, as appropriate, shall be identified.*

This procedure should reference or contain examples of any tags and/or labels used.

Documentation

The ISO 9000 series is vague as to the nature and extent of this required documentation. MIL-STD-1520C contains an identical requirement, but with much more specific detail. It requires that documentation of nonconforming material include the following:

a. *Contract number (P.O. Number, Job Number, Work Order, etc.)*

b. *Initiator of the document*

c. *Date of the initiation*

d. *Identification of the document for traceability purposes (indexing number)*

e. *Specific identification (e.g., part number, name, National Stock Number) of the nonconforming material*

f. *Quantity of items involved*

g. *Number of occurrences*

h. *The place in the manufacturing process where the nonconformance was detected*

i. *A detailed description of the nonconformance*

j. *Identification of the affected specification, drawing, or other document*

k. *A description of the cause(s)*

l. *Disposition of the nonconforming item (return to supplier, rework, repair, scrap, or refer to Material Review Board)*

m. Identification of personnel responsible for making the disposition decision

While MIL-STD-1520C exceeds the requirements of ISO 9000 in this area, it can be a useful reference in developing your own documentation requirements. The sample "Nonconforming Material Report" form in Figure 4.13-1 was derived from the requirements contained in MIL-STD-1520C, clause 5.7, "Nonconforming material documentation."

Remember, "product that does not conform to specified requirements" can be:

• Discovered by a worker

• Discovered by an inspector

• Discovered during an internal audit

• Returned by a distributor

• Returned by the customer

Ensure that your procedure addresses each possible source. In many instances, customer returns require a "Return Material Authorization" (RMA) number.

ABC Company

Nonconforming Material Report

Number # _____

Initiator Name: _____ Date: _____/_____/_____

Contract / Job No.: _____ Part No.: _____

Location Detected : _____ Quantity: _____

Drawing No.: _____ Number of Occurrences: _____

Detailed Description of the Nonconformance:

_____
_____
_____
_____

Description of the Cause(s):

_____
_____
_____
_____

Disposition: ☐ Return to Supplier ☐ Rework ☐ Repair ☐ Scrap

☐ Refer to Material Review Board—Describe Final Disposition:

_____
_____
_____
_____

Dispositioned by: (To be completed by person responsible for making disposition decision)

Name: _____ Date: _____/_____/_____

C:\QUALITY\FORMS\NMR-1094.DOC

Figure 4.13-1: Sample "Nonconforming Material Report" Form

Evaluation

In many industries, the value of nonconforming material is so low that it simply is not cost-effective to address each instance. But cost should not be the only issue. If we reference ISO 9001/2/3, clause 4.14, we can easily develop the following intent:

> *Control of nonconforming material, components, and subassemblies should be to a degree appropriate to the magnitude of problems and commensurate to the risks encountered.*

The ISO 9000 series provides very little guidance on this point. However, MIL-STD-1520C and MIL-HDBK-350 clarify this concept in a way that, I believe, is consistent with the intent of ISO 9000.

> *MIL-STD-1520C, Section 1.1* Purpose:
> *. . . The primary purposes of the corrective action and disposition system are to identify and correct causes of nonconformances, prevent the recurrence of wasteful nonconforming material, reduce the cost of manufacturing efficiency, and foster quality and productivity improvement.*

> *MIL-HDBK-350, Section 1.1,* Implementation note:
> *3. MIL-STD-1520C recognizes that investigation and corrective action for every instance of nonconforming material as if they are of equal significance or consequence is not cost-effective. Focusing corrective action effort is one extremely important feature of this standard. Nonconformances impacting safety, performance, high rate manufacturing processes or delivery schedules require immediate corrective action to prevent further recurrence. While every nonconformance can offer the opportunity to improve, for isolated non-recurring nonconformances the cost of investigation and corrective action could exceed the loss. An effective corrective action and disposition system directs resources toward those nonconformances with the greatest impact and potential for quality improvement. Pareto analysis offers one effective method of focusing on the significant few with the greatest potential return.*

Recognizing that defective noncritical, low-value stock items identified as isolated, nonrecurring nonconformances may exceed the cost of investigation and corrective action, they could be excluded from the formal corrective action and disposition system. In this situation, you should define how certain specific items are to be dispositioned. For example:

> *Production employees are authorized to disposition defective noncritical, low-value stock items (including fuses, resistors, capacitors, etc.) identified during the production process as scrap, provided that they*

are judged by the employee to be isolated non-recurring nonconformances. These items are not required to be introduced into the formal corrective action and disposition system for nonconforming material. Documentation is not required.

Some auditors will question how it is possible to determine whether nonconformances are recurring when product is being dispositioned by individuals keeping no record (a log or count) of each instance. Therefore, it must be clear that the cost of these "low-value" items is so low that several instances must occur during the course of a single shift before the situation justifies the cost of formal disposition. This is a business decision. Threshold values of product should be established when using this approach.

Where applicable, I suggest developing a corrective action and disposition system with defined "minor" and "major/critical" categories of nonconformance. Again referring to MIL-STD-1520C:

3.6.1 Minor nonconformance. *A nonconformance which does not adversely affect any of the following:*

a.   *Health or safety*

b.   *Performance*

c.   *Interchangeability, reliability, or maintainability*

d.   *Effective use or operation*

e.   *Weight or appearance (when a factor)*

NOTE: Multiple minor nonconformances, when considered collectively, may raise the category to a major/critical nonconformance.

3.6.2 Major/critical nonconformance. *A nonconformance other than minor that cannot be completely eliminated by rework or reduced to a minor nonconformance by repair.*

NOTE: Where a classification of defects exists, minor defects are minor nonconformances. Major and critical defects which cannot be completely eliminated by rework or reduced to a minor nonconformance by repair are major/critical nonconformances.

Segregation (Where Practical)

As addressed in Section 4.12, "Inspection and Test Status," there are a number of approaches that can be taken toward identifying, and/or segregating, nonconforming product. One that I did not mention previously is the use of movable posts connected by rope or plastic chain. These barricades are an ideal solution for companies where production surges (nonconformance surges) are common. As your need for a "Nonconforming Area" increases, so does your actual area. As the need decreases, so does the area.

While segregation is preferred, in some instances nonconforming material is of a size, weight, or other condition that it simply is not practical. The standard recognizes this situation. I suggest that your procedure also recognize this possibility. Don't paint yourself into a corner.

I suggest including the following wording, where appropriate, in your procedure:

> *Nonconforming product shall be segregated, when practical, by being placed in a clearly identified and designated "Nonconforming Material" (NCM) area until properly dispositioned. When segregation is impractical or impossible because of physical conditions such as size, weight, environmental stability, or access limitations, other precautions shall be employed to preclude the inadvertent use or installation of nonconforming product.*

Disposition

The most efficient, cost-effective method of disposition can vary greatly from one company or product to another. For a small manufacturer, I suggest including the following wording, as appropriate, in your procedure:

> *When product is initially found to be nonconforming, it shall be immediately reported to Quality personnel. Unless otherwise specified, the responsibility for review and disposition of nonconforming product is assigned to the quality manager. While this authority may be delegated, ultimate responsibility will remain with the quality manager.*

A larger manufacturer may assign responsibility for review and disposition to a "Material Review Board" (MRB), which meets periodically to disposition nonconforming material, identify and analyze trends, evaluate suppliers, etc. An MRB normally includes representatives from several different functions including, but not limited to, Quality, Purchasing, Production, Engineering, and Operations.

A combination of both approaches is common depending upon the cost or criticality of the nonconforming material.

Notification

Most notification issues are typically addressed by either a Material Review Board (MRB) or a Corrective Action Board (CAB). Internally this requirement relates to notifying processes "upstream" that may be producing the nonconforming product or processes "downstream" that may need to repair or rework the nonconforming product.

This requirement includes nonconforming product supplied by subcontractors. A feedback loop is typically developed to notify any subcontractors providing nonconforming product with a request for corrective action (Supplier Corrective Action Request—SCAR). This system is typically developed and administered by the purchasing department.

When nonconforming product is produced by a supplier, it is common to return that product to the supplier. Some companies in Europe even bill their suppliers for the time taken by their employees to identify, disposition, and handle the nonconforming product. A few companies have tried this approach in the U.S. with very little success. But I ask you, if you had a competitive supplier so confident in their product that they allowed you to bill them for their supplying you nonconforming product, wouldn't you be impressed? Wouldn't you prefer them over other suppliers?

◇ *Customer Notification/Product Recall*

If nonconforming product has already been sent to the customer, some auditors contend that this clause implies that "customer notification" would be required. To do this you would need product traceability. Referencing clause 4.8, "Product identification and traceability," *traceability* is not a requirement unless *specified*. Therefore, "customer notification and/or product recall" is not required unless specified.

This clause should be interpreted as addressing those "functions concerned" (the supplier or subcontractor) prior to delivery of the product.

QUALITY MANUAL

13.2 Review and Disposition of Nonconforming Product

The responsibility for review and authority for the disposition of nonconforming product will be defined.

Nonconforming product will be reviewed in accordance with documented procedures. It may be:

(a) reworked to meet the specified requirements,

(b) accepted with or without repair by concession,

(c) regraded for alternative applications, or

(d) rejected or scrapped.

Where required by the contract, the proposed use or repair of product (see 13.2b) that does not conform to specified requirements will be reported for concession to the customer or customer's representative. The description of the nonconformity that has been accepted, and of repairs, will be recorded to denote the actual condition.

Repaired and/or reworked product will be reinspected in accordance with the quality plan and/or documented procedures.

Quality Manual

In reading the first sentence of this clause from the standard, many companies respond by paraphrasing it to list specific job titles of individuals assigned "responsibility for review and authority for the disposition of nonconforming product." Although this approach is completely acceptable, it could also be unnecessarily restrictive. A more flexible approach would be to state:

> *The responsibility for review and authority for the disposition of nonconforming product is defined in the ABC Company Standard Operating Procedure manual.*

When addressing "how" nonconforming product may be dispositioned, don't limit yourself. List all of the possibilities contained in the standard. Even if they are not currently considered options today, they may be later. Also, try not to explain each one in your quality manual. The procedure manual is a much more appropriate document for that level of detail.

The next paragraph of the standard, concerning "nonconforming product accepted with or without repair by concession," should be paraphrased closely to the original text. Many companies state that this will never happen because of the nature of their product. This is where Murphy's law comes into play and the auditor immediately finds an instance where it does happen. Play it safe. Address the requirement in your quality manual.

Procedure

Ensure that your procedure identifies those individuals (by job title) who have the authorization and responsibility for evaluation of nonconforming material. In many instances, you may wish to empower these individuals with the ability to delegate this authority, but they should retain responsibility. If your company has established a Material Review Board (MRB), this will require a detailed procedure defining the MRB and its responsibility in implementing the review and disposition process.

I suggest including the following wording, where appropriate, in your procedure:

Nonconforming product shall be reviewed and dispositioned as follows:

(a) rework to meet the specified requirements;

(b) accept with or without repair by concession (approval);

(c) regrade for alternative applications;

(d) reject or scrap;

(e) return to supplier or subcontractor.

Your procedure should address each possibility in detail.

Although option (e), "return to supplier or subcontractor," is not included in the standard, I believe that you should leave yourself this option. I've seen several instances where product was purchased from a subcontractor for evaluation, only to discover the product to be nonconforming. This resulted in the nonconforming product being sent back to the subcontractor for a refund of the price without replacement.

(a) Rework vs. Repair

MIL-STD-1520C defines both rework and repair. MIL-HDBK-350 provides the following implementation note:

An example of a repair is a hole mistakenly drilled oversize that requires filling and redrilling to correct the size. An example of rework is a hole that is undersized and can be redrilled to the correct dimension.

A book prepared by the ASQC Chemical and Process Industries Division—Chemical Interest Committee, "ANSI/ASQC Q90/ISO 9000 Guidelines for use by the Chemical and Process Industries," offers another example:

In the process industry, reworking may include reprocessing or adjusting of mixtures, including blending.

For a service provider, where no tangible product is involved, "rework" could also be interpreted as amending or correcting a certificate or report (calibration and testing laboratories, etc.).

Rework activities should follow documented procedures that include reinspection to ensure that the resulting product fully complies with specified requirements.

(b) Accepted with or without Repair by Concession

In some instances, a documentation change may be in order as it may be more efficient and economical to change an unnecessary requirement or overly stringent specifications than to identify, document, analyze, and disposition a recurring nonconformance. Occasionally, Engineering may design a product that contains tighter specifications than can be realistically achieved by Production (it happens). By changing the documented specifications of the product, a larger percentage of product may now be accepted.

If product is being manufactured for a specific customer (under contract), the example above may still be a viable option. Another example of a potentially acceptable nonconformance is color variation. The customer may agree to accept product with slight variations. The standard states:

Where required by the contract, the proposed use or repair of product (see 4.13.2b) which does not conform to specified requirements shall be reported for concession to the customer or customer's representative. The description of the nonconformity that has been accepted, and of repairs, shall be recorded to denote the actual condition (see 4.16).

Your procedure should address *who* is delegated responsibility for reporting nonconforming product to the customer for concession and *how* such product is "accepted" by the customer. The "Nonconforming Material Report" form discussed earlier could be used for describing the nonconformity and denoting the actual condition of product accepted by concession.

(c) Regraded for Alternative Applications

Regrading product for alternative applications is common in the chemical and process industries [as described in (a)], but can also apply to other industries.

Another common example is semiconductors and microchips, which are graded for military or commercial applications.

The grading system that you use should be clearly documented with details relating to how product is regraded.

(d) Rejected or Scrapped

The last option given in the standard is for product to be rejected or scrapped. This is total waste. Many companies track such waste for evaluation and eventual introduction into your corrective action system.

◈ Scrap Bins

Some auditors have demanded that scrap bins be identified as such. The reasoning for this is, of course, to eliminate scrap being placed in an unidentified bin or container and later inadvertently reintroduced to the system. This objective can also be accomplished by color-coding containers (bins) or even using trash containers for scrap (excluding hazardous waste). My point here is that the word "scrap" does not have to appear on the bin or container, provided that it is identified through some other means described in your quality system.

Reinspection

In every instance where product is repaired and/or reworked, it must be reinspected in accordance with the quality plan and/or documented procedure requirements.

♡ Limiting Reinspection

Many large manufacturing companies have learned that occasionally they will manufacture a product that repeatedly fails inspection (a lemon). I've heard accounts of a single item failing inspection more than fifty times! Although these items can be repaired and eventually pass inspection, some companies have decided that they are not worth the expense and limit reinspection to some reasonable number (3–5 is common). When that number is reached, the item is dispositioned as scrap.

⫯ Quality Systems Requirements

QS-9000 contains additional requirements in the following clauses: "Control of Reworked Product—4.13.3" and "Engineering Approved Product Authorization—4.13.4" (see the AIAG "Production Part Approval Process" manual).

🗀 *Records*

It is difficult to identify a specific record required by this element. All of its requirements could be contained on a single form or a combination of records.

Concerning documentation of nonconforming product, clause 4.13.1 states that:

> *Control shall provide for identification, documentation, evaluation, seg-regation (when practical), disposition of nonconforming product and for notification to the functions concerned.*

Concerning nonconforming product reported for concession, ISO 9001/2/3, clause 4.13.2, states:

> *Where required by the contract, the proposed use or repair of product (see 4.13.2b) which does not conform to specified requirements shall be reported for concession to the customer or customer's representative. The description of nonconformity that has been accepted, and of repairs, shall be recorded to denote the actual condition. (See 4.16.)*

This element concludes by requiring inspection records documenting that repaired and/or reworked product has been reinspected in accordance with the quality plan and/or documented procedure requirements.

☞ *Guidance*

For further guidance, refer to:

ISO 9000-2:1993, Quality Management and Quality Assurance Standards—Part 2: Generic guidelines for application of ISO 9001, ISO 9002, and ISO 9003
Section 4.13—"Control of nonconforming product"

ISO 9004-1:1994, Quality Management and Quality System Elements—Part 1: Guidelines
Section 14—"Control of nonconforming product"

Military Standards

MIL-STD-1520C, Corrective Action and Disposition System for Nonconforming Material

MIL-HDBK-350, A Guide for MIL-STD-1520C Corrective Action and Disposition System for Nonconforming Material

⟢ *Questions Your Registrar May Ask*

4.13.1 General

☑ How do you ensure that product which does not conform to specified requirements is prevented from unintended use or installation?

☑ How do you provide for identification, documentation, evaluation, segregation (when practical), disposition of nonconforming product, and for notification to the functions concerned?

4.13.2 Review and Disposition of Nonconforming Product

☑ Who is authorized and responsible for review and the disposition of nonconforming product? Where is this defined (documented)?

☑ Are the repair or rework instructions accessible and utilized by the appropriate personnel?

☑ When required by contract, how do you report the proposed use or repair of
product that does not conform to specified requirements for concession to
the customer or customer's representative?

☑ How do you ensure that customer authorization is received prior to shipping nonconforming material?

☑ How is the description of nonconformity that has been accepted, and any
repairs, recorded to denote the actual condition?

☑ How is reinspection of repaired and/or reworked product documented?

4.14 Corrective and Preventive Action

At a Glance

You must do the following:

9001	9002	9003
✓	✓	L

- Establish and maintain documented procedures for implementing corrective and preventive action

- Implement and record any changes to the documented procedures resulting from corrective and preventive action

QUALITY MANUAL

14.0 CORRECTIVE AND PREVENTIVE ACTION

14.1 General

ABC Company has established and maintains documented procedures for implementing corrective and preventive action.

Any corrective or preventive action taken to eliminate the causes of actual or potential nonconformities will be to a degree appropriate to the magnitude of problems and commensurate to the risks encountered.

ABC Company will implement and record any changes to the documented procedures resulting from corrective and preventive action.

Quality Manual

When developing your quality manual, I suggest paraphrasing this wording as it appears in each clause of this element of the standard. Some minor tailoring may be required, but again remember you only need to state broad policy in your Quality Manual.

Procedure

The initial issue of ISO 9000 was generally criticized for not addressing continuous improvement. The standard has always required an effective corrective action system. This is actually the basic cornerstone for continuous improvement. Before writing your procedure for corrective action, consider the long-term benefits from this form of continuous improvement.

An effective corrective action system generally addresses four separate areas:

- Nonconforming product
- Customer complaints
- Quality system nonconformances identified through internal audits
- Quality system nonconformances identified through other means

As mentioned in Section 4.13, single or limited instances of nonconforming product do not necessarily require a formal corrective action. This action may be reserved for addressing trends or other problems which may recur.

This intent is clearly evident in ISO 9000-2, clause 4.14, Note 3:

Corrective action is not necessarily required for every occurrence of a nonconformance, but periodic analysis of patterns of nonconformance should be considered to uncover opportunities for process improvement.

If, for example, you are experiencing a recurring problem of paint being scratched in the same general area on the finished product, noting these occurrences over time may make it apparent that a formal corrective action is necessary.

If you have never developed a formal corrective action system, don't struggle with reinventing the wheel. I suggest referencing both MIL-STD-1520C, "Corrective Action and Disposition System for Nonconforming Material," and MIL-STD-2155 (AS), "Failure Reporting, Analysis, and Corrective Action System." The concepts can easily be expanded to address your entire quality system.

Evidence of a complete, fully functional, corrective action process should be available for review. This is usually documented on "Corrective Action Request" forms (see example in Figure 4.14-1).

☹ *Product Liability*

Companies rushing to implement ISO 9000 typically do not give due attention to the procedures addressing "nonconformances" and the use of "Corrective Action" forms (Figure 4.14-1). This required documentation can leave companies vulnerable to litigation.

Mr. Gregory G. Scott, a Minneapolis trial lawyer and consultant who chairs the International Law subcommittee of the American Bar Association's Product Liability Committee, agrees that ISO 9000's heavy emphasis on documentation could be disastrous for the unprepared. Companies can limit their exposure to litigation by avoiding certain language in documentation that may directly or indirectly imply wrongdoing. According to Scott, words that should be avoided include these:

- "Defect" or "defective"

- "Negligent"

- "Unsafe"

- "Unreasonably dangerous"

- "Hazardous"

- "Reckless"

- "Misrepresentative"

Use the word "nonconforming" instead, Scott suggests. Often, the most damaging evidence in a product liability case comes from written criticisms of a product

ABC Company

Corrective Action Request

CAR/RMA Number # _____

(This section is to be filled out by the person discovering the nonconformance / requesting corrective action. Or, if this is a customer complaint, by the person in contact with the customer.)

Name: _____ Date: _____/_____/_____

Customer Complaint (If applicable)

Company Name : _____ Location : _____

Customer Contact : _____ Phone: (   ) _____

Complaint : RMA Issued: ☐ Yes ☐ No

_____

_____

_____

Nonconformance / Problem Description

Details / Explanation:

_____

_____

_____

Problem Resolution (Attach Appropriate Supporting Documents)

"Root Cause" Investigation and Impact Analysis:

_____

_____

Action(s) Taken To Resolve And Prevent Recurrence:

_____

_____

_____

Nonconformance/Customer Complaint Closed (To be completed by Quality Manager)

Follow-up performed? ☐ Yes—Date: _____/_____/_____   ☐ None Needed

Closed By: _____ Date: _____/_____/_____

C:\QUALITY\FORMS\CAR-1094.DOC

Figure 4.14-1: Sample "Corrective Action Request" Form

by design engineers or sales representatives. Be sure to pass this information to those departments as well.

✍ Note

Mr. Gregory G. Scott is a partner in the law firm of:

Popham, Haik, Schnobrich & Kaufman, Ltd.
3300 Piper Jaffray Tower
Minneapolis, MN 55402
Tel: (612) 333-4800

🏳 Escalation

Part of defining a corrective action system should include a quality escalation process. Here's an example of a generic escalation process:

Escalation Process
Upon discovery of a quality problem or concern, the following process must be followed.

1. *The initiator (any employee) must report the problem or concern to the department quality representative.*

2. *If the concern is determined to be valid, the initiator must complete a Corrective Action Request form documenting the discovery and submit it to the department quality representative.*

3. *The quality representative should first attempt to resolve the problem personally. (This may require seeking technical advice.)*

4. *If the quality representative cannot resolve the problem or concern, then the department supervisor must be advised of the problem or concern.*

5. *If the supervisor cannot resolve the problem or concern, then the department manager must be advised of the problem or concern.*

6. *If the department manager cannot resolve the problem or concern, then the quality manager must be advised of the problem or concern.*

7. *Should anyone in this process feel that reasonable, timely, proper corrective action is not being implemented, they are obligated to notify the quality manager.*

8. *If, at this point, reasonable, timely, proper corrective action is not being implemented, the quality representative is obligated to notify the general manager.*

Failure to report quality problems or concerns can result in disciplinary action up to and including dismissal.

Of course your escalation process may be different. It should be tailored to your specific operation.

Q U A L I T Y   M A N U A L

14.2 Corrective Action

ABC Company procedures for corrective action include:

(a) the effective handling of customer complaints and reports of product nonconformities;

(b) investigation of the cause of nonconformities relating to product, process, and quality system, and recording the results of the investigation;

(c) determination of the corrective action needed to eliminate the cause of nonconformities;

(d) application of controls to ensure that corrective action is taken and that it is effective.

Procedure

Let's address each requirement in this clause of the standard individually.

(a) Customer Complaints

Companies often confuse "customer complaints" with "customer support." Let's define the differences.

Customer complaint:

- A report of customer dissatisfaction (expectations not met)
- A report of nonconforming product or service
- Inconsistencies with the accepted contract (early or late product delivery, overage or underage of product quantities, billing issues, etc.)

Customer support:

- A request for (technical) assistance (answering product- or service-related questions)

- A request for clarification of user instructions

- A request for product-related guidance (product configuration, compatibility or interfacing with other products, etc.)

Although a customer support department can receive customer complaints, they are typically responding to customer questions which, if handled improperly, could escalate into a customer complaint. Make sure that employees working in these areas understand the difference.

Customer complaints and reports of product nonconformities should be formally documented or logged for analysis and corrective action.

(b) Cause Investigation

All too often a corrective action system is ineffective due to incomplete root cause investigation. For example: If a problem was caused by an employee not following a procedure, don't stop there. Ask why the employee didn't follow the procedure:

- Was the procedure available to the employee?

- Was the employee properly trained to follow the procedure?

- Was the employee qualified to perform the assigned task?

- Was there adequate manpower available so that all procedures could be properly followed?

Recurring problems are often due to new or different people working in an area. In other words, workers were not informed about the problem or corrective action (or trained in new procedures), and so it continues.

♀ Cause-and-Effect Diagrams

The cause-and-effect diagram, also called a "fishbone diagram" because of its appearance, allows you to map out a list of factors thought to affect a problem or desired outcome. This type of diagram was invented by Kaoru Ishikawa, and hence is also called an "Ishikawa diagram."

While writing this book, I spoke with one company that has printed "fishbone" charts on the back of its "Corrective Action Request" form and is requiring it to be completed as part of the corrective action process.

(c) Eliminating the Cause of Nonconformities

Corrective action can be short-term or long-term. If you eliminate the cause of the nonconformity, you are implementing a long-term solution. An example of a short-term, or immediate, "fix" would be to issue a "Quality Alert" correcting the problem during a current production run. The long-term solution may be in revising the affected procedures and/or work instructions for use in future orders.

(d) Applying Controls

Once a corrective action has been taken, how do you ensure that it is effective? Can you measure its effectiveness? If a nonconformance was producing waste, you should be able to monitor and detect a decrease in waste if your corrective action was effective. If you detect an increase in waste, you may need to reevaluate the corrective action. In some instances you may not be able to adequately measure the effectiveness of a corrective action.

Q U A L I T Y   M A N U A L

14.3 Preventive Action

The procedures for preventive action include:

(a) the use of appropriate sources of information such as processes and work operations which affect product quality, concessions, audit results, quality records, service reports, and customer complaints to detect, analyze, and eliminate potential causes of nonconformities;

(b) determination of the steps needed to deal with any problems requiring preventive action;

(c) initiation of preventive action and application of controls to ensure that it is effective;

(d) confirmation that relevant information on actions taken is submitted for management review.

🗐 Procedure

Often, the greatest cost savings associated with a quality system is directly linked to an effective corrective action system. The key is not just to correct the obvious problem(s), but rather to determine the root cause of a problem and correct it in such a way as to prevent its recurrence. As problems are solved, you should see the number of corrective action requests drop. If you don't, then you're probably overlooking something. You may be neglecting one of these:

- Informing or involving other related departments experiencing similar problems
- Analyzing corrective action requests for trends

As we did with the earlier section, let us address each requirement in this clause individually.

(a) Appropriate Sources of Information

An ISO 9000 auditor will expect you to define "appropriate" sources of information. This may include the following:

- Processes and work operations that affect product quality
- Concessions
- Audit results
- Quality records
- Service reports
- Customer complaints

These sources of information should allow you to "detect, analyze, and eliminate potential causes of nonconformities." Although all of this information can be recorded onto a "Corrective Action Request" form, I suggest that you attach copies of all supporting data to develop a complete "package" (file).

(b) Determination of Preventive Action

As mentioned earlier, cause-and-effect diagrams (fishbone or Ishikawa diagrams) may be used in determining the preventive action to eliminate the cause of the nonconformance. Responsibility for this determination should also be defined. While this may be individuals (by job title) in a small company, a larger company may have a formal "Corrective Action Board" (CAB—as described in MIL-STD-1520C) or "Failure Review Board" (FRB—as described in MIL-STD-2155). A CAB or FRB may have representatives from several functions within the business, such as Design, Engineering, Purchasing, Processing (Production), Quality, and Human Resources.

(c) Initiation of Preventive Action

Initiation of preventive action must be followed by the application of controls to ensure that it is effective. This can include a follow-up internal audit of the affected area, monitoring of the area concerned, etc. In each instance, the application of controls and responsibility should be defined.

(d) Management Review

As a minimum, a summary of the corrective actions implemented must be submitted for management review. This could include an item-by-item review of each completed CAR. Many companies experimenting with decentralized business units absorb incredible hidden costs through redundantly "reinventing the wheel." An effective corrective action system is most often centralized, with one individual or group evaluating problems with respect to the total organization. This may be the reason behind ISO 9000 requiring this information for management review. In some cases, specific types of problems may be coded and entered into a computer that tracks historical trends. This type of analysis may be required in order to determine the true effectiveness of some corrective actions.

♀ Cost of Quality

While assessing a company in the U.K., I observed that they had added a column on their "Corrective Action Request" form addressing the cost of quality. This column was used for recording details relating to the following:

- Time spent—letters, phone calls, etc.

- Delay incurred

- Parts used or scrapped

- Other related expenses—repair or rework labor, shipping and handling, etc.

Next, an approximate cost of the noncompliance was computed. This allowed management to see the costs associated with poor quality and to realize that this cost could be multiplied if preventive action was ineffective. Management also realized that the most significant expense was virtually impossible to calculate: the loss of a valued customer.

☺ When Is a Corrective Action Request Considered Closed?

Many companies have difficulty in defining *when* and *how* a corrective action request (CAR) is "closed." For example, would it be considered acceptable to close out a CAR by stating "to be discussed at next engineering meeting," or is it required to have CARs completed in the past tense with follow-up?

Corrective actions cannot be closed out until they have been verified as being effective in addressing the problem for which they were originally written. Many CAR forms include a final sign-off field for closure (Figure 4.14-1). All completed CARs should be carried on a summary list that is reviewed in the management review meeting. That meeting passes the final judgment on whether or not the CARs are truly complete and effective.

Keep in mind that you should not get bogged down in the management review meeting discussing all corrective actions. You want to know about the ones that are closed out and if those are effective. A last point in the corrective action meeting would be to make an assessment of the effectiveness of the overall corrective action system.

🗀 *Records*

The "Corrective Action System" should include documented records of the following:

- Customer complaints, product nonconformities (4.14.2a)

- Results of "cause" investigation (4.14.2b)

- Corrective action needed to eliminate cause (4.14.2c) and prevent recurrence (4.14.3b)

- Measures taken to ensure that corrective action is effective (4.14.2d & 4.14.3c)

- Confirmation that corrective actions are submitted for management review (4.14.3d)

All of this information can be included on one form.

☞ *Guidance*

For further guidance, refer to:

> ISO 9004-1:1994, Quality Management and Quality System Elements— Part 1: Guidelines
> Section 15—"Corrective Action"

U.S. Military Standards

> MIL-STD-2155 (AS), Failure Reporting, Analysis, and Corrective Action System

If you are manufacturing a complex, expensive, and/or safety-related device where continued operation is critical, I suggest also referring to:

> MIL-STD-1629A, Procedures for Performing a Failure Mode, Effects, and Criticality Analysis

¦ĭ *Quality Systems Requirements*

If you are planning to comply with QS-9000, I suggest that you also refer to the AIAG document FMEA-1 (Potential Failure Mode & Effects Analysis Manual). Information on the AIAG is located in Appendix A.

ᦏ *Questions Your Registrar May Ask*

4.14.1 General

☑ What criteria is taken into account when determining whether the corrective or preventive action taken is to a degree appropriate to the magnitude of problems and commensurate to the risks encountered?

☑ How are any changes to the documented procedures resulting from corrective and preventive action recorded and implemented?

4.14.2 Corrective Action

☑ How do you ensure the effective handling of customer complaints and reports of product nonconformities?

☑ Who is responsible for investigation of the cause of nonconformities relating to product, process, and quality system, and recording the results of the investigation? Where is this documented?

☑ Who is responsible for determination of the corrective action needed to eliminate the cause of nonconformities? Where is this defined?

☑ Who is responsible for the application of controls to ensure that corrective action is taken and that it is effective? How is this demonstrated?

4.14.3 Preventive Action

☑ What have you defined as "appropriate" sources of information (such as processes and work operations that affect product quality, concessions, audit results, quality records, service reports, and customer complaints) to detect, analyze, and eliminate potential causes of nonconformities?

☑ Who is responsible for determination of the steps needed to deal with any problems requiring preventive action? How is this determination made?

☑ Who is responsible for initiation of preventive action and application of controls to ensure that it is effective?

☑ How is the "effectiveness" of preventive action determined or measured?

☑ How is relevant information on actions taken submitted for management review? What form does this take? How can I verify this?

4.15 Handling, Storage, Packaging, Preservation, and Delivery

At a Glance

9001	9002	9003
✓	✓	✓

You must do the following:

- Establish and maintain documented procedures for handling, storage, packaging, preservation, and delivery of product

- Provide methods of handling product that prevent damage or deterioration

- Use designated storage areas or stock rooms to prevent damage or deterioration of product, pending use or delivery

- Stipulate appropriate methods for authorizing receipt to and dispatch from designated storage areas

- Assess the condition of product in stock at appropriate intervals in order to detect deterioration

- Control packing, packaging, and marking processes (including materials used) to the extent necessary to ensure conformance to specified requirements

- Apply appropriate methods for preservation and segregation of product when the product is under your control

- Arrange for the protection of the quality of product after final inspection and test. Where contractually specified, this protection shall be extended to include delivery to destination.

> Q U A L I T Y   M A N U A L
>
> **15.0** HANDLING, STORAGE, PACKAGING, PRESERVATION, AND DELIVERY
>
> **15.1** General
>
> ABC Company has established and maintains documented procedures for handling, storage, packaging, preservation, and delivery of product.

📖 Quality Manual

I suggest paraphrasing the standard throughout this section. Wording should closely resemble text from the standard to avoid distorting the intent. Some minimal tailoring may be required, but specifics should be left in your procedure(s).

An excellent opportunity to exceed ISO 9000 requirements would be to address your policies toward safety in this section as well.

📄 Procedure

This area often receives far less attention than it deserves. There are many local, state, and federal laws (DOT, EPA, HAZMAT, OSHA, etc.), as well as a proactive environmental responsibility (reusable shipping containers, biodegradable packing material, etc.), that a company could address here.

☠ Hazardous Material

Hazardous materials and substances must be handled, stored, packaged, and transported in accordance with all local, state, and federal regulations, codes, and laws. Refer to Title CFR 49, "Transportation—Hazardous Materials," for further guidance. If transporting hazardous materials and substances internationally, there are additional requirements that you may need to be aware of and communicate to the appropriate functions within your company. Copies of CFR 49 with the HM 181 revision—"Hazardous Materials"—can be obtained from a U.S. Government bookstore.

⛴ Shipping Hazardous Material on Cargo Vessels

If you ship hazardous material on cargo vessels, you should obtain and be familiar with the "International Maritime Dangerous Goods Code," available from:

International Maritime Organization
4 Albert Embankment
London, U.K. SE1 7SR
Tel: 011-44-71-735-7611
Fax: 011-44-71-587-3210

✈ *Shipping Hazardous Material by Air*

If you ship hazardous material by air, you should obtain and be familiar with the "International Air Transportation Association" (IATA) "Dangerous Goods Regulations," available from:

International Air Transportation Association
IATA Building
2000 Peel Street
Montreal, Quebec H3A 2R4
Canada
Tel: (514) 844-6311
Fax: (514) 844-9089 (Publications Department)

as well as the "International Civil Aviation Organization" (ICAO) "Technical Instructions for the Safe Transportation of Dangerous Goods by Air," available from:

International Civil Aviation Organization
1000 Sherbrooke Street, West
Montreal, Quebec H3A 2R2
Canada
Tel: (514) 285-8221
Fax: (514) 286-6376

🖥 *SHiP-HAZMAT Software*

The Bureau of Dangerous Goods, Ltd. (a company), has developed an internationally accepted, automated document and package preparation computer program titled "SHiP-HAZMAT" (DOS-based). It is designed specifically to assist shippers of air cargo hazardous goods to comply with ICAO and IATA Dangerous Goods regulations.

Simply tell SHiP-HAZMAT what net quantity of any "UN number" you want to ship, and the program helps you complete the Shipper's Declaration for Dangerous Goods form in full compliance, as well as demonstrating how to pack, mark, and label your shipment.

Some of the program's features include the following:

- Accurate applications of ICAO/IATA and U.S. Dangerous Goods Regulations

- Application of Special Provision Numbers

- Listing of State and Operator variations, including U.S. Government variations integrated as part of the software logic (non-USA versions also available)

- Printed IATA Shipper's Declaration Form for Dangerous Goods

- Details of inner and outer packaging and packing guidelines

- 3-D graphic of outer package with label and marking requirements

- Customer Product Code and Consignee Databases

SHiP-HAZMAT is regularly updated to ensure continued compliance. To obtain a demo disk, or more information, contact:

Bureau of Dangerous Goods, Ltd.
P.O. Box 190
North Brunswick, NJ 08902 USA
1-800-367-1879
Tel: (908) 422-0700
Fax: (908) 422-8398

Bureau of Dangerous Goods, Ltd.
99 Applegarth Road
Cranbury, NJ 08512-9548 USA
Tel: (608) 860-0300
Fax: (609) 860-0096
Fax: (609) 860-0285

Q U A L I T Y   M A N U A L

15.2 Handling

ABC Company provides methods of handling product that prevent damage or deterioration.

Procedure

This procedure should be specifically tailored to your product/industry. Methods for handling should consider the use of the following:

Fork trucks	Conveyors	Containers	Tongs
Pallets	Cranes	Vessels	Robotics
Pallet jacks	Hooks	Tanks	Trucks
Carts	Slings	Pipelines	Trailers

Handling procedures should ensure the following:

- Product is not damaged

- Product is not inadvertently mixed

- Contamination or deterioration does not occur

- Safety of workers is maintained

Handling certain products may require the use of personal protective equipment, including these:

Hard hats   Steel-toed boots   Eye and face protection

Respirators   Hearing protection   Protective clothing

♀ *Lifting Techniques*

Second only to the common cold, problems with the lower back are a leading cause of lost work time and compensation for adults under the age of 45. Back pain causes approximately 30 million doctor visits resulting in more than $16 billion in compensation and medical costs each year. Many of these problems can be avoided by practicing simple lifting techniques. Consider describing these in your handling procedure. Another idea is to add the following requirement in regard to packaging:

Palletizing
Containers weighing more than 45 kg (100 lb.) must be fitted with hand slots in the transport container for ease of handling. Containers weighing in excess of 70 kg (150 lb.) must be fitted with pallets.

☠ *Hazardous Material*

When handling hazardous materials, U.S. companies are required to comply with 29 CFR 1910.120, "Hazardous Waste Operations and Emergency Response" (HAZWOPER). This regulation deals specifically with spills of chemicals and hazardous waste. Your procedures should contain contingency plans which address the following points:

- Use of personal protective equipment and clothing

- Emergency response teams

- Evacuation plans

- Use of spill carts and spill control stations

- Decontamination procedures
- Emergency follow-up

☝ *Cleaning*

Maintenance, repair, and servicing operations often receive product that has been in use and requires cleaning. Handling procedures should address cleaning methods and the use of solvents, abrasive brushes, etc. that avoid damaging the product. If the water used to clean a product becomes contaminated during that process, procedures should address its proper disposal.

⚡ *ESD (Electrostatic Discharge)*

If ESD (electrostatic discharge) is a concern in your operation, you should develop an ESD Control Program. Many companies reference MIL-STD-1686B, "Electrostatic Discharge Control Program for Protection of Electrical and Electronic Parts, Assemblies, and Equipment," for guidance, along with DOD-HDBK-263, "Electrostatic Discharge Control Handbook for Protection of Electrical and Electronic Parts, Assemblies, and Equipment." Another excellent source of information on this topic is the ESD Association, Inc. (See Appendix A for more information.)

Q U A L I T Y   M A N U A L

15.3 Storage

Designated storage areas or stock rooms will be used to prevent damage or deterioration of product, pending use or delivery. Appropriate methods for authorizing receipt to and dispatch from such areas will be stipulated. In order to detect deterioration, the condition of product in stock is be assessed at appropriate intervals.

▤ *Procedure*

Your procedure should begin by describing *how* designated storage areas or stock rooms are identified. Prevention of damage or deterioration, depending upon the product, could raise additional issues such as environmental control, pest control, security, or sterilization. Your procedure should reflect adequate storage control, addressing the appropriate concerns. If applicable, you should also address how "special" storage requirements are communicated to the warehouse staff when invoked in customer contracts.

"Appropriate methods for authorizing receipt and the dispatch to and from such areas . . ." should address the following:

- **Who** is authorized (usually warehouse personnel and supervisory staff)

- **How** receipt and dispatch is performed (no record required)

Assessment of stock at *appropriate* intervals can be accomplished through internal audits of storage areas and stock rooms or formal inventories. Some companies cycle stock so rapidly that neither of these methods is needed. If this is your situation, describe why no assessment of stock is necessary in your procedure and justify. As a minimum, you may be expected by your registrar to monitor the cycle of stock, alerting you to any change that would require an assessment.

Another source for guidance in this area is the American Production and Inventory Control Society (APICS—reference Appendix A for more information).

Secure Storage Areas or Stock Rooms

While this clause was changed in the 1994 revision of ISO 9000 to remove the word "secure," some regulatory requirements may specify that hazardous material be kept in locked areas. In many instances, you may be required to have an up-to-date inventory of these hazardous chemicals and substances (local, state, and federal laws).

Inventory Methods

The intent of this last sentence:

> *In order to detect deterioration, the condition of product in stock shall be assessed at appropriate intervals*

can be addressed in several ways. For example:

- FIFO (first in—first out inventory systems)

- Routine audits

- Cycle counts

Some accounting considerations may also need to be addressed.

Shelf Life

Many items in inventory have a limited shelf life (organic substances, chemicals, adhesives, O-rings, some gaskets, etc.). Each item should be labeled or otherwise identified as to its expiration date (see Section 4.11). This may require a little research.

> QUALITY MANUAL
>
> **15.4** Packaging
>
> ABC Company will control packing, packaging, and marking processes (including materials used) to the extent necessary to ensure conformance to specified requirements.

Procedure

The best approach any company can take in developing a packaging procedure is to obtain a copy of the "National Motor Freight Classification 100-T." The classes and rules detailed in that classification should address most of your commercial shipping needs. It even contains guidance on how to develop a "short form bill of lading."

For "marking processes," refer to "National Motor Freight Classification 100-T, Item 580, Marking or Tagging Freight."

A copy of "National Motor Freight Classification 100-T" may be purchased from:

The American Trucking Association, Inc.
2200 Mill Road
Alexandria, VA 22314
Tel: (703) 838-1810
Fax: (703) 683-1094

Specific packaging requirements are often defined by the Design and Engineering function(s) to protect the finished product through delivery. Considerations may include compliance with local, state, and federal regulations, codes, laws, and international (UN) requirements. One excellent source for guidance is:

The Handbook of Package Engineering
By Joseph F. Hanlon
Published by McGraw-Hill Book Co., New York, NY

ISBN 0-07-025994-1   (2nd edition)

Over the years, the U.S. DoD has developed several procedures for packaging and packing parts and equipment. Take full advantage of this work. Most may be obtained from the U.S. Naval Publications and Forms Center (see Appendix C). Here is a list of a few:

MIL-P-116J	Military Approved Packaging Methods
MIL-STD-129M	Marking for Shipment and Storage

MIL-STD-147D	Palletized Unit Loads
MIL-STD-1367A	Packaging, Handling, Storage, and Transportability Program Requirements (for Systems and Equipments)
MIL-STD-2073-1B	DoD Materiel Procedures for Development and Application of Packaging Requirements (Part 1 of 2 Parts)
MIL-STD-2073-2	Packaging Requirement Codes (Part 2 of 2 Parts)

You may also wish to refer to the following:

- ASTM D 3950, Strapping, Plastic (and Seals)

- ASTM D 3951, Standard Practice for Commercial Packaging

- ASTM D 3953, Strapping, Flat Steel, and Seals

- ASTM D 4675, Selection and Use of Flat Strapping Materials

Other commercial workmanship standards are also available from a variety of sources. You should list them in your procedures for guidance and reference only, *not* necessarily compliance.

When developing your packaging procedures, be flexible. Consider adding a statement such as:

Where necessary and appropriate, packaging standards may be altered to meet special specified customer requirements.

Obviously, you can't anticipate every possibility. But you can make a good effort.

◻ *Container Certification*

Many products must be packaged in accordance with local, state, federal, and international (UN) regulations, codes, and laws. In these instances the containers may require certification. For more information, and a listing of certified "transit testing" laboratories, contact the International Safe Transit Association (ISTA)—see Appendix A for address and telephone numbers. (Also refer to: ASTM D 4169, Practice for Performance Testing of Shipping Containers and Systems.)

◌ *Servicing and Repair Companies*

Service companies that receive equipment or instruments from their customers for servicing or repair often return those items in the original packaging supplied by the client. There are several reasons for this. Some customers may have supplied customized or reusable shipping containers. If damage were to occur in shipping, this can also resolve the issue of boxes having insufficient bursting strength. To address these issues, many service and repair companies include the following paragraph in their procedure (SOP):

All materials (equipment/instruments, etc.) supplied to the company shall be returned in their original packaging, if practical. All reused shipping containers must have all previous addresses or routing information removed or covered prior to reuse.

This statement is also handy in establishing a practice toward receiving components that may be ESD-sensitive.

📄 *Uniform Packaging and Labeling Regulation (UPLR)*

In an effort to help U.S. consumers make the transition to the metric system and make packaged goods more acceptable to the international marketplace, the National Conference on Weights and Measures Uniform Packaging and Labeling Regulation (UPLR) was revised to conform with the 1992 amendments to the "Fair Packaging and Labeling Act" (FPLA). The new amendments to the FPLA require the use of both the inch–pound (avoirdupois) and SI ("Le Système International d'Unités") units of measure on specific packages of consumer commodities.

The FPLA was amended to bring it in conformity with the "Metric Conversion Act" that designated the metric system as the preferred system of measurement for U.S. trade and commerce. For purposes of international trade, the metric system is more than just SI. It includes the product standards and preferred sizes that are accepted by industries and governments throughout the world.

I suggest that your procedures and practices reflect compliance with this regulation where required. Details concerning the UPLR can be found in the latest edition of NIST Handbook 130, "Uniform Laws and Regulations," available from:

National Conference on Weights and Measures
P.O. Box 4025
Gaithersburg, MD 20885
Tel: (301) 975-4004
Fax: (301) 926-0647

✍ **Note**

Mexico's Federal Law on Metrology and Standardization stipulates that all weights and measurements must be metric. Manufacturers of products for sale in Mexico should familiarize themselves with the Mexican Certification and Labeling Decree of March 7, 1994, as well as all of the applicable NOMs.

☠ *Hazardous Material*

Hazardous materials and substances must be identified (marked) in accordance with all local, state, and federal regulations, codes, and laws. Attention should also be given to compliance with the NFPA (National Fire Protection Association) 704 Standards System for "Identification of the Fire Hazards of Materials." The purpose of the standard is to provide an easily understood system for identifying the health, flammability, reactivity, and specific hazards of a material that may be presented by *short-term, acute exposure* in situations such as fires, chemical spills, and other emergencies.

⚡ *ESD (Electrostatic Discharge)*

Proper *packaging and marking* of ESDS (electrostatic discharge–sensitive) circuit boards, subassemblies, and parts is essential. The examples given in Figure 4-15.1 and 4-15.2 are very generic and are easily tailored to meet your specific industry needs.

⏳ *Quality Systems Requirements*

If you are planning to comply with QS-9000 requirements, refer to section I, clause 4.15. It requires suppliers to develop a system that also complies with the AIAG "Shipping/Parts Identification Label Standard" (AIAG B-3).

> Q U A L I T Y   M A N U A L
>
> **15.5** Preservation
>
> ABC Company will apply appropriate methods for preservation and segregation of product when the product is under its control.

▤ *Procedure*

Many products (food, chemicals, etc.) require special precautions (such as refrigeration) to ensure their preservation. Preservation should prevent the following:

- Spoilage
- Deterioration
- Corrosion
- Contamination

ABC Company		STANDARD OPERATING PROCEDURES	
Computer File:	C:\QUALITY\SOP-15.DOC	Revision:	2.0
Quality Mgr.:	*Jane Doe*	Date:	5-DEC-94
Section:	15.4	Page:	6 OF 15
Title:	PACKAGING OF ESDS CIRCUIT BOARDS		

Packaging   All ESDS (Electrostatic Discharge Sensitive) circuit boards, subassemblies, and parts will be handled, stored, processed, and transported/shipped in electrostatic-shielding bags, containers, conductive Dual In-line Package (DIP) rails, envelopes, packaging, pouches, or conductive tote boxes or storage bins. Unless otherwise specified, ESD protective packaging shall be in accordance with MIL-E-17555 for ESDS items. In addition:

- ESD protective caps shall be used on equipment external connectors that are connected to ESDS parts and assemblies within the equipment.

- Minimize handling of ESDS components and hold them by the body, not the leads.

- Paper and/or generic plastic bags shall not be used to transport/ship ESDS material.

- Bags and envelopes containing ESDS items shall not have ends closed with staples or non–ESD-safe tape.

- Static retentive styrofoam particles shall not be used in shipping any ESDS equipment. Static-dissipative styrofoam particles (peanuts) which comply with MIL-B-81705B are acceptable.

Desiccator storage boxes in which ESDS items are stored shall be clearly identified as an ESDS container, preferably by placing an ESD symbol in the upper left-hand corner of the box lid. Desiccator storage boxes are not considered ESD work stations and do not require a certification label. ESDS items contained in static-shielding bags may be stored in non-ionized storage boxes.

Figure 4.15-1: Sample of ESDS Protective Packaging Procedure

ABC Company	STANDARD OPERATING PROCEDURES		
Computer File:	C:\QUALITY\SOP-15.DOC	Revision:	2.0
Quality Mgr.:	*Jane Doe*	Date:	5-DEC-94
Section:	15.4	Page:	7 OF 15
Title:	PACKAGING OF ESDS CIRCUIT BOARDS		

Marking

EIA-471 LABEL
Figure 1

MIL-STD-1285 LABEL
Figure 2

Assemblies

ESDS (Electrostatic Discharge Sensitive) assemblies shall be marked with either the RS-471 symbol, as illustrated in Figure 1, or the MIL-STD-1285 sensitive electronic device symbol as illustrated in Figure 2. The symbol shall be located in a position readily visible to personnel when the assembly is incorporated in its next higher assembly (a circuit board into its motherboard, for example). When physical size or orientation of the assembly precludes compliance with this requirement, alternative marking procedures shall be developed.

Equipment

Equipment containing ESDS parts and assemblies shall be marked with either the RS-471 symbol or the MIL-STD-1285 sensitive electronic device symbol. The symbol shall be located on the exterior surface of the equipment and readily visible to personnel prior to gaining access to ESDS parts and assemblies within the equipment.

Figure 4.15-2: Sample of ESDS Protective Marking Procedure

This is often accomplished through the following methods:

- Environmental control (temperature, humidity, lighting, etc.)
- Pest control (use of biocides, insecticides, traps, introducing natural predators of insects or rodents into storage areas, etc.)
- Special packaging (use of preservatives, amber bottling, electrostatic-shielding or conductive bags, etc.)

This clause also requires that product be segregated. An example of this is the cleaning of any reusable container, apparatus, or area in which, or through which, a product is transported or stored. This could include the following:

Tank cars	Trucks	Bags
Hopper cars	Barges	Boxes
Airplane or ship cargo bays	Pipelines	Drums
Volumetric glassware	Tanks	Vats

In both areas, your procedure should define and document "appropriate methods" in which "preservation and segregation of product" is to be achieved.

QUALITY MANUAL

15.6 Delivery

ABC Company will arrange for the protection of the quality of product after final inspection and test. Where contractually specified, this protection will be extended to include delivery to destination.

Procedure

This clause is applicable to companies that deliver the final product to their customers in their own trucks, and to those that use subcontracted shipping companies. In the case of using your own trucks, your procedure should ensure that your drivers are properly licensed and trained in the proper handling (including loading and unloading) of the product to its final destination.

Should Freight Carriers be Qualified as Subcontractors?

Some auditors have interpreted the standard in such a way as to require that your freight carriers be assessed and qualified as subcontractors. This is *not* necessarily a requirement. As this clause clearly states, they need only be categorized as subcontractors when a contract requires that "protection" extend to the destination. In other words:

If you ship:

F.O.B. Shipping Point Freight carriers *are not* required to be qualified as subcontractors.

F.O.B. Destination Freight carriers *are* required to be qualified as subcontractors.

☠ *Transporting Hazardous Material*

When transporting hazardous material, the carrier should utilize identification placards as required by the D.O.T.'s HM-181. These placards must be in compliance with 49 CFR 172.500 with preprinted ID numbers as required by 49 CFR 172.332 (c). Canadian placards are not required to be preprinted. Mexican placards should contain the image only. No words are currently allowed.

✍ *Note*

The requirements for placards contained in 49 CFR 172.519 through 172.560 are based on UN Recommendations and may be used for international as well as domestic shipments.

🗁 *Records*

As a minimum, you should have records indicating that the condition of stock is assessed at "appropriate intervals."

Additional records may be generated in the "receipt and dispatch" of product from designated storage areas, and in documenting "segregation" (cleaning of tank cars before next use, etc.), depending upon your approach toward addressing this clause of the standard.

If packaging requires certification, records documenting acceptability (certificates or test reports) should be maintained.

☞ *Guidance*

For further guidance, refer to:

ISO 9000-2:1993, Quality Management and Quality Assurance Standards—Part 2: Generic guidelines for application of ISO 9001, ISO 9002, and ISO 9003
Section 4.15—"Handling, storage, packaging, and delivery"

NIST Handbook 130, "Uniform Laws and Regulations"

NMF 100-T, National Motor Freight Classification 100-T

U.S. Military/U.S. DoD Standards

MIL-P-116J, Military Approved Packaging Methods

MIL-STD-129M, Marking for Shipment and Storage

MIL-STD-147D, Palletized Unit Loads

MIL-STD-1367A, Packaging, Handling, Storage, and Transportability Program Requirements (for Systems and Equipments)

MIL-STD-2073-1B, DoD Materiel Procedures for Development and Application of Packaging Requirements (Part 1 of 2 Parts)

MIL-STD-2073-2, Packaging Requirement Codes (Part 2 of 2 Parts)

MIL-B-81705B, Barrier Materials, Flexible, Electrostatic-free, Heat Sealable

MIL-STD-1686B, Electrostatic Discharge Control Program for Protection of Electrical and Electronic Parts, Assemblies, and Equipment

DOD-HDBK-263, Electrostatic Discharge Control Handbook for Protection of Electrical and Electronic Parts, Assemblies, and Equipment

Hazardous Material

International Air Transportation Association (IATA) Dangerous Goods Regulations

International Civil Aviation Organization (ICAO) 9284-AN/905
Current Technical Instructions for the Safe Transport of Dangerous Goods by Air

International Maritime Dangerous Goods Code

UN Recommendations on the Transport of Dangerous Goods
Volume I—General Requirements
Volume II—UN Testing and Marking for Performance Oriented Packaging Requirements

U.S. Department of Transportation—DOT P 5800.5
Guidebook for First Response to Hazardous Materials Incidents

Title CFR 49, "Transportation—Hazardous Materials"

D.O.T. HM-181 (Hazardous Material)

Other Industry and Commercial Standards

AIAG B-3, Shipping/Parts Identification Label Standard

ASTM D 3950, Strapping, Plastic (and Seals)

ASTM D 3951, Standard Practice for Commercial Packaging

ASTM D 3953, Strapping, Flat Steel, and Seals

ASTM D 4169, Practice for Performance Testing of Shipping Containers and Systems

ASTM D 4675, Selection and Use of Flat Strapping Materials

ISO Guide 41:1984, Standards for Packaging—Consumer Requirements

Bellcore Technical Advisory TA-TSY-000870, Electrostatic Discharge Control in the Manufacture of Telecommunications Equipment

Questions Your Registrar May Ask

4.15.2 Handling

☑ What methods have you adopted/developed for handling product that prevent damage or deterioration? Where is this defined (documented)?

☑ Are special containers properly approved prior to use (as applicable)?

☑ Are the weight limitations and safe loads of all cranes, hooks, and slings known? Is this information posted or otherwise communicated to those employees using them?

☑ If forklifts are used, are their drivers designated and trained? How?

☑ Is special handling required in any area? Does that involve the use of any Personal Protection Equipment (PPE)? If so, where is this defined?

4.15.3 Storage

☑ How are storage areas or stock rooms designated or identified to prevent damage or deterioration of product, pending use or delivery? Does this include any staging, quarantine, and holding areas?

☑ How are appropriate methods for authorizing receipt to and dispatch from designated storage areas stipulated?

☑ Are intervals established for assessing the condition of product in stock? Does this include identifying the following:

• Product that has exceeded its shelf-life?

• Wet or water-stained boxes or containers?

- Damaged or crushed boxes or containers?

- Improper stacking of boxes, containers, or pallets?

- Open containers?

- Spoilage?

- Corrosion?

- Contamination?

☑ Who is responsible for assessing the condition of product in stock in order to detect deterioration? How is this accomplished and documented?

☑ What criteria are used in assessing the condition of product in stock in order to detect deterioration? Do any records substantiate that this has occurred?

4.15.4 Packaging

☑ How are packing, packaging, and marking processes (including materials used) controlled to the extent necessary to ensure conformance to specified requirements? What evidence supports that this control is in place and effective?

4.15.5 Preservation

☑ What are the appropriate methods for preservation and segregation of product when the product is under your control? How are they applied?

☑ Is product segregated according to type (different aisles, racks, shelves, etc.)?

4.15.6 Delivery

☑ How do you arrange for the protection of the quality of product after final inspection and test? Where contractually specified, does this protection extend to include delivery to destination (e.g., use of approved subcontractors)? How can this be verified?

4.16 Control of Quality Records

At a Glance

9001	9002	9003
✓	✓	L

You must do the following:

- Establish and maintain documented procedures for

    1. identification,

    2. collection,

    3. indexing,

    4. access,

    5. filing,

    6. storage,

    7. maintenance, and

    8. disposition of quality records

- Maintain quality records to demonstrate conformance to specified requirements and effective operation of the quality system

- Maintain pertinent subcontractor quality records

- Ensure that quality records are legible

- Store and retain quality records in such a way that they are readily retrievable in facilities that provide a suitable environment to prevent damage or deterioration and prevent loss

- Establish and record retention times for quality records

- Make quality records available for evaluation by the customer or the customer's representative, where agreed by contract, for the agreed period

> ### QUALITY MANUAL
>
> **16.0** CONTROL OF QUALITY RECORDS
>
> ABC Company has established and maintains documented procedures for identification, collection, indexing, access, filing, storage, maintenance, and disposition of quality records.
>
> Quality records are defined as those records maintained to demonstrate conformance to specified requirements and the effective operation of the quality system. Pertinent subcontractor quality records will be an element of these data. Records can be in the form of hard copy, or they can be in electronic or other media.
>
> All quality records must be legible and will be stored and retained in such a way that they are readily retrievable in facilities that provide a suitable environment to prevent damage or deterioration and to prevent loss. Retention times of quality records will be established and recorded. Where agreed contractually, quality records will be made available for evaluation by the customer or the customer's representative for an agreed period.

Quality Manual

Before we begin this section, let's take a moment to discuss what constitutes a "Quality Record." Although ISO 9000 does not specifically define quality records, section 17 of ISO 9004-1:1994 does offer guidance in describing the intent behind keeping quality records in the first place. From that we can formulate the following definition:

> *Quality Records—Hard copy, electronic, or other media that demonstrate conformance to specified requirements and verify effective operation of the quality system.*

Quality records are often confused with quality documents. A quality record is evidence of compliance with a requirement. Records shouldn't be changed, since they contain "event" data (facts or history). However, you expect documents (procedures, instructions, plans, schedules, etc.) to be changed and controlled.

The policy contained in the sample quality manual was developed paraphrasing as much actual text as possible from ISO 9001, clause 4.16. The only significant change needed was to reword the second paragraph to define quality records, taking into account note 19 from the bottom of ISO 9001/2/3, clause 4.16.

This policy, and the associated procedure(s), can easily be expanded to include other records that either do not directly relate to the quality system or are debatable in their relationship (records relating to compliance with various regulatory requirements). The OSHA 200 Log (required by 29 CFR 1904) is a good example of this. Obviously, there is no good reason to develop a redundant or parallel system simply to address these other records. I suggest addressing them in the same system while defining the difference between them and quality records.

Procedure

Many large companies are attempting to follow the decentralization bandwagon into virtually every aspect of the business. This is particularly tempting when addressing something spread throughout an organization such as quality records. I suggest that you keep this a single procedure. If each organization creates their own, they will reinvent the wheel simply to state the specifics relating to their organization alone (typically only two or three lines of text). I support decentralization when and where it makes a company more efficient and effective, but not where it creates non–value-added redundancy just for the sake of decentralization. Simply have each organization provide input to this central procedure. In most organizations, this procedure rarely requires significant change.

I suggest that you begin developing this procedure by briefly restating the policy and listing (identifying) the more significant quality records. For example:

> *This procedure establishes instructions for the identification, collection, indexing, access, filing, storage, maintenance, and disposition of quality records. All definitions and responsibilities not explained here are detailed in the ABC Company Quality Manual.*
>
> *Quality records include, but are not limited to, the following:*
>
> - *Management reviews*
> - *Contracts/customer purchase orders*
> - *Design input data*
> - *Design reviews* (a.k.a. Engineering Reviews)
> - *Design output data* (Drawings, Schematics, Bill of Materials— BOMs, etc.)
> - *Design verification data*

- *Design validation data*

- *Design change orders (a.k.a. Engineering Change Orders—ECOs)*

- *Subcontractor/vendor records (basis for selection/usage)*

- *Purchase orders*

- *Records of customer-supplied product* (Inventory)

- *Process equipment maintenance records*

- *Inspection checklists*

- *Inspection* (receiving, in-process, and final) *records**

- *Test reports* (where applicable)

- *First article inspection reports* (where applicable)

- *Inspection, measuring, and test equipment calibration records*** (Certificates of Calibration, Certificates of Conformance/Analysis for standard reference materials)

- *Records of use* (as necessary to comply with ISO 9001/2, clause 4.11.2 f)

- *Nonconforming material disposition records* (Material Review Reports)

- *Corrective action records*

- *Customer complaints*

- *Internal audit reports*

- *Employee qualification records* (employee résumés, diplomas, degrees, certifications, licenses, etc.)

- *Training records* (Including course descriptions/outlines)

- *Servicing records*

- *Statistical data/results*

*If you use controlled stamps (including signature stamps), you should include:
- *Controlled stamp logs*

**If you perform alignment, calibration, or verification activities internally, you should also include:
- *Completed "Alignment/Calibration/Verification Data Sheets"*

If you acknowledge customer purchase orders, these may also be considered quality records:

- *Acknowledgments*

If special processes (ref. ISO 9001/2, clause 4.9) are identified, you may also need to include the following:

- *Process qualification records*

- *Equipment qualification records*

- *Special process employee qualification records*

Remember that "Pertinent quality records from the subcontractor shall be an element of these data." This can include the following:

- *Laboratory reports*

- *Inspection/test reports*

- *Statistical reports*

- *Certificates of Analysis (C of A)*

- *Process control charts*

- *Reports or Certificates of Calibration*

The "but not limited to" statement allows you to continue to operate under this procedure without revision as you add quality records to your system. For example, ISO 9001/2/3, clause 4.8, "Product identification and traceability," requires you to address traceability *where specified* by contract. This could include additional quality records. For a contract of short duration, these quality records could be addressed in an associated quality plan. Using this approach, you wouldn't have to revise your procedure to add quality records only to go back later and remove them when they no longer apply.

You can easily expand this listing into a chart indicating where each record resides (who is responsible for collection, indexing, filing, storage, and maintenance). The chart in Figure 4.16-1 is only an example. If your company is small, you probably aren't structured into the different departments listed, or yours may have different names. But you get the general idea. All of the examples given are generic. The number of quality records listed could easily be increased as required to better reflect your specific company or industry needs. This chart could also be expanded to include retention times beside each record for further ease of use.

Quality Record Chart	
Quality Record	Responsible Area
Management Reviews	Quality Department
Contracts / Customer Purchase Orders	Contract Administration / Production Control
Design Input Data	Engineering Department
Design Output Data	Engineering Department
Design Reviews (a.k.a. Eng. Reviews)	Engineering Department
Design Verification Data	Engineering Department
Design Validation Data	Engineering Department
Design Change Orders (a.k.a. ECOs)	Engineering Department
Subcontractor / Vendor Records	Purchasing Department
Purchase Orders	Purchasing Department
Records of Customer Supplied Product	Purchasing Department / Production Control
Process Equipment Maintenance Records	Maintenance Department
Inspection Records (Checklists, Reports, etc.)	Quality Department
Test Reports (where applicable)	Quality Department (Testing Lab)
Equipment Calibration Records	Quality Department (Calibration Lab)
Material Review Reports	Quality Department
Corrective Action Records	Quality Department
Customer Complaints	Quality Department (Customer Service)
Internal Audit Reports	Quality Department
Employee Qualification Records	Personnel Department
Training Records	Personnel Department (Training Dept.)
Service Records	Quality Department (Customer Service)
Statistical Data / Results	Quality Department

Figure 4.16-1: Sample Quality Record Chart with Responsible Areas

Filing

Many quality records are compiled into a "Customer File" or "Work Order File." During an audit, it is common for the auditor to ask what a complete finished "file" consists of. The workers usually know, but can't find this addressed in their procedure manual. Filing is often overlooked. Some companies identify certain files in their procedure with a list of all the required documents and quality records. For example:

Customer Files

Customer files include as a minimum, but are not limited to:

- *Customer purchase orders*

- *Any customer correspondence*

- *Work orders*

- *Inspection records/reports*

- *Shipping documents*

- *Invoices*

Some companies have gone so far as to create documentation checklists for their filing system to assist in training administrative staff and/or new hires. I've also seen some very creative systems using different-colored file folders.

An ISO 9000 auditor will, of course, ask to see specific records (customer files). In a large company, it is not uncommon for someone to have removed those files for some purpose (e.g., to resolve an invoicing dispute or verify shipment). You must have some way of controlling these files. This is most easily accomplished by that person placing an identifying "name" card in the empty file folder (particularly when your administrative staff member plans to remove those records from the record room). This allows you to track down the record by knowing who has it. Some companies use different-colored identifying name cards to facilitate this process. The colors may represent different departments or shifts. I've also seen companies where the staff would simply tape their business card to an $8\frac{1}{2} \times 11$ piece of paper which they placed in the empty file folder. Be creative and do whatever works best. Of course, you also need to address *who* has access to quality records. In many instances, this can be by department rather than specific individual (job title).

Sign-out Logs

Some companies have responded to this "file control" issue by developing a sign-out log for records and documents. Although this works, it leaves a permanent record of access which you may not want. For example, in reviewing your sign-out log an auditor may find a record that had been returned even though the user did not log the record back in. Common oversights can result in minor noncompliances casting doubt on the effectiveness of this approach.

Document Control as It Relates to Quality Records

Many quality records consist of forms that, when completed, document facts relating to a specific event, person, subcontractor, customer, process, product, etc. Revision control should extend to the blank forms used in order to assure that only the most current revisions are available. Likewise, changes made to quality records (data) should "be reviewed and approved by the same function or organization" that completed the original record (form).

Blank Spaces on Forms

Another common pitfall is leaving blank spaces on forms. If a form requires a section to be completed, don't just leave it blank. That implies to an auditor that it was an oversight and required data is missing. You should identify those areas to be completed "Where Applicable" or enter "N/A" in sections when they do not apply to the situation.

 Indexing

Companies often forget that *all* quality records must be indexed. This is most often accomplished by sequential numbering. Index numbers can be preprinted on various forms or assigned as needed.

I have encountered some interesting indexing methods in which a single form was used for multiple purposes. For example:

Quality Record:	Indexing Sequence:
Corrective action requests	CA-001-94
Customer complaints	CC-001-94
Measurement standard found out-of-tolerance	MS-001-94

The first two alpha characters represent the type of quality record, the following numbers are sequential to each record, and the last two digits represent the year. At the end of each year, the sequential numbers in the middle begin again at 001. This allows ease of maintenance in assuring that all of the records for the past year have been addressed.

 Fax Records

Although quality records may be in the form of a faxed document, care should be taken if these records have been generated on thermal fax paper (plain-paper fax machines are OK). Thermal paper faxes stored in an office environment may fade and degrade to the point of being unreadable in as few as three years. Thermal paper faxes stored in an uncontrolled environment, such as a warehouse, may darken from the heat until they are a solid black, unreadable image. It only takes a few hot summer days for these records to be completely destroyed (completely black).

While thermal fax paper is obviously not specifically addressed in ISO 9000, the intent of the standard's requirement to "provide a suitable environment to prevent damage or deterioration and to prevent loss" still applies.

I suggest that you address quality records on thermal fax paper by limiting retention time to one year or less, and specifying that they must be maintained in a suitable environment to minimize deterioration or damage.

Alternatively, you can require that quality records be transferred from thermal fax paper to a more stable medium within a specified time period (e.g., photocopy, electronically scanned image, microfiche).

🖥 *Computer Security*

As computer-based paperless systems become commonplace, more and more quality records are taking the form of electronic data. As we begin reading this clause, we see that access to quality records must be controlled:

> *The supplier shall establish and maintain documented procedures for identification, collection, indexing,* access, *filing, storage, maintenance, and disposition of quality records.*

If you maintain quality records on a computer, then this means that you must establish procedures limiting access to those records (i.e., programs, files, screens, fields). File protection can be accomplished by password-encrypting (protecting) specific files (typically to read-only) in a small company. For larger companies, this is usually handled by having your system administrator establish and maintain computer security levels for those individuals who require access to various hard drive (network) directories. Consider listing those job functions that require access to quality records in your procedure. This level of control should also protect files (quality records) from unauthorized update.

Each specific approach toward setting up security systems depends on both the organization and structure of the business, and on the software or hardware being used. A great deal of expert guidance is available from such organizations as:

The Computer Security Institute
600 Harrison Street
San Francisco, CA. 94107

Tel: (415) 905-2370
Fax: (415) 905-2218
BBS: (405) 905-2480

CompuServe
   71702.402@compuserve.com

National Computer
   Security Association
10 South Courthouse Ave.
Carlisle, PA. 17013

Tel: (717) 258-1816
Fax: (717) 243-8642
Virus Helpline: 1-900-555-NCSA
($1.90/min. Must be 18 or older.)

CompuServe: GO NCSAFORUM
   75300.2557@compuserve.com

Process data is increasingly recorded by various computer systems. If these records are to be used as part of your quality system, you should do the following:

- Verify that the software meets the quality system needs

- Verify the accuracy and precision of recorded values

You may even wish to periodically review records for missing or erroneous data.

💾 *Electronic (Computer) Data Back-ups/Virus Scanning*

The ISO 9000 requirement to

> . . . *provide a suitable environment to minimize deterioration or damage and to prevent loss*

also applies to computer and other electronic data that serve as quality records. Hard drives crash; therefore, this requirement must be translated into computer terminology to mean that you are required to create archives of files (quality records) to assure recovery if inadvertently lost.

This is most easily accomplished through the routine of backing up such data files (e.g., onto floppy disk or tape). Provide details such as these in your procedure:

- **Who** is responsible for running back-ups (even if they are automated)

- **How** often they are generated

- **Where** they are kept

This procedure should also address periodic scanning for computer viruses. Before you dismiss this suggestion by saying "We just won't allow outside access to our computer system," beware. If *any* of your employees does work at home on a personal computer, they are exposing your system to outside influences. According to a 1992 study performed by USA Research, monetary losses attributed to computer viruses reached about $1 billion in 1991. I've only found one virus on my computer. I got it by transferring data from a computer that others were also using. The bottom line here is—if you have computers, you *are* vulnerable to viruses. Scanning once a month is usually a reasonable effort and, believe me, well worth the time spent.

The software for running such scans must be constantly updated to identify new viruses. Computer network servers and mainframes often require a special version of scanning software.

🖎 *Note 1*

NCSA members receive a "Corporate Computer Virus Prevention Policy" manual that they are allowed to incorporate into their own quality system.

✍ Note 2

Most virus scanning software programs have the capability to create a report or "scan log" documenting each scan activity along with its results. I suggest that you utilize this feature to create a *quality record* documenting your scanning activities.

The NCSA also offers a certification program for anti-virus vendor's software products. These vendors voluntarily submit their products to NCSA to be tested and certified (this can be used as a basis for anti-virus software vendor selection, satisfying ISO 9001/2/3, clause 4.6.2). To obtain a current listing of certified products, contact the NCSA.

⧖ Retention Times

Although ISO 9000 doesn't specify minimum retention time(s), it does require you to establish them. If you are conducting business with government agencies and/or regulated industries, many require specific record retention times (typically invoked in their contracts through referencing various codes and federal regulations). This is another good reason to place specifics in your procedure manual rather than your quality manual. If you unexpectedly win a government or regulated-industry contract, you may only need to revise one procedure.

Consider these factors when establishing retention times:

- Requirements of various contracts with customers

- Applicable regulatory requirements

- Product liability and other legal issues

- The stated (documented) useful life of the product

If longer time periods are not prescribed by legislation or in contracts, retaining records five to seven years is common practice.

If you plan to seek ISO 9000 registration, you must have sufficient quality records available to verify to your registrar that your quality system is functioning. This would automatically require a minimum retention time from the date of the registrar's last visit to the next. This time period may vary from one registrar to the next.

⋈ Quality Systems Requirements

If you are planning to comply with QS-9000, reference section I, clause 4.16, for specific record retention requirements.

☠ *Hazardous Waste*

Since there is currently no statute of limitation under the SuperFund (CERCLA) for hazardous waste liability, many companies retain all hazardous waste files (records) indefinitely.

▦ *Fire-Rated File Cabinets*

Many quality auditors have been trained that there are only two ways to ensure safe record storage:

- Fire-rated file cabinets
- Off-site storage

While these practices certainly meet the requirements of the standard, it must be recognized that they may be considered extreme precautions in today's office environment. These practices have been promoted by a previous generation of auditors based on "common sense." Several years ago fire codes were less stringent. Sprinkler systems were not nearly as prevalent as they are today. I can certainly understand an auditor taking this position if records are stored in an old wooden frame structure, but now most buildings are designed to resist, retard, and even respond to a fire. Fire suppression systems are now common in many computer rooms where electronic data is stored (reference NFPA 75, *Protection of Electronic Computer/Data Processing Equipment*, and NFPA 2001, *Clean Agent Fire Extinguishing Systems*).

As you define your procedure and practices for record storage, consider your position. You must determine whether a reasonable effort has been made in addressing the requirement and, possibly, justify that position to your auditor. If you are a large company with multiple sites, you may wish to use the following example:

Hard copy quality records
Hard copy quality records shall be stored in various commercial grade file storage cabinets inside the work area or office section of each facility. Fire-rated file cabinets may be required in some facilities as directed by the quality manager.

Electronic quality records
Back-ups of electronic data (i.e., disks, tapes, etc.) shall be stored in commercial grade storage enclosures (e.g., desk drawers, file cabinets, disk storage containers, etc.) inside the work area or office section of each facility. Fire-rated storage containers designed specifically to protect electronic storage media may be required in some facilities as directed by the quality manager.

Electronic data can easily be stored off-site by simply uploading the data to another computer. Such routines can be automated to occur at regularly scheduled intervals.

✍ Note

Try not to use the term "fireproof." Virtually no file storage device is truly fireproof. Fire-resistant file cabinets are rated to withstand maximum temperatures for a specified period of time. Hence, they are "fire-rated."

Integrated Imaging Technology

Varian Associates, Lexington, MA, once maintained rows of file cabinets to store all of their paper quality records. Now they have eliminated the vast majority of paper (e.g., purchase orders, contracts, internal audits, etc.) and keep images of those records on one computer network server. These records are readily accessible and can be printed back to hard copy at a moment's notice.

Varian is using a Microsoft Windows–compatible program developed by Wang Laboratories called OPEN/image—Windows (OPEN/server for networks). The information captured in image form can include typed text, handwritten forms, printed documents annotated with text and drawings, line drawings, and photographs. This system can easily address all of the ISO 9000 requirements relating to indexing, access, filing, and storage. If you already have a Windows-based computer system, this technology allows you to use a great deal of your existing hardware, making it surprisingly affordable.

Wang also publishes a magazine titled *Integrated Image* that features stories about how different industries are using this technology. Really interesting stuff! For more information on this technology, contact:

Wang Laboratories, Inc.	Tel: 1-800-New-Wang
One Industrial Ave.	(1-800-639-9264)
Lowell, MA 01851	Tel: (508) 459-5000
U.S.A.	Fax: (508) 967-2819

Customer Access to Quality Records

Remember that you also need to address the following requirement:

Where agreed contractually, quality records shall be made available for evaluation by the customer or his representative for an agreed period.

While this customer must have access to quality records relating to the work you performed for him, you generally wouldn't want that customer to have access to any other customer's files. You may want to address this by placing a brief statement in your procedure as follows:

Customer access to quality records
Quality records pertaining to a specific customer's work shall be made available for inspection by that customer or that customer's representative. A customer audit is limited in access to only those records relating to the work performed for that specific customer.

☞ Guidance

For further guidance, refer to:

ISO 9000-2:1993, Quality Management and Quality Assurance Standards—Part 2: Generic guidelines for application of ISO 9001, ISO 9002, and ISO 9003
Section 4.16—"Quality records"

ISO 9004-1:1994, Quality Management and Quality System Elements—Part 1: Guidelines
Section 17—"Quality records"

OSHA

Recordkeeping Guidelines for Occupational Injuries and Illnesses

A Brief Guide to Recordkeeping Requirements for Occupational Injuries and Illnesses

ᴄᴬ Questions Your Registrar May Ask

Most of the questions relating to quality records will have already been answered in your documentation review. The remaining concerns will be focused on demonstrating compliance. Many questions will have been asked while in other areas.

☑ Who is responsible for the collection of each quality record? (Remaining questions are usually directed toward the appropriate person in each area.)

☑ How are quality records identified, indexed, and filed? Can you show me an example in process?

☑ How do you ensure that quality records are legible?

☑ What does a complete finished "Customer File" consist of?

☑ How do these quality records demonstrate conformance to specified requirements and effective operation of the quality system?

☑ Who has access to these records? Are all of the quality records stored here? (To determine whether off-site storage is used.)

☑ What is the retention time for each quality record? Were applicable regulatory and legal requirements taken into consideration in establishing these retention times? If so, can you show me the applicable regulatory and legal requirements that were consulted?

☑ Who is responsible for maintaining these records? Does that person also dispose of quality records? Where is this process defined in your quality plan and/or documented procedures?

☑ How do you store and retain quality records in such a way that they are readily retrievable in facilities that provide a suitable environment to prevent damage or deterioration and prevent loss?

☑ Do you keep electronic (computer) quality records? Do you create back-ups of this data? How often? Who is responsible for initiating these back-ups? Can you load a recent back-up (bring up the header) so that I can verify the date? Where is this process defined in your quality plan and/or documented procedures?

☑ Do you maintain pertinent subcontractor quality records? Can you show me examples of this?

☑ Are quality records available for evaluation by the customer or the customer's representative, where agreed by contract, for the agreed period? How is this accomplished?

4.17 Internal Quality Audits

At a Glance

You must do the following:

9001	9002	9003
✓	✓	L

- Establish and maintain documented procedures for planning and implementing internal quality audits

- Schedule internal quality audits

- Provide personnel independent of those having direct responsibility for the activity being audited to carry out the audits

- Record the results of the audits

- Bring the results of the audits to the attention of the personnel having responsibility in the area audited

- Ensure that management personnel responsible for the area audited take timely corrective action on deficiencies found during the audit

- Conduct follow-up audit activities that verify and record the implementation and effectiveness of the corrective action taken

> QUALITY MANUAL
>
> **17.0** INTERNAL QUALITY AUDITS
>
> ABC Company has established and maintains documented procedures for planning and implementing internal quality audits to verify whether quality activities and related results comply with planned arrangements and to determine the effectiveness of the quality system.
>
> Internal quality audits will be scheduled on the basis of the status and importance of the activity to be audited and will be carried out by personnel independent of those having direct responsibility for the activity being audited.
>
> The results of the audits will be recorded and brought to the attention of the personnel having responsibility in the area audited. The management personnel responsible for the area shall take timely corrective action on deficiencies found during the audit.
>
> Follow-up audit activities will verify and record the implementation and effectiveness of the corrective action taken. The results of internal quality audits form an integral part of the input to management review activities

Quality Manual

I suggest paraphrasing the standard throughout this section. Wording should closely resemble text from the standard to avoid distorting the intent. Address specific details in your procedure. I have incorporated ISO 9001/2, clause 4.17—Note 20, into the sample quality manual in order to clarify that internal audits will be an element of the management review.

Procedure

Before developing your internal quality audit program, ask yourself (and perhaps management), the following questions:

- What should the audit accomplish?
- What form of information from the audits is most valuable to management?
- What is the best way to communicate "findings" to the various elements while retaining their support and cooperation?

ISO 9001/2/3, Clause 4.17—Note 21, states:

> *Note 21*
> *Guidance on quality-system audits is given in ISO 10011-1:1990, ISO 10011-2:1991, and ISO 10011-3:1991.*

I suggest following that guidance. Some companies are hung up on developing work instructions for *everything*. I've found, in most instances, that work instructions for this section can easily be included in a procedure (second level). If you aren't convinced and still want a third level, then address intervals, scheduling, qualifying internal auditors, notification to areas of upcoming audits, etc. in the second level and place emphasis on the details of how to conduct the audit in the third level. These details could include the following:

- How to conduct the opening meeting (who should be there, what to say, etc.)

- How to conduct the actual audit (can vary from one company, or location, to another—may even involve leading a team)

- How to use internal audit forms

- How to conduct the closing meeting (who should be there, what to say, etc.)

- How to compile an internal audit report

If you are referencing the ISO 10011 series in your procedure, say so. I do *not* suggest stating that your internal audit program is in compliance with ISO 10011 or any other guidance document. (One typically states compliance with standards, not guides.)

☺ *Lead Assessor vs. Internal Audit Courses?*

Just like any other employee performing a job function, auditors must be trained and qualified. You will also need to have a record of the training. ISO 9000 does not state any specific qualifications for internal auditors other than they be independent from the function that they are auditing. It is entirely up to each company to define the minimal qualifications and training required. The sample "Record of Lead Auditor Qualification" form in Figure 4.17-1 was developed based on a similar sample contained in ASME NQA-1-1989, "Quality Assurance Program—Requirements for Nuclear Facilities." This example can be altered to fit the requirements you deem most satisfactory.

Many companies new to ISO immediately send their quality manager to an ISO 9000 Lead Assessor course. This is generally a bad idea, especially if you expect to learn how to conduct an internal audit from this course. Many of the organizations offering Lead Assessor courses have not gone out of their way to

ABC Company

Record of Lead Auditor Qualification

Name:	Date:

QUALIFICATION REQUIREMENTS		CREDITS
Education—University/Degree/Date 4 Credits Max.		
1. Undergraduate Level 2. Graduate Level		
Experience—Company/Dates 9 Credits Max.		
Technical (0-5 credits) and Related Industry (0-1 credit), or Quality Assurance (0-2 credits), or Auditing (0-4 credits)		
Professional Accomplishment/Certificate/Date 2 Credits Max.		
1. P.E. 2. Society		
Management—Justification/Evaluator/Date 2 Credits Max.		
Explain: Evaluated by: (Name and Title)	Date	

Total Credits:

AUDIT COMMUNICATION SKILLS	
Evaluated by: (Name and Title)	Date:

AUDIT TRAINING COURSES

Course Title or Topic: 1. 2.	Date

AUDIT PARTICIPATION

Location	Audit	Date
1.		
2.		
3.		
4.		
5.		
EXAMINATION:	SCORE:	DATE:
AUDITOR QUALIFIED AND CERTIFIED BY: (Signature and Title)		Date Certified

Figure 4.17-1: Sample for Record of Lead Auditor Qualification

fully inform potential students that this course is intended for experienced quality auditors who plan to conduct second- and/or third-party audits leading a team of auditors. Many of the basics will *not* be covered.

Some companies believe that if they send their quality managers to this training course, it will give them insight as to what their registrar's auditors will be looking for. Again, this is not necessarily the case. This course focuses on the dynamics of leading a team of auditors on an ISO 9000 compliance audit. It does *not* focus on interpretation of the ISO 9000 series as it relates to any specific industry.

If you are implementing an ISO 9000 system, I suggest attending an Internal Audit course instead. This course is much more beneficial. One of the frustrations experienced by registrars is the large number of companies conducting poor internal audits. A common source of this problem is internal auditors who have taken the Lead Assessor course without learning the basics.

⌛ *Scheduling Internal Audits*

The topic of scheduling is often filled with pitfalls. Don't use phrases such as

Internal audits will be conducted annually.

Many auditors interpret this to mean that if you audit an area in June of this year, another audit is due during June of next year. If you are auditing several different areas at different times of the year, you're asking for trouble. It's very easy to lose track of when you did which area. Keep it simple. Say something like

At least one complete internal quality audit will be conducted each calendar year.

While the difference may seem subtle on the surface, this second statement allows you to audit any area at any time during the year. The most important concern, obviously, is that you complete a full internal audit of every area during the time you have established.

Your "Internal Audit Schedule" should also be under document control (with approval and revision control).

💣 *Scheduling Specific Audit Dates*

A common pitfall is to tie oneself down to a specific audit date. These are often missed. Don't paint yourself into a corner. Schedule them to be done during specific weeks or months (refer to Figure 4.17-2: Sample Internal Audit Schedule). Scheduling by quarter would be a bit too vague. Unexpected circumstances almost always arise to cause specific dates to be missed. Include in

ABC Company
Internal Audit Schedule

Area	JAN	FEB	MAR	APR	MAY	JUN	JUL
Sales Dept.	Team 1						Team 1
Engineering Dept.		Team 2					
Purchasing Dept.					Team 2		
Production Line(s)		Team 1					
Servicing				Team 1			
Shipping & Receiving	Team 3						
Calibration Lab.		Team 3					
Quality Dept.						Team 2	
Training (HR)			Team 3				

Approved By:　　　　　　　　　　　　　　Date Approved:

Figure 4.17-2: Sample Internal Audit Schedule

your procedure what actions will be taken in the event that you need a variation in the schedule. You can set a specific date in the notification sent to each department just prior to their audit.

Does Your Dog Bite?

There was once a young man traveling through a rural area who came upon an old country store. Deciding to stop and get some refreshments, he approached the store. A rather large, mangy-looking dog was lying across its entrance, and an old farmer was on the porch in a rocking chair. The dog rose up emitting a low, menacing growl. Somewhat intimidated, the young man asked the farmer, "Does your dog bite?" The farmer responded, "No, sir, he might growl at strangers, but he won't bite." Reassured, the young man continued to approach the store. Suddenly, the dog rose up and savagely bit the young man's leg, drawing blood. Retreating rapidly toward his car the young man yelled back at the farmer, "I thought you said your dog didn't bite!" The old farmer stood up and yelled back, "That's not my dog!" The moral of the story is to be sure you ask the right people the right questions.

Some quality organizations send a copy of their internal audit checklist to each department or location they plan to audit in advance. They then request that the responsible manager or supervisor conduct a preliminary internal audit and return the completed checklist. This ensures that the department or location is prepared and understands what is expected of them. Surprisingly, these preliminary internal audits rarely reduce the number of nonconformances identified in the internal audit.

Their real value lies in identifying differences of interpretation between the department or location and the internal audit team. With misinterpretations identified, the correct information can be clarified and lead to much more productive results in future internal audits.

💣 *Auditing the Quality Function*

Neglecting to include the quality department in the internal audit schedule is a common oversight. Audits of the "Internal Audit" system must be carried out, by someone who is not responsible for *directing* internal audits, to ensure that the requirements of this clause are met.

This audit should verify the following:

- An authorized internal audit schedule is both available and being followed

- Persons conducting the internal audits are properly qualified and trained

- Internal audits are carried out by personnel independent of those having direct responsibility for the activity being audited

- Internal audits are documented

- All applicable elements of ISO 9000 are addressed in the internal audits

- Management personnel responsible for the areas audited take timely corrective action on the deficiencies found during the audit

- Follow-up activities are performed

- All internal audits are properly "closed"

☹ *Don't audit to ISO 9000*

This may sound confusing at first, but don't set up your internal audit program to audit against ISO 9000 alone. Your *procedures* should meet all of the requirements of ISO 9000. Audit for compliance with them. This is most easily accomplished through the use of an Internal Audit Plan Matrix (see Figure 4.17-3).

	Sales Dept.	Engineering Dept.	Quality Dept.	Purchasing Dept.	Prod. Lines	Cal. Lab.	Shipping & Receiving	Service	Training (HR)
4.1	X	X	X	X	X	X	X	X	X
4.2			X						
4.3	X								
4.4		X							
4.5	X	X	X	X	X	X	X	X	X
4.6				X					
4.7					X		X		
4.8					X				
4.9					X				
4.10			X		X				
4.11					X	X			
4.12			X		X				
4.13					X				
4.14			X						
4.15							X		
4.16	X	X	X	X	X	X	X	X	X
4.17									
4.18									X
4.19								X	
4.20			X		X				

Figure 4.17-3: Sample Internal Audit Plan Matrix

Ideally, you realize that ISO 9000 is a very minimal standard and will be expanding your quality system to embrace a more comprehensive TQM philosophy. At such time you will, of course, want to ensure compliance with those additional requirements.

While it is true that a registrar's auditors will be referencing the ISO 9000 standard, they will also be auditing compliance with your own procedures. Your procedures contain the details of *how* you are meeting the ISO 9000 requirements.

Paperless Systems

Many quality system auditors are inexperienced in auditing computer security systems (4.5 and 4.16). Fortunately, the National Computer Security Association (NCSA) offers a series of "Security/Audit Program Kits." Each kit contains the following:

- A statement of purpose and scope of the audit

- A list of the necessary preparatory steps

- A complete set of questions (checklist)

✓ *Internal Audit Checklists*

Although ISO 9000 does not specifically require you to use an internal audit checklist, I suggest that you do. By completing a checklist, you can show objective evidence verifying whether quality activities and related results comply with planned arrangements (the intent of the internal audit). The internal audit is also used to determine the effectiveness of the quality system. Therefore, it should document areas of compliance, as well as noncompliance. This is essential for the management review process.

A friend of mine, who is a pilot, once told me that he felt checklists were for aircraft, not quality systems. These are two entirely different uses of a checklist. For aircraft, there is a specific sequence and number of items to be checked that doesn't vary. This requires an *inspection* checklist. When conducting an internal quality audit, there are a number of specific items that will not vary, but unlike aircraft, each one of these items may send the auditor in a different investigative direction. A quality system should constantly be changing and improving. Your audit checklist should grow and evolve as well. Develop your audit checklist so that the minimum criteria are covered, but space is left for additional questions that may surface at the time of the audit.

Documenting objective evidence is essential to any audit. Objective evidence is that which can be retrieved and proven. For example, when reviewing purchase orders, document the P.O. numbers that you examined. This provides specific information that can be referenced in the future, as well as an indication of the sample size of P.O.s examined during the audit.

"Lack of objective documented evidence supporting internal audit activities" is a common noncompliance. Remember, to a good auditor, "Nothing is self-evident."

♀ *Internal Audit Reports*

Massive detailed reports with numerous noncompliances are often overwhelming, and demoralizing to the auditee. I suggest that after a manageable number of noncompliances are identified (say, five or six), stop the audit. This allows the department audited to focus full attention on the problems. After corrective action is complete, resume the audit with a follow-up to the previous audit. Initial internal audits often surface misunderstandings and miscommunication that, once resolved, lead to more fluid, productive internal audits. Remember, you and the auditee are both on the same side working toward a common goal.

Internal Audit "findings" can be issued on the same form on which corrective action is described. The example in Figure 4.17-4 is very generic and by no means the only acceptable format. You may prefer to have the department quality representatives respond to your internal audits instead of department managers. If you take this approach, be sure to keep those department managers plugged in to the internal audit process. Care should also be taken in training the auditees to provide sufficient detail in their responses.

In the example, I have noted that the auditor should close each internal audit. Some companies prefer to have the quality manager oversee and close internal audits in order to avoid any disputes with department managers. This implies to me that the internal auditors have not been properly trained if they must be overseen. Train them—and let them stand on their own. How can they take pride in their work as auditors if you rob them of the total responsibility? I suggest that the quality manager only become involved when a dispute occurs. This in itself may require some form of corrective action to be taken.

The other side of this coin, however, occurs when you have cross-trained employees acting as internal auditors. Some may attempt to issue noncompliances as a form of retribution for other disputes. It happens. Some companies have developed systems in which the auditor issues "observations" only. These are then submitted to the quality manager, who determines which observations should be reclassified as noncompliances before the report is issued.

The standard states:

Follow-up audit activities shall verify and record the implementation and effectiveness of the corrective action taken (see 4.16).

I've included a section at the bottom of the form in Figure 4.17-4 to address this requirement as well. It is common for internal audit "findings" to remain open until the next internal audit of that area. At that time, a follow-up is performed and previous "findings" are closed prior to beginning each new audit cycle.

Management Review of Internal Audits

At the end of ISO 9001/2/3, clause 4.17, Note 20, states:

The results of internal quality audits form an integral part of the input to management review activities (see 4.1.3).

Some companies include a field at the bottom of their "Internal Audit Corrective Action Requests" to be signed off at the time of the management review.

Records

Required internal audit quality records include the following:

- Internal audit reports and results

- Internal audit corrective actions and follow-up activities

- Internal auditor qualifications (see ISO 9001/2/3, clauses 4.1.2.2 and 4.18)

ABC Company

Internal Audit Corrective Action Request

Number # _____

Dept. / Shift :_____ Date: _____/_____/_____

Procedure / Policy #_____ Response due date: ___/___/___

Nonconformance (Attach Appropriate Supporting Documents / Objective Evidence)

Description / Details:

_____

_____

_____

_____

_____

Cause (Attach Appropriate Supporting Documents)

"Root Cause" Investigation and Impact Analysis:

_____

_____

_____

_____

_____

Corrective Action (Attach Appropriate Supporting Documents)

Action(s) Taken to Resolve and Prevent Recurrence:

_____

_____

_____

_____

_____

Anticipated completion date: ___/___/___

Dept. Mgr._____ Date: _____/_____/_____

Nonconformance Closed

(To be completed by Auditor)   Follow-up performed?   ☐ Yes   ☐ No

Closed By: _____ Date: _____/_____/_____

C:\QUALITY\FORMS\ICAR-994.DOC

Figure 4.17-4: Sample Internal Audit Corrective Action Request Form

Also, an "Internal Audit Plan" must exist as a quality record, a procedure, or other controlled document, depending upon the approach taken.

☞ *Guidance*

For further guidance, refer to:

ISO 9000-2:1993, Quality Management and Quality Assurance Standards—Part 2: Generic guidelines for application of ISO 9001, ISO 9002, and ISO 9003
Section 4.17—"Internal quality audits"

ISO 9004-1:1994, Quality Management and Quality System Elements—Part 1: Guidelines
Section 5.4—"Auditing the quality system"

ISO 10011-1:1990, Guidelines for Auditing Quality Systems—Part 1: Auditing

ISO 10011-2:1991, Guidelines for Auditing Quality Systems—Part 2: Qualification Criteria for Auditors

ISO 10011-3:1991, Guidelines for Auditing Quality Systems—Part 3: Managing Audit Programs

ANSI/ASQC Q1-1986, Generic Guidelines for Auditing of Quality Systems

Canadian Standards

CAN/CSA-Q10011-91, Guidelines for Auditing Quality Systems
(Adopted ISO 10011-1:1990, 10011-2:1991 and ISO 10011-3:1991)

CAN3-Q395-81, Quality Audits

ᕦ *Questions Your Registrar May Ask*

☑ Who is responsible for maintaining and managing your internal audit program?

☑ Have training and qualification requirements for auditors been defined and documented? Are records available that detail the training and qualification of each internal auditor?

☑ Are "noncompliance" and/or "observation" definitions established and understood by each auditor?

☑ How are internal audits planned? Is a "scope" defined?

☑ What criteria do you use for determining the effectiveness of the quality system?

☑ How are internal audits scheduled? (On the basis of status and importance of the activity?)

☑ Is a formal schedule for internal quality audits prepared and authorized? May I see it? How can I verify that this schedule is being followed?

☑ How do you ensure that internal audits are carried out by personnel independent of those having direct responsibility for the activity being audited?

☑ How are the results of internal audits recorded? How can I verify that all of the applicable requirements of ISO 9000 have been audited?

☑ How are the results of the audits brought to the attention of the personnel having responsibility in the area audited?

☑ How do you ensure that management personnel responsible for the area audited take timely corrective action on deficiencies found during the audit? How do you define the word "timely"?

☑ When do you conduct follow-up audit activities that verify and record the implementation and effectiveness of the corrective action taken? How is this documented?

☑ How are the results of the audits input to management review activities?

4.18 Training

At a Glance

You must do the following:

9001	9002	9003
✓	✓	L

- Establish and maintain documented procedures for identifying training needs

- Provide for the training of all personnel performing activities affecting quality

- Qualify personnel performing specific assigned tasks on the basis of appropriate education, training and/or experience, as required

- Maintain appropriate records of training

> **QUALITY MANUAL**
>
> **18.0** TRAINING
>
> ABC Company has established and maintains documented procedures for identifying training needs and provides for the training of all personnel performing activities affecting quality. Personnel performing specific assigned tasks will be qualified on the basis of appropriate education, training, and/or experience, as required. Appropriate records of training will be maintained.

📖 *Quality Manual*

The quality manual should cover all of the requirements stated by paraphrasing as much actual text from the standard as possible.

≡ *Deming*

Here is another area where followers of W. Edwards Deming will find that his philosophies are directly applicable. The seventh of his fourteen points can be addressed here:

> • *Institute training*

Too often, workers have learned their jobs from other workers who were never trained properly. They are forced to follow unintelligible instructions. They can't do their jobs because no one tells them how. If procedures were never properly documented, then all training is based on "tribal knowledge": traditions passed from one worker to another.

And Deming's thirteenth point:

> • *Institute a vigorous program of education and retraining*

Both management and the work force will have to be educated in your new quality program and retrained as it changes and evolves.

Far too often, those responsible for training find themselves begging for time from production. Priority is disproportionately given to activities that directly affect short-term production gains, rather than those supporting the long-term growth and expansion of an organization. This is typical of a business focused on surviving for the month or quarter vs. one planning to become an industry leader.

Procedure

Larger companies often have a separate "Human Resources" (HR) or "Personnel" Department with its own procedure manual containing corporate job descriptions and perhaps even some training programs. Smaller companies generally find it easier to keep everything in one "Standard Operating Procedure" (SOP) manual that may also contain related "Job Descriptions."

Your training procedure should describe, as applicable, the following:

Employee indoctrination and orientation:

- **Who** is responsible for administering the indoctrination and orientation

- **When** it will be administered (usually within the first thirty days)

- **Where** it will be administered

- **How** it will be communicated to each new employee

Training program:

- **Who** is responsible for directing the training program

- **Who** should be trained

- **What** form of training is available

- **When** training is available or required

- **Where** training is conducted

- **How** training (classes) will be scheduled

- **How** employees should go about requesting additional training

- **How** departmental supervisors or managers determine that an employee should attend training

Tuition reimbursement programs:

- **Who** is responsible for directing the tuition reimbursement program

- **What** form of training is available

- **When** the employee is eligible for participation

- **How** employees should go about requesting tuition reimbursement

Your training procedure should begin by describing how you identify training needs (see Figure 4.18-1). This is typically done through the use of job

Clause/Title	Who/What
4.1 Management Responsibility	All employees must be trained to understand the company's quality policy.
4.2 Quality System	Everyone involved in developing and/or using quality plans.
4.3 Contract Review	All personnel involved in contract review processes.
4.4 Design Control	All personnel involved in design and engineering processes.
4.5 Document and Data Control	Everyone involved in creating and/or controllng quality documents or data, including personnel authorized to review and approve documents or data for adequacy.
4.6 Purchasing	All personnel involved in subcontractor selection and purchasing activities.
4.7 Control of Customer-Supplied Product	Everyone involved in control of customer-supplied product.
4.8 Product Identification and Traceability	Everyone coming in contact with the product from receipt and during all stages of production, delivery, and installation.
4.9 Process Control	Everyone involved in identifying, planning, and/or controlling the production, installation, and servicing processes that directly affect quality. This includes training individual workers in the use of their work instructions.
4.10 Inspection and Testing	Everyone involved in inspection and/or testing activities.
4.11 Control of Inspection, Measuring, and Test Equipment	All personnel involved in the control or use of inspection, measuring, and test equipment.

Figure 4.18-1: Who Should be Trained in What

Clause / Title	Who / What
4.12 Inspection and Test Status	Everyone coming in contact with the product from receipt and during all stages of production, delivery, and installation. Particular emphasis should be placed on those who are authorized to change inspection and test status.
4.13 Control of Nonconforming Product	All personnel empowered and responsible for identifying nonconforming product and everyone authorized to disposition nonconforming product.
4.14 Corrective and Preventive Action	Everyone empowered and responsible for generating corrective action requests and everyone authorized to disposition or close corrective action requests. (Anyone serving on a Corrective Action Board—CAB)
4.15 Handling, Storage, Packaging, Preservation, and Delivery	Everyone responsible for handling, storage, packaging, preservation, and/or delivery of product.
4.16 Control of Quality Records	Everyone responsible for the identification, collection, indexing, access, filing, storage, maintenance, and/or disposition of quality records.
4.17 Internal Quality Audits	Those individuals responsible for directing and/or conducting internal quality audits.
4.18 Training	All personnel responsible for identifying training needs and/or providing training to personnel performing activities affecting quality.
4.19 Servicing	All personnel performing and/or reporting servicing.
4.20 Statistical Techniques	All personnel involved in the use of statistical techniques.

descriptions that detail the minimum qualifications required for assuming a position or performing a work function (see Figure 4.18-4).

Tribal Training

A common pitfall when developing training procedures is to leave out too much detail because it is considered "common knowledge" (a.k.a. tribal knowledge) or "common sense." Often it is not. When auditors find work process procedures lacking detail, they immediately look to the training program to determine whether the amount of detail is adequate.

Undocumented training programs (or minimally documented training programs) in which a large amount of information is passed verbally from one person to another do not meet the intent of this requirement. Poor quality is often caused by differences between workers, between inspectors, and between workers and inspectors. The root cause is a lack of documented or formalized work instructions and procedures. Don't confuse "tribal knowledge" with craftsmanship, however. There are many examples of job functions that involve training through apprenticeship programs (often called "on-the-job training"). These training techniques should be fully defined in your training program.

Who Should Be Trained in What

Companies often have difficulty in clearly defining *who* should be trained in *what* areas. Although each company is unique and may have different training needs, as a minimum those requirements contained in ISO 9000 must be addressed.

Each company should develop a formal training program to address each of the applicable areas found in the standard. Most companies, of course, break down several of the sections to identify specific job functions that individuals should be trained or qualified in performing.

Training Needs Matrix

You can also develop a training needs matrix similar to the internal audit plan matrix in Figure 4.17-3. This just makes sense. If you're going to audit an area, individuals working in that area must first be properly trained. But let's carry this idea a little further. In Figure 4.18-2, I've added a row at the bottom to include OSHA training requirements. Your actual matrix may be different from the example provided.

Of course, all of the training defined in Figure 4.18-2 is in addition to the basic company indoctrination (insurance, benefits, etc.) that all employees receive. Many companies now include their "Quality Policy" as a part of the ini-

	Sales Dept.	Engineering Dept.	Quality Dept.	Purchasing Dept.	Prod. Lines	Cal. Lab.	Shipping & Receiving	Service	Training (HR)
4.1	X	X	X	X	X	X	X	X	X
4.2			X						
4.3	X	X							
4.4		X							
4.5	X	X	X	X	X	X	X	X	X
4.6				X					
4.7	X				X			X	
4.8		X			X				
4.9		X			X				
4.10			X		X			X	
4.11					X	X			
4.12			X		X				
4.13					X			X	
4.14			X						
4.15					X			X	
4.16	X	X	X	X	X	X	X	X	X
4.17			X						
4.18	X	X	X	X	X	X	X	X	X
4.19								X	
4.20			X		X				
OSHA	X	X	X	X	X	X	X	X	X

Figure 4.18-2: Training Needs Matrix

tial indoctrination training. While the example given above uses the numbering system from ISO 9001, your specific "Training Needs Matrix" should be linked to your company's standard operating procedures (SOPs).

In some instances, it is not always possible for every new employee hired or promoted to be trained in every aspect of the job immediately. In these situations, a formal plan should be developed to ensure that training is completed within a reasonable time frame. In some industries, it is common to find an apprenticeship program where employees receive "on-the-job" training under the supervision of a more experienced journeyman. These programs should be fully documented in detail.

◈ *Identifying Training Needs*

Some auditors have interpreted the requirement to "identify training needs" as a formal requirement for what they call a "Training Needs Assessment." In other words, they want to see a formal periodic evaluation of each employee's future training needs. This is a very conservative, and sometimes extreme, interpretation that is very arguable. I believe that "training needs" could be defined as the difference between an employee's current job description and anticipated future job description. Therefore, if you have formal job descriptions, you have met both this requirement and have established the qualifications needed for each job function. This requirement can also be met through developing a "Training Needs Matrix" such as Figure 4.18-2.

✚ OSHA Requirements

Most U.S. businesses are involved in activities that require them to comply with Occupational Safety and Health Administration (OSHA) Regulations. This typically requires them to provide some degree of training to their employees. Figure 4.18-3 is a brief listing of some of the more common regulations that apply to a wide variety of industries. Although ISO 9000 auditors are not currently trained to verify compliance with these regulations, it is still a good idea to include them in your formal training system where records will be generated giving evidence of compliance.

OSHA, Labor	Title
29 CFR 1910.38	Employee Emergency Plans and Fire Prevention Plans
29 CFR 1910.95	Occupational Noise Exposure (Ear Protection)
29 CFR 1910.120	Hazardous Waste Operations & Emergency Response
29 CFR 1910.132	Personnel Protective Equipment
29 CFR 1910.133	Eye and Face Protection
29 CFR 1910.134	Respiratory Protection *
29 CFR 1910.135	Occupational Head Protection
29 CFR 1910.136	Occupational Foot Protection
29 CFR 1910.146	Permit-required Confined Spaces
29 CFR 1910.147	The Control of Hazardous Energy (Lockout/Tagout)
29 CFR 1910.157	Portable Fire Extinguishers
29 CFR 1910.178	Powered Industrial Trucks
29 CFR 1910.211–247 Subparts O & P	Machinery and Machine Guarding Hand and Portable Powered Tools and Other Hand-held Equipment
29 CFR 1910.251–255 Subpart Q	Welding, Cutting, and Brazing
29 CFR 1910.1200	Hazard Communication (HazCom "Right to Know")
	*Reference ANSI Z 88.2-1980, "Practices for Respiratory Protection"

Figure 4.18-3: Common OSHA Requirements

☠ *Hazardous Material*

Hazardous materials and substances must be handled, stored, packaged, transported, and disposed in accordance with all local, state, and federal regulations, codes, and laws. In many states, such as California, these requirements far exceed those mandated by the federal government. These documents require specific training to be provided to your employees. At the state level, there are also differing worker "Right To Know" regulations that must be adhered to.

These include, but are not limited to, the following:

- Development and maintenance of a chemical inventory

- Employee training

- Evacuation and emergency response plans

- Availability of applicable MSDSs to employees

- Identification and classification of hazardous materials

- Maintenance of accurate records

Similar requirements apply in both Canada and Mexico.

If you transport hazardous materials and substances internationally, there are additional requirements that you may need to be aware of and communicate to the appropriate organizations in your company. If shipping dangerous goods by air, IATA* offers an excellent training manual:

IATA

Dangerous Goods Training Programme—Book 1

Shippers; Cargo Agents; Operators' Cargo Acceptance Staff

⬅ *On-the-Job Training/Apprenticeship Programs*

While "on-the-job training" (OJT) is generally considered compliant with ISO 9000, abuse of the term has caused many auditors to be concerned. Too often such programs are plagued with problems. For example:

- An experienced worker may not be a good teacher

- An experienced worker may leave out some of the explanations because of being so accustomed to performing the job

- The new worker may be forced to produce before being fully trained

*See Chapter 4.15 for more information on IATA.

All of these problems can easily be overcome by formalizing and structuring "on-the-job training"/apprenticeship programs. Instructors should be properly qualified and trained, and new workers should be monitored during these programs with positive feedback.

Training the Trainer

Don't forget to train your trainers. This is a common oversight. Define what qualifications are required to be a trainer. A course entitled "Training the Trainer" is available from Industrial Training Corp. (see "Guidance" for address information).

Training Logs

Some companies have established training programs utilizing "Training Log Books" for their inspectors. This concept is similar to the use of SCUBA Dive Logs. The employee keeps the log and has the instructor sign off each level of training as it is accomplished. This approach allows each inspector to take responsibility for his or her own professional advancement, and encourages continuous improvement. It also reduces the amount of documentation that must be administered because the employees are responsible for keeping their own training records.

Retraining

Remember to address retraining of all affected personnel when a procedure is revised or updated. This training must also be documented.

Job Descriptions

"Job descriptions" are often developed to define minimum or necessary employee qualifications required for performing a specific job or work function (see Figure 4.18-4). However, some companies are apprehensive of fully defining jobs for fear of creating a "that's not my job" mentality among their workers. Clearly, a lack of trust exists there that must be overcome before the business can flourish. When employees say, "That's not my job," they may really be saying, "I'm not trained or qualified to perform that job." This statement may be a cry for help rather than a sign of apathy. Rather than lacking "team spirit," a worker may be fearful of injuring another or damaging the product.

When creating job descriptions, I suggest stating both the qualities you would desire in an ideal candidate, and the minimum requirements for performing the job (see Figure 4.18-4). This will allow you to better differentiate between applicants. I also suggest that each job description include a "Work

Summary" that concludes with "Other duties as assigned." This opens the door to cross-training.

You'll notice that I included a revision control level at the bottom of the sample. Job descriptions generally change over time.

While a company typically determines what qualifications are required in order to perform specific job functions, in some instances there may be local, state, or federal requirements. For example, the "Federal Motor Carrier Safety Regulations" (FMCSR) of the U.S. Department of Transportation, Part 391, establishes minimum qualifications for persons who drive motor vehicles as, for, or on behalf of motor carriers. Where appropriate, each job description should address these additional requirements and considerations.

✍ Note

Several companies are concluding their job descriptions with a section for the employee to sign indicating that he understands the duties and requirements of the job (as shown in Figure 4.18-4). For more information on developing job descriptions and related topics, I suggest contacting the Society for Human Resource Management (SHRM—see Appendix A for address).

♿ The Americans with Disabilities Act (ADA)

The Americans with Disabilities Act (effective July 26, 1992, affecting companies with 25 or more employees—expanded on July 26, 1994 to include companies with 15 or more employees) should also be considered when developing job descriptions. Enforced by the U.S. Equal Employment Opportunity Commission (EEOC), the ADA forbids discrimination against the disabled in job-application procedures, hiring, firing, compensation, advancement, and *job training*. Job descriptions should focus on the specific essential tasks required to perform that function. For example, if a specific job requires perfect vision or color differentiation, that associated *task* should be described or referenced in the job description. Otherwise, a person with a visual impairment (varying degrees of blindness or color-blindness) may feel inadvertently discriminated against. In addition, persons with disabilities may be able to perform specific job functions if provided additional special training. A simple formalized job description can serve as evidence of a company's efforts to comply with this act.

📄 "Grandfathering" Existing Employees

For many companies implementing ISO 9000, this is their first formal quality program. When they initially qualified their employees, that may not always have been documented. Later, when an employee received training, that too

---

JOB DESCRIPTION

JOB TITLE: QUALITY ASSURANCE SPECIALIST

JOB LEVEL: 8

IMMEDIATE SUPERVISOR: QUALITY MANAGER

WORK SUMMARY:

Assist in the administration, maintenance, and auditing of the ABC Company quality system. This includes hosting customer audits and conducting vendor audits. Maintain a close working relationship with all ABC Company personnel regarding quality assurance. Assist in all aspects of the business that have an impact on quality.

DESCRIPTION OF WORK PERFORMED:

- Host customer audits of ABC Company.
- Direct responses to customer audits.
- Perform periodic internal audits of ABC Company.
- Conduct supplier/subcontractor audits, as directed by the Quality Manager, maintaining an approved vendors list for ABC Company.
- Assist in resolving operational quality trouble areas.
- Handle customer intervention on quality matters.
- Provide guidance to operations personnel to optimize quality and production.
- Provide guidance to Quality Representatives.
- Review, interpret, and evaluate relevant industry guidelines and standards for compliance and/or inclusion into the ABC Company quality system.
- Develop, schedule, plan, and coordinate quality training within ABC Company.
- Represent ABC Company through participating in related industry forums and activities.
- Assist in writing updates and addenda to the Quality Assurance manual and Standard Operating Procedures manual.
- Maintain, review, and analyze ABC Company Monthly Warranty Reports.
- Maintain quality files and logs as necessary.
- Other duties as assigned.

Page 1 of 2

C:\QUALITY\JOBDESC\QASP-994.DOC

Figure 4.18-4: Sample Job Description

INSTRUCTIONS, METHODS, AND PROCEDURES USED:
Limited supervision. Daily quality decisions relating to ABC Company are
made by the specialist. Most instruction given verbally and/or through
e-mail.

RELATIONS TO OTHERS:
Contact and deal with management, engineers, test personnel, inspectors,
and auditors both in ABC Company and in other companies. Impact of this
is very strong; may have bearing on future business.

DIRECTION RECEIVED FROM OTHERS:
Quality Manager; General Manager

DIRECTION EXERCISED:
Over own work:
Dully quality decisions relating to ABC Company are made by the specialist.

Over others:
Train and guide Quality Representatives on quality procedures and
methods. Stop-work authority when quality violations are discovered.

ESSENTIAL REQUIREMENTS TO PERFORM JOB:
- Successful completion of Internal Auditor training course
- ASQC Certified Quality Auditor (CQA) or IIA Certified Internal Auditor (CIA)
- Experience in statistical analysis techniques and SPC
- Strong working knowledge of ISO 9001
- AAS in Electronic Technology or equivalent experience
- Two years experience in related manufacturing
- Advanced technical writing skills
- Strong interpersonal skills
- Thoroughly familiar with techniques, equipment, limitations, and
  applications of measuring, testing, and inspection equipment
- Ability to develop and execute subject presentations and training courses
- Strong working knowledge of computer software: word processing, data-
  bases, spreadsheets, communications, and presentation packages

EMPLOYEE ACCEPTANCE
I have read and understand this job description, including the essential
requirements to perform the job.

_____   _____

Employee's signature   Date

Page 2 of 2

C:\QUALITY\JOBDESC\QASP-994.DOC

Figure 4.18-4: Sample Job Description (cont'd)

may not have been properly documented. How do you document all of this history for compliance with ISO 9000? Easy.

Forms: One way is to create a form (or a formatted letter) to complete in documenting each employee's qualifications, past experience, and training. These letters may be signed-off by supervisory personnel and/or various management personnel attesting to the information being correct, then placed in that employee's file.

Updated Resumes: Another way is to have each employee update his or her résumé to include all of the employee's qualifications, past experience, and training. The updated résumé is then placed in the employee's training file.

Either approach should bring your program up to the present and allow your formal training systems to take over in documenting new training.

👁 *Color Blindness*

Many inspection and testing activities require the ability to differentiate varying colors (using "color chips," representative samples, etc.). In these instances the inspector may be required to pass an eye examination. It should be noted that color blindness is a fairly rare hereditary condition that mostly affects males. Once the condition and degree of severity is identified, it should not deteriorate or worsen.

Where visual inspection is critical, employees should be sent to an ophthalmologist for vision testing. If visual (color) inspection occurs, but is not detailed or critical, you may choose to conduct your own color-blindness tests using:

Ishihara's Tests for Colour-Blindness
Concise Edition 1994

By: Dr. Shinobu Ishihara
Professor Emeritus of University
of Tokyo

Approved by:
Isshinkai Foundation

Published by:
Kanehara & Co., Ltd.
(Medical Book Publisher)
P.O. Box No. 1   Hongo P.O.,
Tokyo 113-91, Japan

🚶 *Temporary Employees*

Most companies will at some point employ temporary workers. These workers must also be trained. Instead of viewing this as another burden for their training department, smart companies are calling on temporary agencies to provide basic training to these workers as a prerequisite for their business. This indoctrination training can include your quality policy, quality system, safety program, work functions, etc. Progressive temporary employment agencies have responded by viewing this as a competitive edge. Another benefit from this approach is that the temporary agency becomes more inclined to send you the same people the next time you need them. This allows them to control the amount of training they are performing and provides you with experienced workers. In the end, you both have a win–win situation.

State Licensing and Certification Programs

Many states offer licensing and certification programs for workers in a variety of skills and professions including, but not limited to, these:

Accountants	Electricians	Recruiters
Barbers/cosmetologists	Lawyers	Tool makers
Crane operators	Pipe fitters	Welders

In addition to these programs, many industry organizations offer both training and certification programs for a variety of job functions. See Appendix A for more detail.

Quality Auditors

A common oversight in this area is neglecting to qualify or train quality auditors. This often applies to both internal and supplier auditors (if applicable). You can define these criteria yourself, use the criteria established by recognized auditor certification programs, or require all of your auditors to participate in an auditor certification program.

It may be difficult for your employees to participate in a recognized "Lead Assessor Certification" program, as most ISO 9000 registrars require of their auditors, unless they are performing multiple supplier audits (internal audits are not typically accepted or recognized in such programs).

I suggest that companies review the Institute of Internal Auditors "Certified Internal Auditor" Program (see Appendix A). Another option is the ASQC Certified Quality Auditor (CQA) Program. I believe the IIA and CQA programs to be far more valuable to most companies in that the central concepts are the same.

Playing Games

With training costs on the rise, some companies are searching for cheaper, more effective methods. Many are turning to games. Yes, games. Off-the-shelf games designed to build teams, improve service, and teach interpersonal and leadership skills. Most games share a common goal—they attempt to link competitive play to active, or *experimental*, learning. Experimental learning occurs when participants become actively involved in developing their own understanding of training objectives, as opposed to simply being told what to learn. Microsoft Corp., for example, uses games to build interpersonal and team skills. Martin Marietta Corp. has developed a board game called "Gray Matters" to build ethics awareness among employees.

Some companies have developed games (such as ISO Jeopardy and ISO Pictionary) to assist in training their employees in the area of quality. Because adults learn in "chunks" of information, these games are often developed as a series of questions and answers based on relationships among company procedures, policies, and the ISO 9000 standard. This concept, called mind mapping (or learning through relationships), is considered the hottest concept in training right now.

These games are rarely available "off-the-shelf" because they are developed to focus on each company's specific, unique quality system.

 ## Records

This clause simply states that *"Appropriate records of training shall be maintained."* While training records can take many different forms, they are typically derived from stated qualifications or job requirements. As the standard states:

> *Personnel performing specific assigned tasks shall be* qualified *on the basis of appropriate education, training and/or experience, as required.*

First, you must have records that define the necessary qualifications for each job function (training needs). This is typically done by way of a "Job Description" (a.k.a. "Position Description"). Training records must then document that the stated qualifications have been met as "appropriate education, training and/or experience, as required."

This may be in the following forms:

- Certificates, degrees, diplomas, licenses, etc.

- Course descriptions and course outlines, along with instructor identification and qualifications to teach assigned courses or skills

- Letters, memos, etc., documenting experience.

Larger companies typically have a designated HR (Human Resources) or Personnel Department that maintains training records in a central location. The choice is yours, but my experience has shown that a centralized approach to maintaining records results in fewer inconsistencies and fewer noncompliances being issued.

🖳 *Employee Training Database*

If you insist on decentralizing control of these records, then I suggest storing and maintaining them on a centralized computer database (like the example shown in Figure 4.18-5). Such a database will allow you to compile reports listing all of the training an individual employee has received for assessment of future training needs. In fact, such a database could be linked to a "Training Needs" (Job Descriptions) file for comparison.

☺ *Maintenance of Training Records*

This clause of the standard ends by referring to 4.16 (quality records), which indicates that training records are to be considered as quality records. This means that you must provide for their "identification, collection, indexing, access, filing, storage, maintenance, and disposition." While much of this can easily be addressed by referring to "Training Records" in your "Quality

---

Training Database

Employee: _____

Course Title: _____

Course
Description: _____

Length of
Course: _____

Date of Course _____ / _____ /_____

Name of
Instructor: _____

Figure 4.18-5: Employee Training Database (Computer Screen or Card File)

Records" procedure, you should also address *who* is responsible for maintaining these records and *where* they will reside in your "Training" procedure.

Companies promoting decentralization tend to place responsibility on each departmental supervisor. This produces both positive and negative results. While departmental supervisors are typically the most qualified to determine ongoing training needs, they are also typically more concerned with production than with maintaining training records.

☞ ## *Guidance*

For further guidance, refer to:

ISO 9000-2:1993, Quality Management and Quality Assurance Standards—Part 2: Generic guidelines for application of ISO 9001, ISO 9002, and ISO 9003
Section 4.18—"Training"

ISO 9004-1:1994, Quality Management and Quality System Elements—Part 1: Guidelines
Section 18—"Personnel"

ISO 9004-2:1991, Quality Management and Quality System Elements—Part 2: Guidelines for services
Section 5.3—"Personnel and material resources"

ISO 10015, Continuing Education and Training Guidelines (draft)

Other

For guidance in developing job descriptions, I suggest referencing:

The Encyclopedia of Prewritten Job Descriptions and

The Job Descriptions Encyclopedia: An ADA Compliance Manual.

Each manual is available from:

Business & Legal Reports, Inc.   Tel: (203) 245-7448
Customer Service Department   1-800-7-ASK-BLR
64 Wall Street   (1-800-7-275-257)
Madison, CT 06443-1513   Fax: (203) 245-2559

Title CFR 29—Labor (available from U.S. Government bookstores*)

Title CFR 49, Vol. 100–199, "Transportation—Hazardous Materials" with the HM 181 revision—"Hazardous Materials" (available from U.S. Government bookstores*)

Some great sources for Safety, OSHA, EPA, and HazMat compliance training materials are:

J.J. Keller
3003 W. Breezewood Lane
P.O. Box 368
Neenah, WI 54957-0368
Tel: (800) 327-6868 (U.S. & Canada)
Fax: (414) 727-7516
Request the "OSHA / Environmental Compliance Products Catalog" and the "Transportation Catalog"

Labelmaster
An AMERICAN LABELMARK Co.
5724 N. Pulaski Road
Chicago, IL 60646-6797
Tel: (800) 621-5808
Fax: (800) 723-4327
EDI Accounts available
Request the "Industrial Compliance Products" catalog

American Society of Safety Engineers
1800 East Oakton Street
Des Plains, IL 60018-2187

Tel: (708) 692-4121   Ext. 231
Fax: (708) 296-3769

Industrial Training Corp.
13515 Dulles Technology Drive
Herndon, VA 22071
Tel: (703) 713-3335
     (800) 638-3757
Fax: (703) 713-0065

Questions Your Registrar May Ask

 ☑ Are minimum job qualifications (training needs and requirements) defined (by position or job title or work area)? Where are they documented?

☑ Who is responsible for administering the "Training" portion of your business?

☑ Do training records provide documented evidence of a specific employee's

*For a free catalog of U.S. Government publications, write to:
Free Catalog   Tel: (202) 783-3238
P.O. Box 37000   Fax: (202) 512-2250
Washington, DC 20013-7000

qualification to perform a specific job or work function? Can you show me an example demonstrating this?

☑ If employee training has been "grandfathered," what was the basis for that grandfathering? What supporting objective documented evidence exists?

☑ Do you have an on-the-job training or apprenticeship program? If so, how is it detailed?

☑ Are the methods for qualification of personnel in special processes and operations (e.g., welding, brazing, soldering) documented?

☑ What are the qualification requirements for instructors or trainers? Who are they?

☑ Who has responsibility for maintenance and storage of training records? Where is this defined?

4.19 Servicing

At a Glance

9001	9002	9003
✓	✓	✗

Where servicing is *a specified requirement*, you must establish and maintain documented procedures for the following:

- Performing servicing in accordance with specified requirements

- Verifying that the servicing meets the specified requirements

- Reporting that the servicing meets the specified requirements

QUALITY MANUAL

19.0 SERVICING

Where servicing is a specified requirement, ABC Company will establish and maintain documented procedures for performing, verifying, and reporting that the servicing meets the specified requirements.

Quality Manual

This clause does not necessarily refer to the normal service or technical assistance activities you provide (although it is a good idea to include them in your quality system), or to the provision of a service, unless specified in a contract. As we see in referencing ISO 9000-2, this requirement primarily applies to manufactured products that require regular maintenance in certain specific areas. This maintenance is sometimes referred to as "after-sales service." The following are some practical examples of "servicing":

- Manufacturing machinery maintenance

- Computer repair and maintenance

- Inspection, measuring, and test equipment repair and calibration services

- Process control instrumentation maintenance, repair, and calibration services

- Truck and vehicle fleet maintenance

If your primary business is manufacturing, contractual requirements for "servicing" may define your responsibility to help your customer ensure proper use of the product following delivery. Servicing means repair, maintenance, upgrading, etc.

Many manufacturers will have a separate business unit or division to provide servicing for their product. For example: It's common for inspection, measuring, and test equipment manufacturers to have their manufacturing plant acting as one business unit while another, consisting of several smaller satellite offices, provides calibration and repair services to their customers.

If your primary business is servicing various products (calibration laboratory, computer repair center, etc.), then I suggest developing your policy to describe how you will address *additional* servicing requirements. In the earlier example, the company is in a reactive mode awaiting a contract specifying the details. As a servicing company that has already defined its service, your customers already know what you will be doing. But they may require additional servicing activities. In this instance, your quality system would need to address these additional requirements. This clause can easily be tailored to do just that:

> Servicing
> *Where additional servicing beyond that which is normally provided, as described in this quality system, is a specified requirement, ABC Company shall establish and maintain documented procedures for performing, verifying, and reporting that the servicing meets the specified requirements.*

 ## Not Applicable

This clause is usually interpreted from the standpoint of a manufacturer, but many companies are registered to ISO 9002 whose sole activity involves providing services that do not involve servicing a product. In this case, the clause may very well be *not applicable* to your company. In this instance, you still must address the clause. You can't simply ignore it. I suggest the following text:

> Servicing
> *The scope of the ABC Company quality system does not include servicing.*

This statement removes all doubt concerning the requirement and should not impede a company from achieving registration. The registrar would simply note that "Servicing" is excluded from the scope of registration. This would then be indicated on the company's certificate of registration.

 ## Procedure

After your contract review function has accepted a contract where servicing is a specified requirement, your "Servicing" procedure should begin by defining the following:

- **Who** communicates the *specified requirements* for servicing to the appropriate organization(s)

- **How** the *specified requirements* are communicated (documented in the form of a "customer-specific" work instruction, procedure, quality plan, quality bulletin, memo, etc.)

Servicing contracts, like any other contract, can take many different forms. The following listing is an example of areas servicing agreements can address:

- Specialized handling and test equipment needed (including maintenance and control)

- The particular operating, control, inspection, and testing procedures used to verify the performance of the servicing

- Turnaround times

- Backup provisions including technical assistance and the availability of alternate equipment or materials

- How complaints are resolved

- Training the customer's personnel

- How to contact your personnel in case of an emergency

If your primary business is servicing a particular range or type of products, you may wish to refer to existing service plans in your procedure rather than duplicate them. This will allow you to revise only the service plan (a.k.a. quality plan) when changes are needed, rather than both the plan(s) and the procedure.

☺ *Service Infrastructure*

Whether you use your own or second-party service providers, ensure that you have the infrastructure in place to adequately support them. In planning these activities you should do the following:

- Clarify servicing responsibilities

- Validate the design and function of necessary servicing tools and equipment

- Ensure the control of measuring and test equipment

- Ensure the availability of spare parts (kits)

- Ensure that the necessary trained staff is available (define required training)

This plan can include access to controlled documents such as these:

- Schematics and drawings

- Parts lists

- Product bulletins

- Product updates (hardware and software) and "Change Notices"

- Product servicing procedures and instructions

Coordinate the various organizations that need to support the servicing element. This can include, but is not limited to, the following:

- "Dispatch" operations

- Engineering support/technical assistance

- "Warranty" repair services

"Dispatch" operations could be subcontracted, in which case they would need to be qualified and approved as required by clause 4.6, "Purchasing" ("Dispatch" operations would be considered a purchased *service*).

Normal "Warranty" repair services could be considered a part of this element (the standard does not state *who* made servicing a specified requirement). Your procedure should define *who* is responsible or authorized to award or reject such warranties, and *how* this is communicated to the customer.

Supporting a manufacturer is very different from providing a service such as calibration or testing. You have to decide which elements apply and how.

Authorized Service Representatives/Centers

It is common for manufacturers to "authorize" second-party service providers to maintain their product. These types of agreements can cover many areas and have many different conditions. For example, a second party may be authorized to service any of the following:

- All products

- Specific product lines

- Only "out-of-warranty" products

- Products in certain regions or countries only

It is wise to address these second-party service providers in your quality system up-front. Doing it later can be difficult. These second-party providers may be thought of as subcontractors in that they are representing your company or are functioning as an extension of it.

🗁 Records

The records related to this clause can take many different forms, depending on the nature of the servicing, and there may be more than one record required.

As a minimum, although it may have a different title, this would typically be a servicing report.

☞ *Guidance*

For further guidance, refer to:

ISO 9000-2:1993, Quality Management and Quality Assurance Standards—Part 2: Generic guidelines for application of ISO 9001, ISO 9002, and ISO 9003
Section 4.19—"Servicing"

ISO 9004-1:1994, Quality Management and Quality System Elements—Part 1: Guidelines
Section 16.4—"Servicing"

ISO 9004-2:1991, Quality Management and Quality System Elements—Part 2: Guidelines for services

Another source for guidance is the Association for Services Management International (AFSM International). This organization provides conferences, exhibitions, and training programs throughout the world.

Ꮳ *Questions Your Registrar May Ask*

Since this clause is very vague, many of the following questions may not apply. I have included them here to provide insight for you in developing this procedure.

☑ Who is responsible for administering the "Servicing" portion of your business?

☑ How are contracts invoking servicing requirements communicated to that department? Can you show me an example where this has happened?

☑ What mechanisms do you have for verifying and reporting that such services meet the specified requirements?

☑ What does a complete, finished "Servicing Record" consist of?

☑ What mechanisms do you have for ensuring that product updates and change notices are distributed to those performing servicing work?

☑ How do you validate the design and function of special-purpose tools or equipment for handling and servicing products after installation?

☑ How do you control measuring and test equipment used in field servicing and tests? (if different from other inspection, measuring, and test equipment)

☑ How do you control the issue of spare parts kits? How do you replenish them when needed?

☑ Do you authorize second-party "Service Representatives"? Who are they?

☑ What does it mean to be an "Authorized Service Representative" for your company?

☑ How do you qualify second-party "Authorized Service Representatives"?

☑ How do you disqualify second-party "Authorized Service Representatives"?

☑ When are second-party "Authorized Service Representatives" used?

4.20 Statistical Techniques

At a Glance

You must do the following:

9001	9002	9003
✓	✓	✓

- Identify the need for statistical techniques required for establishing, controlling, and verifying process capability and product characteristics

- Establish and maintain documented procedures to implement and control the application of statistical techniques

> **QUALITY MANUAL**
>
> **20.0** STATISTICAL TECHNIQUES
>
> **20.1** Identification of Need
>
> ABC Company will identify the need for statistical techniques required for establishing, controlling, and verifying process capability and product characteristics.
>
> **20.2** Procedures
>
> ABC Company will establish and maintain documented procedures to implement and control the application of the statistical techniques.

Quality Manual

Statistical techniques can be useful in virtually every aspect of an organization's operation. Although I support their use, I suggest leaving yourself open to using statistical techniques rather than identifying specifics in your quality manual.

Procedure

Statistical techniques can be applied to many of the areas addressed in ISO 9000. For example, they may be used to do the following:

- Report on the performance of the quality system (clause 4.1.2 b)
- Identify improvement opportunities (clause 4.1.2 b)
- Validate designs through the use of DOE (Design of Experiments) techniques (clause 4.4.8)
- Assess and monitor subcontractor acceptability (clause 4.6.2)
- Forecast production requirements and scheduling plans (clause 4.9)
- Monitor and control key process parameters and product characteristics (clauses 4.9 d and 4.20.1)
- Ensure continuing process capability (clauses 4.9 g and 4.20.1)
- Perform receiving inspection (clause 4.10.2)
- Perform in-process inspection (clauses 4.2.3 f and 4.10.3)

- Perform final inspection (clause 4.10.3)

- Assess measurement capability (clause 4.11)

- Investigate the cause of nonconformities (clause 4.14.2 b)

- Evaluate customer complaints (clause 4.14.3 a)

You can easily add more applications for statistical techniques as your quality system evolves beyond ISO 9000. Statistical techniques are typically used to replace inspection activities by continuously monitoring a process (build quality in rather than inspect it in). Documented statistical data can then be used to demonstrate conformance to quality requirements.

☰ *The Basics*

The topic of statistics goes well beyond the scope of this book, so I will only touch on a couple of the basics. Statistical techniques focus on two types of data, attribute and variable.

Attribute Data

Attribute data states whether a characteristic, or attribute, exists or doesn't exist. When you use a Go/No Go gage, or inspect for visual defects, or check to make sure a certain component has been installed, you can get one of two answers: yes or no, go or no-go. An item either *conforms* to quality standards or it does not. An item that does not conform is considered a *nonconforming item.*

Attribute data:

Good / Bad

Yes / No

Pass / Fail

Go / No-Go

Attribute data is often displayed in a "P" chart. A "P" chart displays the fraction of nonconforming items, expressed as a percentage of all items produced. "P" stands for percentage.

Variable Data

Most statistical applications involve specific data points that vary. Hence the term variable data. Manufacturers concerned with the dimensions of a part or precision of adjustments and controls would collect variable data to statistically gage and measure their process.

Variable data might be collected from the historical point data of a standard voltage cell, for example, in order to determine actual drift rates and true uncertainty.

Whichever statistical techniques you decide to adopt, document them thoroughly or reference the source (industry standards, military standards, etc.).

🖥 *"Off-the-Shelf" Statistical Software*

There are many inexpensive "off-the-shelf" statistical software packages available for a variety of applications. There are far too many available to list individually here, but for more information check out the ads in some of the magazines listed in Appendix B. There are some packages available that constantly monitor a process, generating a real-time graphic representation.

A great source for both freeware (free software) and shareware (try before you buy software) statistical software is the "Statistics BBS." This computer bulletin board is sponsored by the Statistical Applications Institute and operated by the Analytical Consulting Group, Inc.:

Statistics BBS (electronic bulletin board)
(316) 687-0578
Character format: TTY using 8,N,1
System Operator: Brad Brown, (316) 648-5093

The Statistics BBS is operated for the primary purpose of disseminating knowledge relating to statistics and its use in industry, medicine, and society in general. Anyone and everyone interested in statistics and its applications is welcome to access this board. Any other technical subject (i.e., engineering, physics, chemistry, astronomy, biology) is welcomed for discussion.

💡 *Deciding Which Control Chart to Use*

Many people want to use control charts but are uncertain about which one to use. Jill A. Swift, an assistant professor in the Engineering Department at the University of Miami in Florida, has developed a unique flow chart (Figure 4.20-1) to assist in making this decision. Her flow chart has several distinguishing features:

- It is simple to use

- Only a basic understanding of statistics is required

- All levels of personnel can use and, more important, understand it

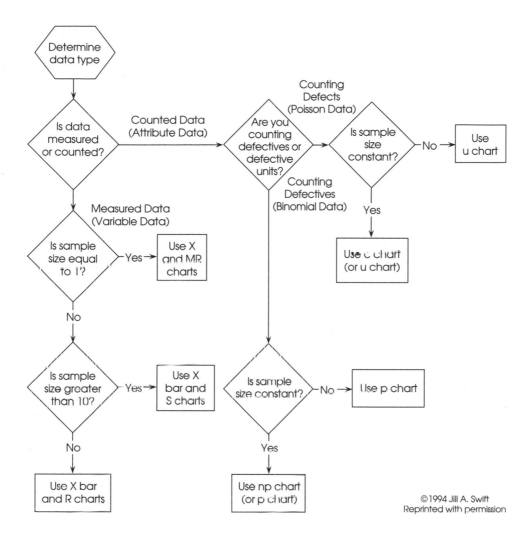

Figure 4.20-1: Control Chart Decision Maker Flowchart

⅃Ⅹ *Quality Systems Requirements*

The Automotive Industry Action Group (AIAG) has published a standard reference manual for statistical process control entitled "Fundamental Statistical Process Control Reference Manual" (SPC-1). This manual was prepared by the quality and assessment staffs at Chrysler, Ford, and GM, under the auspices of the Quality Requirements Task Force. It can be used by any supplier to develop statistical data in accordance with QS-9000. This manual should be considered an introduction to statistical process control.

To obtain further information on ordering this book, call the AIAG at (810) 358-3570. Multiple copy discounts and discounts for suppliers are available.

📁 *Records*

The records relating to this clause depend on the statistical techniques you use. Statistical results are normally depicted graphically in the following forms:

- Histograms
- Control charts (including precontrol charts, if used)
- Run charts
- Scatter plots

Any record relating to statistical techniques used in "controlling and verifying process capability (C_p) and product characteristics" will need to be addressed.

☞ *Guidance*

Once you've established a need, you must describe the statistical techniques used throughout your procedures. While you may need to tailor a technique to suit your specific application, don't reinvent the wheel.

For further guidance, refer to:

ISO 9000-2:1993, Quality Management and Quality Assurance Standards—
Part 2: Generic guidelines for application of ISO 9001, ISO 9002, and ISO 9003
Section 4.20—"Statistical techniques"

ISO 9004-1:1994, Quality Management and Quality System Elements—
Part 1: Guidelines
Section 20—"Use of statistical methods"

ISO 9004-2:1991, Quality Management and Quality System Elements—
Part 2: Guidelines for services
Section 6.4.3—"Statistical methods"

ISO2602:1980, Statistical Interpretation of Test Results—
Estimation of the Mean—Confidence Interval

ISO 2854:1976, Statistical Interpretation of Data—
Techniques of Estimation and Tests Relating to Means and Variances

ISO 2859-1:1989, Sampling Procedures for Inspection by Attributes—
Part 1: Sampling Plans Indexed by Acceptable Quality Level (AQL) for Lot-by-Lot Inspection

ISO 2859-2:1985, Sampling Procedures for Inspection by Attributes—Part 2: Sampling Plans Indexed by Limiting Quality (LQ) for Isolated Lot Inspection

ISO 2859-3:1991, Sampling Procedures for Inspection by Attributes—Part 3: Skip-lot Sampling Procedures

ISO 3207:1975, Statistical Interpretation of Data—Determination of a Statistical Tolerance Interval

ISO 3301:1975, Statistical Interpretation of Data—Comparison of Two Means in the Case of Paired Observations

ISO 3494:1976, Statistical Interpretation of Data—Power of Tests Relating to Means and Variances

ISO 3951:1989, Sampling Procedures and Charts for Inspection by Variables for Percent Nonconforming

ISO 7870:1993, Control Charts—General Guide and Introduction

ISO 7873:1993, Control Charts for Arithmetic Average with Warning Limits

ISO 7966:1993, Acceptance Control Charts

ISO 8258:1991, Shewhart Control Charts

ISO 8422:1991, Sequential Sampling Plans for Inspection by Attributes

ISO 8423:1991, Sequential Sampling Plans for Inspection by Variables for Percent Nonconforming (Know Standard Deviation)

ISO/TR 8550:1994, Guide for the Selection of an Acceptance Sampling System, Scheme, or Plan for Inspection of Discrete Items in Lots

ISO 8595:1989, Interpretation of Statistical Data—Estimation of a Median

Additional ANSI/ASQC and U.S. military standards relating to statistical techniques are listed under the guidance section of chapter 4.10.

Another great source for guidance or information on this topic is the American Statistical Association. See Appendix A for more information on this organization.

Questions Your Registrar May Ask

Because this clause is very vague, many of the following questions may very well not apply. I have included them here to provide insight for you in developing this procedure.

4.20.1 Identification of Need

☑   How is the need for statistical techniques required for establishing, controlling, and verifying process capability and product characteristics determined?

4.20.2 Procedures

☑   Which statistical techniques are employed?

☑   How are statistical techniques implemented and controlled?

☑   Who is responsible for data collection?

☑   What data is collected? At what intervals?

☑   Who is responsible for processing statistical data? Reporting results?

☑   If statistical control is not maintained, is corrective action taken?

Chapter 5
Registration

The ISO 9000 series was originally conceived as first-party and second-party documents. ISO 9004 is intended to be used as a first-party document by organizations to develop and evaluate their own internal quality management system. ISO 9001, ISO 9002, and ISO 9003 are intended to be used as second-party documents between a buyer and seller. Compliance with any element of ISO 9000 can be voluntary; however, ISO 9001/2/3 can be required by a contract. Such contracts generally require some form of additional evidence that the supplier is compliant with the appropriate ISO standard. This is where registration comes into play.

What is Registration/Certification?

A system has evolved in which many independent third parties, known as "registrars," use the ISO 9000 series standards to evaluate quality systems. When a supplier's quality system is confirmed as conforming with a registrar's interpretation of an ISO 9000 series standard, that registrar issues the supplier a "Certificate of Registration." The supplier is then listed in a directory of registered suppliers and awarded the right to use the facility registration symbols of that registrar in advertising and other printed matter. The symbols may not be used on a product or in any way that might imply product certification, since the registration is of the supplier's quality system, not of an individual product.

ISO 9000 registration alone does *not* mean that a company is an industry leader, nor is it a symbol of quality excellence. ISO 9000 registration simply means that a company has demonstrated continued compliance with ISO 9000 to a quality system registrar.

When Is the Due Date for Registration?

There is no due date for compliance or registration. Anyone who implements the ISO 9000 series may state compliance. However, in the current world market, a statement of compliance may be meaningless without third-party verification by an accredited registrar.

Why Register?

ISO 9000 registration was initially being driven by the EC. To understand why, one must understand the EC and its objectives. The EC was officially established in 1958 with a goal of creating an integrated, community-wide market free of restrictions on the movement of goods, services, people, and capital. This process was taking place very slowly. Then the CEC (Commission of the European Community) White Paper, in 1985, set out the actions needed to be accomplished to remove the remaining barriers and constraints to a single market by December 31, 1992. To achieve this, several directives were adopted by the EC Council of Ministers.

Under the "Product Liability Directive," established by the EC in 1986, the producer is liable for damage caused by a defective product. Additionally, use not intended by the manufacturer is not a viable defense if the use is "reasonably foreseeable." One of the most important aspects of this directive is its reversal of "burden of proof." That is, the injured party does not have to prove producer negligence. Furthermore, in the event the producer cannot be identified, other persons in the supply chain may be liable, including nonmanufacturing importers and distributors.

While a certified quality system will not provide a company with immunity from liability, it will decrease the risks. Third-party registration provides Europeans with confidence in their suppliers. Suppliers outside the EC are, of course, not bound by these directives. This makes registration of importers much more important to an EC customer. For this reason, North American manufacturers who are not registered may have increased difficulty in exporting to the EC.

As many of the first U.S. companies achieved registration, they quickly realized benefits resulting in significant cost savings. Recognizing that these same benefits could be realized by their suppliers, potentially resulting in further cost savings, they have chosen to require many of their suppliers to implement ISO 9000. Following the lead of industry, many U.S. government agencies have adopted ISO 9000 and are invoking it on their contractors (NASA is requiring some contractors to become ISO 9000 certified).

The Decision to Seek Certification/Registration

If a customer invokes ISO 9000 with evidence of third-party certification as a contract requirement, the decision is obvious. Seek registration or start refusing business. Rather than find yourself in this reactive situation, you can look to what your customers are doing. If they are either already registered or are seeking registration, it's a sure bet that they will eventually expect the same from their suppliers.

This is the bottom line:

- Compliance with ISO 9000 is a quality issue

- Certification/registration is a marketing issue

The following list contains just a few of the reasons companies give for seeking registration:

- Registered companies typically have an effective edge in global markets and a profitable advantage over competitors who are not registered. As customers recognize the value of a certified quality system, those not registered may experience a declining market share.

- Registered companies can tender for ISO 9000 contracts (where registration is required) at home and abroad.

- There is a potential reduction in customer audits.

The decision to seek ISO 9000 registration should involve all levels of management, including the marketing/sales element of the organization. Registration provides your company with a competitive edge that must be fully understood by all elements in order to realize the true benefits.

After choosing to seek registration, there are more questions that must be answered. Specifically, *what* should be registered *where* and *when*?

Product Lines

You can register specific product lines (services) with others excluded. While this may sound rather silly at first, it can be the ideal solution for operations where you are phasing out specific product lines. Your scope of registration would simply exclude the product lines you select. It is also a possibility to seek registration to ISO 9001 or 9002 excluding the "Servicing" function. This must be discussed and agreed upon with your registrar in advance.

Multiple Sites and Corporate-Wide Registration

Registration does not automatically extend to other plants under the same quality system manufacturing the same product elsewhere. Each location must be assessed separately. This having been said, many registrars offer a "sampling plan" where a specified number of locations are selected and assessed for compliance with ISO 9000. Based on that activity, and the effectiveness of your internal auditing program, all locations could then be registered without a site visit to each. This must be discussed and agreed upon with your registrar in advance.

Time Frame

Bear in mind that the registrar you select may have a three- to four-month back-log before he or she can schedule your assessment.

Preparation for Registration

The most common pitfalls in achieving registration are obvious:

- Lack of management commitment
- Poor planning (time schedules that are too aggressive)
- Lack of coordination/involvement with other elements
- Lack of adequate resources
- Lack of training and experience

Lack of management commitment is clearly the most serious problem to address. This places the quality function in a very difficult position.

Many of the remaining obstacles, should they exist, can be addressed by a good consultant.

Should You Use a Consultant?

Here's what the *National ISO 9000 Support Group* recommends to consulting clients.

ISO 9000 Group Cautions Consulting Clients

Companies hoping to get ISO 9000 certification with the assistance of a North American consulting organization may want to do a little home-work before signing on the dotted line.

The National ISO 9000 Support Group has announced preliminary find-ings from their survey of 300 consulting organizations in North America in an attempt to dispel rumors concerning the actual cost of obtaining ISO 9000 certification. The study found that the cost of hir-ing a consultant for one eight-hour day can range from $320 to $2,000, but companies who had achieved at least one successful client registra-tion to ISO 9000 were charging an average of 58 percent more than con-sultants who had not yet had a client successfully registered.

Out of 660 total individual consultants represented in the survey only 111 had been formally trained in ISO 9000 assessments. The client base of the respondents, however, totaled 2,025 companies seeking certification.

"We have to repeat our warning issued late last year about consultants," says ISO 9000 Support Group Chairman Richard Clements. *"There are still a large number of consultants that have no formal training in the ISO 9000 standard. Always be sure to ask for qualifications and references."*

This article was reproduced from *Quality Digest* magazine, August 1993.

I agree with this advice, but would like to emphasize that most companies don't use consultants correctly. Consultants are for "consulting." Many companies hire consultants to develop and implement their entire quality program. When this happens, the company does not have ownership of the program; it belongs to the consultant. These companies generally have a difficult time keeping their registration because they have not adopted ISO 9000 into their company culture.

Consultants can be great, when used properly. Consultants should provide the following:

Insight	Coordination	Training
Planning	Assistance	Review

Only you can decide whether you need a consultant. But if you do, choose wisely. Remember clause 4.6.2:

The supplier shall evaluate and select subcontractors on the basis of their ability to meet subcontract requirements including quality system and any specific quality-assurance requirements.

This requirement should certainly apply to ISO 9000 consultants. Here are some standard questions (criteria) to help you get the right one.

Consultant Questionnaire

1. Have you helped any other companies achieve registration?

A consultant who has not gone through this experience must be considered questionable. If a consultant has helped other companies achieve registration, ask for this information:

- Company name

- Number of locations (where)

- Type of industry

- Contact name

- When

- Who was the registrar (try to select a consultant who has experience with the registrar that you have selected—there are differences)

- What role did you play (scope of consulting assignment)

Immediately follow up by calling the registered company and verifying the information given. Ask whether the company would use the consultant again.

If a consultant has assisted other companies, ask what role they played in that process:

- Gap analysis

- Documentation development/preparation

- Manual reviews

- Quality system development

- Training

- Internal audits

- Preassessments

2. Is your company registered or are you individually certified?

It has become quite common for consultanting companies in the U.K. to seek registration as well. They believe that before they can help others achieve ISO 9000 registration, they themselves must achieve registration.

The British Quality Consultants Association was formed in the U.K. to certify *individuals* as "qualified" consultants. A similar program has been established in the U.S. by the American Quality Consulting Association (AQCA).

3. Are the individual consultants registered (lead) assessors?

Many consultants have taken the Assessor and/or Lead Assessor courses, but are not actually registered assessors or lead assessors. There is some advantage to having taken the course in that they will have some basic understanding of how the registrar's assessors will be performing the assessment. But the real concern here is whether the consultant has ever conducted an audit! Registered assessors are provided a card attesting to their status—ask to see it.

If they are not a registered assessor, then ask for a listing of the quality audits in which they have participated. The more the better. Then verify a few of them. If they have not been involved in the audit process themselves, how can they help you through one?

4. Do you currently have any relationship with a registrar?

Some consultants are periodically hired as "contract" assessors to assist registrars. This is a very strong qualification for a consultant. If they have, then follow that question with these:

> Which registrar(s) have you worked with?
>
> In what capacity?
>
> • Manual reviews
>
> • Preassessments
>
> • Assessments
>
> • Surveillance visits
>
> How long have you worked with a registrar?
>
> How many assignments have you accepted from each registrar?

This last question is very important. Obviously, because this person was an employee, you would not be able to call the registrar and ask if they continue to use this person, or how they performed. By asking the consultant how many assignments they have accepted you can gage that number against how long they have been associated with the registrar and make a determination as to whether the registrar was pleased with their performance. Registrars make mistakes, too. Don't repeat one of theirs.

If a consultant has accepted more than five or six assignments, I would assume that the registrar was happy with his or her performance.

5. What kind of experience do you have with our industry?

Often each industry has specific approaches toward meeting the requirements of ISO 9000. Each company may tailor that approach, but it won't be drastically different. Although industry experience is a plus, I find that many companies tend to place excessive emphasis on this point. The standard is generic. Don't pass on a good consultant because he or she didn't know the particulars of your specific industry.

The American Quality Consulting Association

A concern currently shared by some qualified consultants and many companies is that there are several persons who are consulting but are not qualified. The result is a bad name for consultants, bad experience with the ISO 9000 series standards, lots of lost money, time, and market share.

Consulting with companies is different from assessing companies to the standard. A consultant must be able to adapt to the company environment and help them to mold their quality system rather than imposing a favorite system on the company. A successful consultant will have the fruit of long-term success with clients.

In an effort to provide some level of confidence for the clients and to circumvent some of the bad press consulting is receiving, the American Quality Consulting Association (AQCA) has been formed. The association is initially focusing on providing a significant level of confidence to clients with regard to ISO 9000 consulting.

The program is still in development with input from IQA lead assessors and members of the British Quality Consultants Association, so minor changes are likely. The proposed CIC program is this:

A. Certification

1. Successfully complete the Lead Assessor's training course.

2. Complete two assessments under the direction of a lead assessor.

3. Provide evidence of key involvement with successfully guiding one company through ISO 9000 series registration. Submit a detailed report of this project with application.

4. Have two sponsors who are certified CICs or five references of key contacts from clients whom you have worked with.

5. Provide five personal contacts from companies with whom you've worked as a consultant.

B. Maintenance–Recertification

1. Provide evidence of successful activity. This could be letters from a minimum of two clients and a detailed report of one client project.

2. Perform two assessments per year as part of the assessment team or as lead assessor.

3. Provide three personal contacts from companies with whom you are working as a consultant.

Applications will be evaluated for minimum body of knowledge, experience, ability to work with clients, and effectiveness of service provided to determine acceptance.

Levels of
membership and fee

Provisional $150.000	An individual who demonstrates a minimum body of knowledge but has not yet had the experience required to become an associate.
Associate $175.00	The individual who has demonstrated the required level of knowledge and experience as a quality consultant. The experience criteria include ethics, interpersonal skills, and effectiveness.
Fellow	An individual who the governing board considers to have made a consistent contribution to the industry.

Members of AQCA will be listed on the National ISO 9000 Support Group bulletin board service and newsletter and will be the list of consultants supplied to their membership when consultant inquiries are made.

The AQCA headquarters is:

American Quality Consulting Association
P.O. Box 342
Allendale, MI 49401-0342
Jim Wilkinson—President

Tel: (616) 895-5546
Fax: (616) 892-4606
Business hours:
8:00 A.M. to 5:00 P.M. EST
Mon–Fri.

Selecting a Registrar

Once the decision has been made to seek registration, you must select a registrar. Again, remember ISO 9001/2/3, clause 4.6.2:

The supplier shall evaluate and select subcontractors on the basis of their ability to meet subcontract requirements including quality system and any specific quality-assurance requirements.

This requirement should also apply to ISO 9000 registrars. In many cases, the decision to seek registration is customer-driven. In this instance you may wish to ask your larger customers which registrar(s) they will recognize and which they will not (I know several companies who will not recognize registration by certain registrars).

Every three months, the NIST Office of Standards Services publishes a list of organizations that NIST understands to offer quality system registration services, according to the ANSI/ASQC Q9000, ISO 9000 series, or equivalent criteria, in the U.S., Canada, and Mexico. They note that no attempt has been made to evaluate any of these programs. You can request a copy by contacting:

Office of Standards Services—NIST   Tel: (301) 975-4039
Standards, Code, and Information Program   Fax: (301) 975-2128
Administration 101, A629, Div 211
Gaithersburg, MD 20899

The following "Registrar Questionnaire" should help you in your selection.

Registrar Questionnaire

1. Are you accredited? If so, by whom? (RAB, SCC, DNG, RvC, NACCB, etc.)

Not all registrars are accredited. Selecting a registrar who is not accredited is *strongly discouraged*. It is highly improbable that registration by a nonaccredited registrar would be recognized by your customers or fulfill contractual requirements. In contrast, many of the *legitimate* international registrars are accredited by multiple bodies.

Of the forty registrars in the U.K., only half are accredited by the NACCB. The others operate as second-party registrars with specific scopes relevant to their industry. Some examples are British Railways, British Gas, British Coal, and British Nuclear Fuel. Those registrars accredited by the NACCB have a much broader scope and have greater general acceptance.

Canada (SCC)

The Standards Council of Canada (SCC) operates a registrar accreditation program called *Accreditation of Organizations that Register Suppliers' Quality Systems*. It was approved by the SCC on December 9, 1991.

Mexico (DGN)

In Mexico, a National Accreditation and Certification System for certification bodies and quality system registrars was established under the aegis of the "Dirección General de Normas" (DGN). In regulated areas, the appropriate regulatory body will oversee the accreditation process and will make recommendations to the Ministry of Commerce regarding approval. Registration certificates from registrars not accredited under the National Accreditation and

Certification System will *not* be accepted for regulatory and procurement purposes.

If you are operating or conducting business in Mexico, you should weigh the importance of choosing a registrar who is accredited by the DGN.

United States (ANSI/RAB)

The Registrar Accreditation Board (RAB), an affiliate of the American Society for Quality Control (ASQC), will formally accredit those registrars that meet the requirements in the U.S. In 1994, the ANSI (American National Standards Institute) and the RAB established a joint program known as the *American National Accreditation Program for Registrars of Quality Systems*. Because ANSI is the U.S. member delegate to ISO, its participation in a joint ANSI/RAB program was considered key to enhancing the credibility and worldwide acceptance of the U.S. registration program.

EU Considerations

If you are exporting to the EU (previously the EC—European Community), you should consider a registrar who is accredited by a member of the EAC (see note below). International recognition of all registrars is not yet global. However, I expect to see regional recognition agreements established that will eventually reach that goal.

✍ Note—The EAC Agreement

On May 22, 1991, the EAC (European Accreditation of Certification) established a "Memorandum of Understanding between National Accreditation Bodies Accrediting Certification Bodies." The aims and objectives of the EAC are to promote collaboration, harmonize the operations of participating bodies, and work for general acceptance of the equivalence of certificates issued by certification bodies. Accreditation of such bodies would normally require assessment to ensure compliance with the European Standard EN 45011 for bodies certifying products, EN 45012 for bodies certifying quality systems, and EN 45013 for bodies certifying personnel.

Each European nation typically has a National Accreditation Body. These bodies accredit the certification bodies (Registrars). The EAC "Memorandum of Understanding" members (at the time of this publication) include most of the EU and EFTA (European Free Trade Association) countries. This means that these countries are developing mutual recognition agreements where registration in one country will be recognized by another. If your customers are based in EU and/or EFTA countries, it would be prudent to ensure that the registrar you have selected is accredited by a national accreditation body that is a member of the EAC.

2. How are your auditors (assessors) qualified?

Ask all potential registrars how their assessors (auditors) are trained and by what organization. Ensure that their assessors are trained and certified or registered by recognized authorities or institutions.

The Institute of Quality Assurance (IQA), located in London, operates an international registration scheme for the qualification and registration of quality assessors. This scheme is recognized by the U.K. Department of Trade and Industry and has contributed significantly toward the world-class respect and reputation of integrity held by IQA-trained auditors. In the U.S., the RAB has developed a similar program for auditor registration, with training being administered by the ASQC. Most legitimate registrars operating in North America require that all of their auditors be either IQA- or RAB-registered "Lead Assessors."

✍ Note 1

There has been a problem with mutual recognition among the various organizations administering the training and certification of assessors. In an attempt to address this situation, the first Worldwide Conference of International Registration of Assessors was held in Singapore on September 29–30, 1993. It was attended by delegates from the following countries:

Australia	Hong Kong	Korea	South Africa
Brazil	India	Malaysia	Thailand
Brunei	Indonesia	New Zealand	United Kingdom
China (PRC)	Japan	Singapore	U.S.A.

Consensus was reached that a system should be established in which certifications of quality systems auditors would be internationally recognized through mutual recognitions among national or regional auditor certification bodies.

✍ Note 2

The ASTM (American Society for Testing and Materials) has also developed a guide addressing assessors of laboratory accreditation systems. Refer to ASTM E 1322-90, "Standard Guide for Selection, Training, and Evaluation of Assessors for Laboratory Accreditation Systems."

✍ *Note 3*

Because of the growing demand for registration and the limited number of registered "Lead Assessors," many ISO 9000 registrars are utilizing "contracted" auditors or associates. Legitimate registrars qualify these auditors in the same manner as their full-time staff. However, if this is a concern to you, discuss it with your registrar in advance. Auditors are given a card identifying their status and level by the body which has certified or registered them. If you have concerns, notify the registrar (also in advance) that you would like to see these cards at the opening meeting prior to the assessment.

From personal experience I find that the use of associates has many benefits, provided those associates are properly chosen. Many associates are retired quality professionals with many years of practical experience.

3. Is the registrar accredited to register your industry scope?

Ask each registrar if he or she is "accredited" for your specific industry scope. Registrars seeking accreditation must submit a listing of those areas where they have experience. This is typically done by SIC (Standard Industry Code) number. Legitimate (accredited) registrars must have experience in a specific industry in order to be accredited in that area.

4. Can you provide a list of references that we may contact?

Ask for a list of the companies registered by that registrar and contact a few of them for their impressions of the registrar. Ask them the following questions:

- Is the company satisfied in their relationship with their registrar? Why?

- Are the auditors consistent in their interpretation of the standard? If no, then what have the differences been?

- Did the company research various registrars before making a decision, or was the selection mandated by a corporate directive?

- If other registrars were researched, why were they not chosen?

- Would the company choose the same registrar again today? If not, then who would they choose and why?

The purpose of this questionnaire is to establish consistency of a registrar and differentiators between registrars, not reputation.

5. How long has the registrar been in business?

Extreme caution should be exercised in choosing a registrar new to the business.

6. How many companies have you registered?

It is prudent to ensure that the registrar is established with a solid base of clients. After all, if your registrar goes out of business, your registration expires.

7. Do your auditors use checklists or scoring systems?

This will vary from one registrar to the next. Some feel that this provides a fair, unbiased method of assessment, while others feel that it is too restrictive. Opponents view each company as being unique and feel that each should be assessed as such. Checklists tend to create an artificial "cookie mold" in which all companies should fit.

8. Where are your auditors based?

Geography should also be considered. A registrar with only one office, located in another country, may have difficulty understanding the differences in your management style and organizational hierarchy.

9. Do you offer a preassessment?

Many registrars offer an optional "preassessment" to address any concerns you may have before proceeding with the formal registration. I highly recommend that you take advantage of this option.

10. Price

Inaccurate reports of excessive costs of registration flourish. These reports contain a common flaw: They include the cost of preparation and consultants. If I told you that it cost me more than $20,000 to obtain my driver's license, it would sound incredible, right? I've arrived at that figure by including the cost of the car, reasoning that a driver's license is useless without a car.

Don't confuse the "cost of quality" with the "cost of registration." Registration is optional; having a formal quality system shouldn't be.

Cost can vary substantially from one registrar to another. In many instances, costs are hidden as travel fees and mark-ups. It is important to make sure that all costs are disclosed "up front." In that it helps to ask the right questions, here are some of the most important.

How much will registration cost?

Cost is typically based upon the size of your organization, the ISO 9000 series standard selected (ISO 9001, ISO 9002, or ISO 9003), the scope of registration (one product, a product line, or an entire facility), and the number of facility locations. In instances where a company has multiple locations under the same quality system, it may be possible to achieve registration through an ongoing "sampling" program of the different locations. Know in advance what it is you want to purchase.

Will the cost of surveillance be included in the registration fee?

Initial quotations for registration generally include the first two surveillance visits itemized separately. After registration, each surveillance will represent a separate cost prior to each occurrence. These prices, of course, are subject to being raised over time.

What is the registrar's billing rate?

Some registrars have a daily billing rate. Others compute quotations based on each job individually. Some rates include an estimate of anticipated travel and living expenses associated with the assessment activities. Others list this as a variable.

Are travel expenses and lodging billed at reasonable rates?

Of those registrars that list travel and living expenses as a variable, some mark up these rates by some percentage. Others bill strictly at cost (no markup). Some registrars will discuss travel and living expenses prior to assessment, agreeing to limitations that you set. One option is for you to arrange travel and hotel accommodations with direct billing to your company.

Will assessors be traveling from a location within the U.S. or from Europe?

Many registrars with offices in Europe may, from time to time, use assessors from other offices outside the U.S. When this occurs, be sure the registrar pays the cost of those assessors entering the U.S. Clients normally pay the cost of travel from locations in the continental U.S.

The Registration Process

As the flow chart in Figure 5-1 reflects, the registration process begins with you completing and submitting a registrar's questionnaire (see Figure 5-2). This information allows each registrar to complete a formal quotation for you. This should be the final step in your selection of a registrar. Upon identifying an acceptable quote, you would submit your formal application for registration.

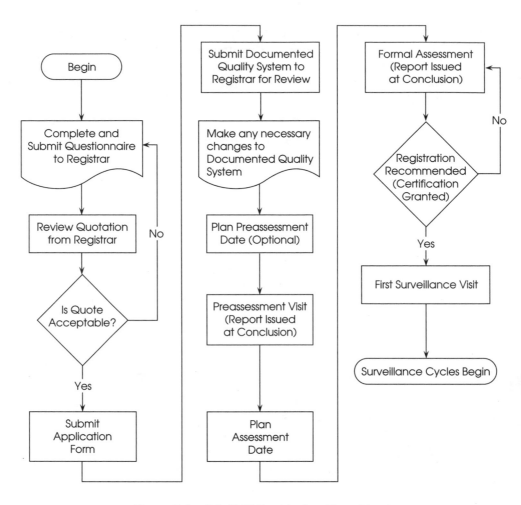

Figure 5-1: ISO 9000 Registration Flow Chart

At that time you would establish a date in which to submit your documented quality system (DQS—quality manual & procedure manual) to the registrar for review. This typically takes two to four weeks. The registrar will then respond with a written report of the DQS review. There may be noncompliances that will need to be addressed before proceeding with scheduling a preassessment (if selected).

The registration process involves a two-stage evaluation:

1. Quality manual & procedures vs. ISO 9000 requirements

2. Objective evidence from site visit vs. quality manual and procedures

QUESTIONNAIRE

This Questionnaire is sent to inquirers to obtain preliminary information which will enable us to confirm an estimate of costs for registration and to process any subsequent application as quickly as possible. The Questionnaire should be completed in as much detail as possible.

1. **Company Name** _____

   Address _____

   _____

   Contact _____

   Position _____

   Tel #/Fax # _____

2. **Employees**—please give details of employees in the following

   a) Total in company _____ Total at main address _____

   b) Total at subsidiary premise(s): 1) _____ 2) _____ 3) _____

   c) Total in organization for which registration is sought _____

3. **Scope of Registration**—please give a description of the products, processes, or services for which Registration is sought:

   _____

   _____

4. **Deletions from Scope of Registration**—please describe the products, processes, or services for which Registration is not sought:

   _____

   _____

5. **Standard Industrial Classification Code (SIC)** - _____

6. **Details of any Quality System Documentation produced**—e.g. None, Policy Manual only, System at Draft Stage

   _____

7. **Have you a specific program/timescale for attaining Registration?**

   _____

   _____

   Quality Documentation ready for review by ____ / ____ / ____ Ready for Assessment by ____ / ____ / ____

8. **Have you used a consultant?** If yes, please give details. _____

   _____

   Form No: 5004/5/93 (E)

Figure 5.2: Sample of Registrar's Questionnaire

The Preassessment (Optional)

If you have concerns about proceeding with the formal assessment because of uncertainty in given functions, a preassessment would identify noncompliances in those areas evaluated with no recommendation being made (there is no pass or fail recommendation given during a preassessment). I am often asked to describe the *real* advantage of a preassessment. If your employees have been working for a year or longer to develop and implement an ISO 9000–compliant quality system, a nonrecommendation during the formal assessment may have devastating consequences for morale.

A preassessment often serves as a period of "expectation management." This allows your registrar to see your operation during a less formal activity, giving you the opportunity to explain why you may have chosen a particular approach toward meeting the requirements, or intent, of ISO 9000. In turn, you would have the opportunity to gain a better understanding of your registrar's interpretation of the standard toward any areas of concern. I must emphasize that this interaction should *not* be viewed as an opportunity to gain consulting from the registrar. There may be noncompliances issued during a preassessment that must be addressed before you schedule your formal assessment.

The Assessment

The first thing you will need to do is to make arrangements for the auditor's arrival. The lead auditor will typically contact you for information regarding flights, hotels, and directions to your company. I recommend having clear, concise directions from the nearest major airport pretyped with a map, if possible. If directions to your company are difficult to follow, consider sending someone to meet and bring the auditor(s) to the company.

The Care and Feeding of Auditors

Most ISO 9000 auditors virtually live "on the road." Travel is a way of life for them. They will appreciate any effort that you may take in making their stay with you more enjoyable. Trying to save a couple of dollars by making reservations for them to stay at the cheapest hotel in town won't impress them. The audit process can be difficult; it is more difficult when your auditors were not able to sleep the night before because their hotel is beside a busy expressway. The most common hotel problem is poor environmental control (too hot or too cold with no middle settings).

I am not suggesting that you reserve the most expensive hotel in town for your auditors. Just don't reserve the cheapest.

If you are located in or near a small town that doesn't have any decent hotels, then I suggest researching the possibility of arranging their stay at a bed and breakfast. These are often reasonably priced and are a welcome change of pace for the auditors.

Food is a constant problem for auditors. They typically perform their audits during the workday and travel to their next client site each night. The hotel you select should either have a restaurant or be situated in an area near several restaurants. I'm not suggesting that you arrange and host all of their meals, but they will need to eat.

The Opening Meeting

The audit team will arrive and immediately wish to conduct an "opening meeting" (see Figure 5-3) to establish the scope of the activity. By this time you should have a pretty good understanding of the audit process.

The Guide

A guide should be assigned to escort each auditor or audit team throughout the audit. As mentioned in the opening meeting, the guide will be responsible for acting as a liaison between the audit team and the company. While summaries of daily activities may be presented at the end of each day, it remains the responsibility of the guide to understand the details of any concerns raised. I strongly recommend that the guide keep detailed notes throughout the audit.

The guide will be introducing the auditor(s) to various employees who may be working on a production line. The guide should have a supervisor or other capable employee standing by to take over on the production line while employees are interviewed. If there are any employees the auditor would like to interview who have special considerations (hearing impairment, visual impairment, illiteracy, language barriers, etc.), this should be brought to the attention of the auditor in advance. This can avoid potentially embarrassing situations for both the auditor and the employee.

As mentioned in Chapter 3, ISO 9000 auditors will be using standard quality terminology. Similarly, your employees may be using terminology unique to your company. Here, too, the guide should provide any clarification of acronyms or terms that may be unfamiliar to either party.

Define Observations, Minor and Major Noncompliances

The Lead Auditor should define observations and minor and major noncompliances in the opening meeting (see Figure 5-4). Most registrars will issue an

OPENING MEETING

INTRODUCTION OF AUDIT TEAM

CONFIRM SCOPE OF ACTIVITY (FULL ASSESSMENT OR LIMITED SURVEILLANCE)

CONFIRM CONFIDENTIALITY
(ALL ASSESSORS' PERSONAL NOTES WILL BE DESTROYED AT END OF ACTIVITY)

ACTIVITY WILL BE PERFORMANCE BASED (WHICH MEANS THAT A SAMPLING OF EMPLOYEES WILL BE INTERVIEWED & RECORDS WILL BE REVIEWED—REQUEST ONLY ONE OTHER COMPANY EMPLOYEE BE PRESENT DURING INTERVIEWS)

CONFIRM IDENTIFICATION OF GUIDES—EXPLAIN ROLE OF GUIDE(S)
• LIAISON BETWEEN COMPANY AND AUDITOR(S)
• INTRODUCE SELECTED COMPANY EMPLOYEES TO AUDITOR(S)
• REVIEW OBSERVATIONS & NONCOMPLIANCES WHEN RAISED BY AUDITOR(S)
• ANSWER QUESTIONS & PROVIDE CLARIFICATION (IF COMPANY USED A CONSULTANT(S)—THE COMPANY IS BEING ASSESSED; NOT THE CONSULTANT(S). CONSULTANT(S) MAY, HOWEVER, PARTICIPATE AS AN OBSERVER.)

DEFINE OBSERVATIONS, MINOR & MAJOR NONCOMPLIANCES

EXPLAIN "EARLY WARNING" IF A MAJOR NONCOMPLIANCE IS IDENTIFIED

A REPORT WILL BE GENERATED AT THE END OF THE ACTIVITY AND LEFT WITH THE COMPANY—A TIME WILL BE SET AND A CLOSING MEETING HELD

REQUEST THAT A CURRENT COPY OF COMPANY'S DQS BE AVAILABLE

CONFIRM OFFICE FACILITIES ARE RESERVED FOR AUDITORS USE

CONFIRM LUNCH ARRANGEMENTS

REVIEW HEALTH & SAFETY REQUIREMENTS (USE OF SAFETY GLASSES, HARD HATS, STEEL TOED SHOES/BOOTS, AREA RESTRICTIONS, ETC.), UNION CONCERNS, SPECIAL EMPLOYEE CONSIDERATIONS (HEARING IMPAIRMENT, VISUAL IMPAIRMENT, ILLITERACY, LANGUAGE BARRIERS, ETC.)

INVITE QUESTIONS

Figure 5-3: Sample of ISO 9000 Auditors' "Opening Meeting" Agenda

---

Categories of Noncompliances

Minor noncompliance—A minor noncompliance relates to a single observed lapse in a procedure.

Major noncompliance—A major noncompliance relates to the absence of a required procedure or the total breakdown of a procedure. A number of minor noncompliances listed against the same clause of ISO 9000 represents a total breakdown of a system and thus are collectively a major noncompliance.

Observation—An observation is a matter about which the assessor (auditor) is concerned but which cannot be clearly stated as a noncompliance. Observations also indicate trends that may cause problems in the future.

Figure 5-4: "Categories of Noncompliances" as Defined by Most Registrars

"early warning" if any major noncompliances are identified that would result in their not being able to recommend registration.

The Interviews

A formal assessment will focus on two areas:

1. Reviewing quality records documenting compliance with the standard

2. Interviewing employees demonstrating compliance with the standard

Proper maintenance of quality records has been discussed throughout this book, but interviews are another matter. Expect several employees throughout your operation to be interviewed. The best preparation for this is to interview employees through your internal audit process. I've found that where many companies begin with nervous employees stuttering and forgetting details, after two or three surveillance visits those same employees are confident and proud. This change occurred for two reasons:

• The employees are more experienced in describing their job functions

• The employees are more comfortable being interviewed

While practice may not "make perfect," it certainly "makes better."

▲ Klingons in Business Suits!

Contrary to popular belief, auditors are not mild-mannered closet Klingons dressed in business suits. Well, maybe a few of them are, but most certainly are not. This myth is driven primarily by fears of inadequacy. Workers are constantly reminded during the preparation for registration of how important the achievement is. If driven too hard, workers fear that giving a wrong answer to an auditor will cost the company its registration, and them their jobs! I personally know of instances in which workers have quit their jobs because of the anxiety associated with going through an upcoming assessment. Ridiculous! Why would workers quit their jobs rather than answer a few simple questions, typically relating to their work functions, asked by someone they had never met? This is a classic case of a company building up an incredible myth of brutal auditors.

First of all, it would be incredibly rare for a single worker to cause a company to fail registration. The only instance I can think of where this could happen is where that worker becomes uncooperative, hostile, and/or adversarial with an auditor. As a lead auditor, I would not subject any of my team to that sort of abusive situation. Auditors are gathering information. If they cannot gather required information from an area, then they cannot verify compliance with the standard. Therefore, that area must be considered as noncompliant.

Auditors are accustomed to workers being nervous and, understanding that, generally make allowances. (This is why in the opening meeting I like to request that only one other company employee be present during interviews—usually the guide.)

The Early Warning

Ideally, your registrar will have a policy of informing you if any major noncompliances are found during the audit. If they are identified, ask the lead auditor to explain any options that you may have. If he or she is unable to discuss this during the assessment, contact the registrar's headquarters and discuss any options that you may have with the program manager, technical director, or equivalent.

The Closing Meeting

At the end of the assessment, the audit team will retire to an office area to compile their final report. Depending upon the size of the company, the size of the audit team, and scope of the assessment, this can take from one to four hours.

Upon completing their report, they will be ready to review their conclusions in a formal closing meeting (see Figure 5-5). At that time, any noncompliances

CLOSING MEETING

THANK COMPANY FOR ASSISTANCE & HOSPITALITY

BRIEF RÉSUMÉ OF SCOPE OF ACTIVITY

CONFIRM CONFIDENTIALITY

DURING THE COURSE OF AN ACTIVITY, AUDITORS MAY STATE EXAMPLES OF COMPLIANCE AND NONCOMPLIANCE TO CLARIFY (THE REGISTRAR'S) POSITIONS AND INTERPRETATIONS REGARDING ISO 9000; THESE SHOULD IN NO WAY BE PERCEIVED BY THE COMPANY AS TRAINING OR CONSULTING—THE PRIMARY ROLE OF THE REGISTRAR IS TO VERIFY THE COMPANY'S COMPLIANCE WITH ISO 9000—NOT DIRECT IT

THE ACTIVITY WAS CONDUCTED ON A SAMPLING BASIS
(WHILE NONCONFORMANCES MAY NOT HAVE BEEN REPORTED IN AN AREA, IT DOES NOT FOLLOW THAT NONE NECESSARILY EXIST THERE)

ACTIVITY REPORTS ARE MADE BY EXCEPTION—RESULTS OF THE REPORT SHOULD NOT BE VIEWED AS A CRITICISM OF THE OVERALL QUALITY SYSTEM—THE ACTIVITY ONLY ASSESSES FOR COMPLIANCE WITH ISO 9000

STATE NUMBER OF OBSERVATIONS AND NONCOMPLIANCES— OFFER TO REVIEW EACH IN DETAIL

CONCLUSION:
- PREASSESSMENT STATUS
- RECOMMENDATION REGARDING REGISTRATION
  (DISCUSS USE OF LOGO / RIGHT OF APPEAL IF NONRECOMMENDATION)
- CONTINUING SURVEILLANCE STATUS

EXPLAIN USE OF CORRECTIVE ACTION PLAN FORM & TIME SCALES
(WHERE APPLICABLE)

ESTABLISH DATE FOR NEXT ACTIVITY

Figure 5-5: Sample of ISO 9000 Auditor's "Closing Meeting" Agenda

will be reviewed and a decision announced concerning a recommendation for registration. The lead auditor cannot award registration. He or she makes a recommendation to the President of the Registrar, who actually awards the registration.

Contrary to popular belief, the President of the Registrar doesn't necessarily have the last word in awarding registration. All recommendations and "Certificates of Registration" issued are periodically reviewed by an Independent Control/Review Board (ICB) that can overturn any decision.

Likewise, if a company is not recommended for registration, they have the right to appeal the decision to the ICB for review. The ICB is typically composed of individuals independent of the registrar representing industry and academia. But we can hope you will not need to go through this process.

After Registration

Registration cannot be considered a project to be complete upon certification. The "Certified" or "Registered" status must be maintained, with associated maintenance and reassessment fees. Once a company achieves registration, the registrar schedules periodic surveillance visits.

Surveillance Visits

The type and extent of surveillance programs vary from one registrar to another. These visits are normally not as extensive as the registration process and only focus on a limited number of clauses. The company would *not* be informed in advance as to which areas are to be included in each surveillance, and some areas may be reviewed repeatedly.

Some registrars issue a certificate that is valid for as long as the surveillance activities continue to provide favorable results. Others issue a certificate with an expiration date, typically three years from issue, at which time a complete reassessment will be performed and a new certificate issued.

The duration of each surveillance visit will depend upon the size of your organization, the ISO 9000 series standard selected (ISO 9001, ISO 9002, or ISO 9003), the scope of registration (one product, a product line, or an entire facility), and the number of facility locations. The minimum is generally one day.

Losing your Certification

At any point in the surveillance process where a major noncompliance is found, a registrar can revoke certification. While registrars do have an appeals process, I assure you that this action is not taken lightly. If you have not adopted ISO 9000 into your company culture, you cannot hold onto your registration.

Marketing your Achievement

Once registered, your company will be included in a "Directory of Registered Companies." You will receive "camera-ready" artwork of your registrar's logo and instructions on use of the registration logo in advertising and other printed matter. This logo can be included on the following:

- Advertisements
- Catalogs
- Commercials
- Business cards
- Bills of lading
- Invoices

The symbols may not be used on a product or in any way that might imply product conformity, because the registration is of the quality system, not of an individual product.

Chapter 6
ISO 9000, the EU, and NAFTA

It now appears that the ISO 9000 series has been fully accepted by the EU and will be the governing documents referenced throughout not only Europe, but the entire world, for establishing general guidelines in quality management systems. At the time of this publication, more than eighty-one countries had adopted the ISO 9000 series as their national quality standard.

EU and EFTA Countries

In addition to the EU (European Union—previously known as the European Community) member countries, all of the EFTA (European Free Trade Association) member countries have also adopted the ISO 9000 series (see Figure 6-1).

The United Kingdom

The European movement promoting ISO 9000 compliance and registration was clearly driven by the U.K. According to the British Department of Trade and Industry (DTI) Quality Assurance Register, more than 30,000 companies in the U.K. have already completed the registration process to ISO 9000. It is difficult to determine how many companies are registered in all of Europe, in that most countries do not maintain a complete listing, but the number pales by comparison to the U.K. Virtually every purchase agreement, contract, and specification written by U.K. industries, institutions, and government agencies includes a "boilerplate" requirement that mandates the contractor to demonstrate compliance with ISO 9000.

The accrediting body for ISO 9000 registrars in the U.K. is the *National Accreditation Council for Certification Bodies* (NACCB).

Country	ISO 9000	ISO 9001	ISO 9002	ISO 9003	ISO 9004
Austria	ONORM ISO 9000	ONORM ISO 9001	ONORM ISO 9002	ONORM ISO 9003	ONORM ISO 9004
Belgium	NBN-EN9000	NBN-EN9001	NBN-EN9002	NBN-EN9003	NBN-EN9004
Denmark	DS / ISO 9000	DS / ISO 9001	DS / ISO 9003	DS / ISO 9003	DS / ISO 9004
Finland	SFS-ISO 9000	SFS-ISO 9001	SFS-ISO 9002	SFS-ISO 9003	SFS-ISO 9004
France	NF EN 9000	NF EN 9001	NF EN 9002	NF EN 9003	NF EN 9004
Germany	DIN ISO 9000	DIN ISO 9001	DIN ISO 9002	DIN ISO 9003	DIN ISO 9004
Greece	ELOT EN9000	ELOT EN9001	—	—	—
Iceland	IST ISO 9000	IST ISO 9001	IST ISO 9002	IST ISO 9003	IST ISO 9004
Ireland	I.S./ISO9000	I.S./ISO9001	I.S./ISO9002	I.S./ISO9003	I.S./ISO9004
Italy	UNI/EN 9000	UNI/EN 9001	UNI/EN 9002	UNI/EN 9003	UNI/EN 9004
Netherlands	NEN-ISO 9000	NEN-ISO 9001	NEN-ISO 9002	NEN-ISO 9003	NEN-ISO 9004
Norway	NS-EN 9000	NS-EN 9001	NS-ISO 9002	NS-ISO 9003	—
Portugal	NP EN 9 000	NP EN 9 001	NP EN 9 002	NP EN 9 003	NP EN 9 004
Spain	UNE 66-900	UNE 66-901	UNE 66-902	UNE 66-903	UNE 66-904
Sweden	SS-ISO 9000	SS-ISO 9001	SS-ISO 9002	SS-ISO 9003	SS-ISO 9004
Switzerland	SN EN 9000	SN EN 9001	SN EN 9002	SN EN 9003	SN EN 9004
United Kingdom	BS EN ISO 9000	BS EN ISO 9001	BS EN ISO 9002	BS EN ISO 9003	BS EN ISO 9004

Note: Luxembourg is a member of the EU, but typically references Belgium's National Standards.

Figure 6-1: EU/EFTA Member Countries and the ISO 9000 Series

The TickIT Scheme

With the publication of the ISO 9000:1987 series, the U.K. Department of Trade and Industry (DTI) wished to establish the relevance of these standards to the production of software. The result was "TickIT," a certification scheme developed by Information Technology professionals and supported by the DTI and the British Computer Society (BCS). TickIT stands for "Tick Information Technologies" ("Tick" is a term used in the U.K. that is equivalent to "checkmark").

The scheme may have additional requirements for the company being registered, and the lead assessor must also have additional qualifications (reference ISO 9000-3 for guidance). If you are a company outside of the U.K. who does not intend to serve the U.K., then you can still be registered to ISO 9000 by an NACCB-accredited registrar; you simply will not receive the TickIT accreditation mark/logo.

The single best source of information on this scheme is found in the booklet:

"TickIT: Making a better job of software"
Guide to Software Quality Management System Construction and Certification using EN29001 / ISO 9001

Available from:

TickIT Project Office
68 Neuman Street
London W1A 4SE
Tel: +44 (0)71 383 4501
Fax: +44 (0)71 383 4771

It should be noted that a similar scheme has been considered by ANSI/RAB, but the U.S. Information Technology industry is not yet receptive.

NATO

In February 1993, the North Atlantic Treaty Organization (NATO) adopted supplemented versions of ISO 9001, 9002, and 9003 as part of its Allied Quality Assurance Publication (AQAP) series. AQAP-100, "General Guidance on NATO Quality Assurance," provides information and guidance on NATO quality assurance and its view on quality management. This particular series is also referred to as the "Century" series. The supplements are:

AQAP 110: "NATO Quality Assurance Requirements for Design, Development, and Production"—to be used in conjunction with ISO 9001

AQAP 120: "NATO Quality Assurance Requirements for Production"—to be used in conjunction with ISO 9002

AQAP 130: "NATO Quality Assurance Requirements for Inspection"—to be used in conjunction with ISO 9003

The AQAP 110, 120, and 130 standards also reference ISO 8402, ISO 9000, ISO 9004, and ISO 10012. NATO Guide AQAP-119, "NATO Guide for AQAPs -110, -120, -130," was developed to supplement the guidance standard ISO 9000-2.

However, according to AQAP 100, other AQAP standards and guides such as AQAP 131, "NATO Quality Assurance Requirements for Final Inspection"; AQAP-150, "NATO Quality Assurance Requirements for Software"; AQAP-159, "NATO Guide to AQAP-150," and AQAP-170, "NATO Guide for a Government Quality Assurance Programme" are not based on an equivalent ISO 9000 standards.

NAFTA Countries

With the advent of the North American Free Trade Agreement (NAFTA), participating companies should also be aware of the position each member country has taken toward ISO 9000.

Each NAFTA country has adopted ISO 9000 as their national quality standard according to Figure 6-2.

The United States

The American Society for Quality Control Standards Committee, rather than independently revising and extending its current Generic Guidelines for Quality Systems (ANSI/ASQC Z1.15-1979), elected to join other nations in adopting standards fully consistent with the "ISO 9000–9004 Series" of Quality Management and Quality Assurance Standards in 1987 as the ANSI/ASQC Q-90 series. The title was changed with the 1994 revision to the ANSI/ASQC Q-9000 series to more closely resemble the better-known ISO title.

In order to establish a U.S. authority for accrediting registrars, the Registrar Accreditation Board (RAB) was established as an affiliate of the American Society for Quality Control (ASQC) in late 1989. In 1994, the ANSI (American National Standards Institute) and the RAB established a joint program known as the *American National Accreditation Program for Registrars of Quality Systems*. In that ANSI is the U.S. member delegate to ISO, its participation in a joint ANSI/RAB program was considered key to enhancing the credibility and worldwide acceptance of the U.S. registration program.

ANSI/RAB have initiated talks with the U.S. Department of Commerce to encourage government recognition of the ANSI/RAB program for registrar accreditation. A goal of the ANSI/RAB program is to fit into the structure that is developing in Europe, where the intent is to establish national systems of

Country	ISO 9000	ISO 9001	ISO 9002	ISO 9003	ISO 9004
Canada	CAN/CSA-Q9000	CAN/CSA-Q9001	CAN/CSA-Q9002	CAN/CSA-Q9003	CAN/CSA-Q9004
Mexico	NOM-CC-2	NOM-CC-3	NOM-CC-4	NOM-CC-5	NOM-CC-6
United States	ANSI/ASQC Q 9000	ANSI/ASQC Q 9001	ANSI/ASQC Q 9002	ANSI/ASQC Q 9003	ANSI/ASQC Q 9004

Figure 6-2: NAFTA Countries and ISO 9000

accreditation and registration and, eventually, mutual recognition of these national systems across national boundaries. As a declaration of intent to work toward mutual recognition, ANSI/RAB has signed memoranda of understanding (MOU) with the national accreditation bodies of the Netherlands, Australia, Japan, New Zealand, and the United Kingdom (as of September 1994).

The U.S. Department of Defense

The U.S. Department of Defense (DoD) recognized the advantages offered by ISO 9000 very early. A memorandum from the U.S. Assistant Secretary of Defense, dated in August 1989, stated, ". . . I want to adopt ISO Standards 9001, 9002, 9003 in their entirety and develop supplemental military standards. . . . I expect to see the resulting military standards supersede the current MIL-Q-9858A, MIL-I-45208A and Standard Form 32."

Another memorandum from the Department of the Air Force reads, ". . . DoD adoption is effective Feb. 6, 1991, and the ANSI/ASQC Q90 series of standards should be listed soon in the DoD Index of Specifications and Standards. Changes to the Defense Federal Acquisition Regulation Supplement are currently being developed and when approved, ANSI/ASQC Q91, Q92 and Q93 will replace MIL-Q-9858A and MIL-I-45208A for new contracts. . . ."

On February 14, 1994, the U.S. DoD and NASA jointly issued MIL-HDBK-9000/NASA-HDBK-9000 as a guidance document to assist contracting activities that have decided to use ANSI/ASQC Q91 or Q92 quality system standards with domestic contracts.

Other U.S. government agencies are also in various phases of either adopting or recognizing ISO 9000. Among them are these:

- Department of Energy (DoE)

- Department of Agriculture (USDA)

- Food and Drug Administration (FDA)

- National Institute for Occupational Safety and Health (NIOSH)

- Mine Safety and Health Administration (MSHA)

- General Services Administration (GSA)

- Office of Management and Budget (OMB)

- National Aeronautics and Space Administration (NASA)

- National Oceanic and Atmospheric Administration (NOAA)

- U.S. Coast Guard

- U.S. Postal Service

Both the ISO 9000 Series and ANSI/ASQC Q9000 Series of standards are available from:

The American National Standards Institute (ANSI)
11 West 42nd Street, 13th Floor
New York, NY 10036, USA
Tel: (212) 642-4900
Fax: (212) 398-0023
(212) 302-1286 (Orders Only)
Telex: (212) 42 42 96 ANSI UI

The American Society for Quality Control (ASQC)
Quality Press
611 E. Wisconsin Ave.
P.O. Box 3005
Milwaukee, WI 53201-3005
Tel: (800) 248-1946
(414) 272-8575
Fax: (414) 272-1734

✎ Note

The U.S. Department of Commerce has established an automated information system that can provide information on a number of NAFTA-related subjects. To access call:

NAFTA Facts—Mexico Division: (202) 482-4464

NAFTA Flash Facts—Canada System: (202) 482-3101

Mexico

In 1990, Mexico adopted the ISO 9000 Standard Series as NOM-CC-2, 3, 4, 5, and 6. Development of Mexican standards is under central control of the Secretaria de Comercio y Fomento Industrial (Secretariat for Commerce and Industrial Development—SECOFI). Other ministries, including the Ministries of Health, Agriculture, Environment, Transportation, and Energy, play key roles in developing and enforcing standards.

Mexico now has two types of standards:

NOM (Normas Oficial Mexicanas): These are mandatory technical regulations. All Mexican government technical regulations, regardless of the ministry that issues them, will have this prefix.

NMX (Normas Mexicanas): These are voluntary standards, intended for use as references.

There are currently two categories of mandatory Mexican standards (NOMs) that affect imported products:

1. NOMs on commercial information, such as labeling, that must be made available to the consumer; and

2. NOMs related to product performance and/or safety. These typically require a "certificate of quality" to be presented to Mexican Customs along with all of the other import documents normally submitted. This "certificate of quality" attests that the product has been tested by an accredited Mexican laboratory and found to have complied with the applicable NOM.

These standards may be requested directly from the Mexican Government at:

> Dirección General de Normas (DGN)
> Secretaria de Comercio y Fomento Industrial (SECOFI)
> Dept. de Certificacion y Verificacion de Normas Obligatorias
> Ave. Puente de Tecamachalco No. 6, Piso 1
> Col. Fuentes de Tecamachalco
> Naucalpan, Mex. C.P. 53950
>
> Tel: 011-52-55-40-26-20, or 011-52-55-89-98-77, ext. 130
> Fax: 011-52-56-06-30-86

On July 1, 1992, Mexico passed the Federal Law on Metrology and Standardization. This law also led to the establishment of a National Accreditation and Certification System for certification bodies and quality system registrars under the aegis of the Dirección General de Normas (DGN). The first registrar was accredited in March 1994. In regulated areas, the appropriate regulatory body will oversee the accreditation process and will make recommendations to the Ministry of Commerce regarding approval. Registration certificates from registrars not accredited under the National Accreditation and Certification System will not be accepted for regulatory and procurement purposes.

For further information, contact:

> Dirección General de Normas
> Calle Puente de Tecamachalco No. 6
> Lomas de Tecamachalco
> Seccion Fuentes
> Naucalpan de Juarez
> 53950 Mexico
> Phone: 011-52-55-20-84-94
> Fax: 011-52-55-40-51-53
> Telex: 177 58 40 imceme
> Cable: secofi/147

✍ Note

Mexico has also signed as a member of the NAFTA-like "Group of Three Pact" (G-3). It is hoped that this free trade agreement with Colombia and Venezuela (both of which have also adopted ISO 9000 as their national quality standard) will later expand to include Bolivia, Chile, Ecuador, and Peru.

Canada

The Canadian Standards Association (CSA), rather than replace its current Quality Assurance Program standards (CAN3-Z299—Category 1, 2, 3, and 4), elected to adopt the "ISO 9000–9004 Series" as a separate set of standards, thus establishing two nationally recognized quality standards. The CSA has designated their ISO 9000–compatible standards as the CAN/CSA-Q9000 series (see Figure 6-3). This series complies with the minimum requirements of ISO 9000, but is complemented by additional criteria from the CAN3-Z299 series. This was necessary for acceptance in Canada because the Z299 series had already become the norm used throughout Canadian industry.

Eventually it is anticipated that the CAN/CSA-Q9000 series will completely replace the CAN3-Z299 series.

✍ Note

Canadian companies may be registered to either ISO 9000 or CAN/CSA-Q9000 standards. A CAN/CSA-Q9000 registration would include the additional requirements taken from CAN3-Z299.

The Standards Council of Canada (SCC) operates a registrar accreditation program called *Accreditation of Organizations that Register Suppliers' Quality Systems*. It was approved by the SCC on December 9, 1991.

Canadian Quality Standard Equivalents					
ISO 9000	ISO 9001	ISO 9002	—	ISO 9003	ISO 9004
CAN/CSA-Q9000	CAN/CSA-Q9001	CAN/CSA-Q9002	—	CAN/CSA-Q9003	CAN/CSA-Q9004
CAN3-Z299.0	CAN3-Z299.1	CAN3-Z299.2	CAN3-Z299.3	CAN3-Z299.4	—

Figure 6-3: Canadian Quality Standard Equivalents

Canadian standards may be requested directly from:

Standards Council of Canada
1200-45 O'Connor
Ottawa, Ontario K1P 6N7
Canada
Tel: (613) 238-3222;
1-800-267-8220 (Inside
Canada Only)

Fax: (613) 995-4564

Canadian Standards Association
178 Rexdale Boulevard
Rexdale (Toronto), Ontario, Canada
M9W 1R3
Tel: (416) 747-4368

Business Development Group
(416) 747-4019

Canada's "Supplier Quality Initiative" (SQI)

Canada has established a "Supplier Quality Initiative" (SQI) program, a joint venture between Government Services Canada and Industry and Science Canada, that focuses on the ISO 9000 standards for quality management and the adoption of these standards in federal procurement.

ISO 9000 is being introduced to federal procurement on a sector-by-sector basis. The following are sectors or commodity groups where ISO 9000 is currently being considered as a procurement tool:

- Furniture

- Photocopiers/duplicators

- Maintenance

- CIDA/packaging

- Clothing, footwear, life support, knotwear, and outwear

- Textiles: mattresses, bedding, linens, towels

- Fax machines

- Microcomputers

Monthly updates may be found in the CanadExport newsletter, published by External Affairs.

Canada's National Quality Institute

The National Quality Institute (NQI) is a national, independently incorporated, not-for-profit organization established to promote the principles and practices of total quality and the implementation of new quality policies in the

Canadian workplace. The premise of the NQI is that total quality must become a national priority to enhance Canada's competitive position as a nation.

The National Quality Institute has the responsibility of developing a national strategy for the implementation of quality improvement and related work reorganization principles in all institutions and organizations in Canada. It must ensure that there is a coherent and coordinated approach to the implementation and integration of the national strategy with strategies at other levels of the overall program, and it must avoid duplication of quality programs and services.

Funding for the initiatives financed by the NQI comes from federal government contributions, fees for services, in-kind private sector contributions, and corporate contributions. The funding of the NQI is designed to meet specific program needs so that it will not compete with private- and public-sector funding arrangements for the community-based, sector-based, functional, and provincial initiatives. The ISC Technology Outreach Program has made funds available, on a matching basis, to support NQI quality initiatives. This contribution agreement between Industry, Science and Technology Canada and the National Quality Institute totals $19 million and covers a five-year period starting September 1, 1992. It is allocated to organizations who provide specific services in quality and are participants in the Canadian Network for Total Quality.

Canadian Network for Total Quality

The Canadian Network for Total Quality (NQN—National Quality Network) was formed in early 1992 after a number of organizations had approached Industry, Science and Technology Canada with proposals to deliver services in total quality to Canadian organizations. ISO requested that the organizations sponsoring the proposals join together to provide an integrated proposal for total quality services. A significant part of that proposal was for the establishment of the National Quality Institute. Strong support for a national quality organization also came from the federal government's Prosperity Initiative, whose action plan, "Inventing Our Future," confirmed widespread recognition that a real commitment to total quality is essential to meet the competitive challenges of the nineties.

The NQN is a group of organizations from different sectors and regions of the country that have voluntarily joined forces to improve the use of total quality principles and practices in Canada. The NQI will facilitate awareness and coordinate the delivery of quality services through the NQN.

Although each organization operates in its own sphere, all are linked in a network that facilitates the development and implementation of an integrated strategy to enhance the use of total quality concepts in Canada. The participating organizations will disseminate information, provide training services, and assist organizations in the implementation of quality practices.

The network facilitates partnerships to promote and support the implementation of total principles in all aspects of business in order to strengthen national well-being and international competitiveness. The agreement between Industry, Science and Technology Canada and the Canadian Network for Total Quality to proceed with the implementation of the proposed initiatives was signed in December 1992.

The NQI and the NQN—Partners in Quality

It is the intention of the current participants to encourage organizations with similar goals to join the network. Some of the organizations participating in the NQN receive funding from the NQI. Organizations seeking financial assistance would apply to the NQI. They would then be required to demonstrate that their quality initiative meets a unique need and does not compete with initiatives already in place.

Funding is based on an in-kind contribution, and proposers must demonstrate that they have private-sector financial support equal to 50% of the total cost of the initiative. The NQI has developed guidelines that must be met by organizations requesting funding. An Advisory Board has been established that will assess the proposals.

The NQI will coordinate the efforts of private-sector partners in the NQN in order to facilitate networking and avoid duplication of services. The Network will perform a variety of activities designed to facilitate the availability and delivery of total quality information, services, and training across Canada. It will encourage national partnerships to promote and support the implementation of total quality principles in all aspects of Canadian enterprises in order to strengthen international competitiveness and national prosperity.

The NQI will integrate strategies at various levels in order to ensure a coherent and consistent approach throughout the country. The NQN will help to ensure that Canadians have access to those organizations with the most experience to help them in the transformation to total quality organizations.

The NQI and NQN are part of an integrated approach to promoting quality in Canada and will provide Canadian organizations with the access to the skills they need to develop quality practices. Both of these bodies will pay particular attention to the need for small- and medium-sized enterprises to obtain information and advice on how best to apply total quality principles and practices.

For more information, contact:

Industry Canada
Senior Quality Officer
Regional Services Branch
235 Queen Street,
1st Floor East
Ottawa, Ontario K1A 0H5
Tel: (613) 954-4974
Fax: (613) 954-5463

Government Services Canada
(for information on federal procurement)
Director, Supplier Quality Initiative
Supply Program Management Directorate
Ottawa, Ontario K1A 0S5
Tel: (819) 956-7426
Fax: (819) 953-1057

Organizations You Should Know about

There are a number of organizations, groups, and societies that can offer substantial assistance in developing your quality system to meet and exceed the quality requirements of ISO 9000. This is accomplished by viewing ISO 9000 as several separate elements rather than one large, all-encompassing system unique to itself. As these individual areas are developed, they bring the entire quality system together (the whole being greater than the sum of its individual parts).

In this section I have listed a few of these organizations, groups, and societies along with their address. Figure A-1 is a chart showing how each can be focused toward an individual element.

The American Chemical Society (ACS)

```
1155 16th Street NW      Tel:  (202) 872-4363
P.O. Box 57136                 1-800-227-5558
Washington, DC 20037    FAX: (202) 872-6067
```

The American Electronics Association (AEA)

```
5201 Great American Pkwy.    Tel:  (408) 987-4200
P.O. Box 54990               Fax: (408) 970-8565
Santa Clara, CA 95056-0990
```

The American Management Association (AMA)

```
The American Management
Association Building         Tel: (212) 586-8100
135 West 50th Street              (800) 262-9699
New York, NY 10020-1201    Fax: (212) 903-8168
```

Clause	Clause Title	Organizations, Groups, and Societies	Training	Certification Programs
4.1	Management Responsibility	American Management Association (AMA)	✓	
4.2	Quality System	The National ISO 9000 Support Group		
		The American Society for Quality Control (ASQC)	✓	✓
4.3	Contract Review	The National Association of Purchasing Management, Inc. (NAPM)	✓	
4.4	Design Control	American Society of Mechanical Engineers (ASME)	✓	
		The Institute of Electrical and Electronics Engineers (IEEE)	✓	
		National Fire Protection Association (NFPA)		
		Industrial Fasteners Institute (IFI)		
4.5	Document and Data Control	The Computer Security Institute (CSI)	✓	
		National Computer Security Association (NCSA)	✓	
4.6	Purchasing	The National Association of Purchasing Management, Inc. (NAPM)	✓	✓
4.7	Control of Customer-Supplied Product	—		
4.8	Product Identification and Traceability	—		

Figure A-1: Help for Developing Your Quality System

Clause	Clause Title	Organizations, Groups, and Societies	Training	Certification Programs
4.9	Process Control	The American Production and Inventory Control Society, Inc. (APICS)	✓	✓
		The Instrument Society of America (ISA)	✓	
		The Manufacturers' Alliance for Productivity and Innovation (MAPI)	✓	
	(Special Processes)	The American Welding Society (AWS)	✓	✓
	(Safety)	The American Society of Safety Engineers (ASSE)	✓	✓
		National Safety Council	✓	✓
4.10	Inspection and Testing	—		
4.11	Control of Inspection, Measuring, and Test Equipment	The National Conference of Standards Laboratories (NCSL)	✓	
		The National Conference on Weights and Measures (NCWM)		
		The American Measuring Tool Manufacturers Association (AMTMA)		
4.12	Inspection and Test Status	—		
4.13	Control of Nonconforming Product	—		
4.14	Corrective and Preventive Action	—		

Figure A-1: Help for Developing Your Quality System (*continued*)

Clause	Clause Title	Organizations, Groups, and Societies	Training	Certification Programs
4.15	Handling, Storage, Packaging, Preservation, and Delivery	The American Production and Inventory Control Society, Inc. (APICS)	✓	✓
		The American Trucking Association		
		The ESD Association	✓	
		The International Safe Transit Association (ISTA)		✓
4.16	Control of Quality Records	Association of Records Managers and Administrators, Inc. (ARMA International)	✓	
		The Computer Security Institute (CSI)	✓	
		National Computer Security Association (NCSA)	✓	
4.17	Internal Quality Audits	The Institute of Internal Auditing	✓	✓
4.18	Training	Society for Human Resource Management (SHRM)	✓	✓
		American Society for Training and Development (ASTD)	✓	✓
4.19	Servicing	The Association For Services Management International (AFSM International)	✓	
4.20	Statistical Techniques	The American Statistical Association (ASA)	✓	
		The International Statistical Applications Institute (ISAI)	✓	

Figure A-1: Help for Developing Your Quality System (*continued*)

AMA Affiliated Centers:

CANADA
Canadian Management Centre
150 York Street, Fifth Floor
Toronto, ON. M5H 3S5
Tel: (416) 214-5678
Fax: (416) 214-1453

MEXICO
Management Centre de Mexico A.C.
Paseo de la Reforma 199, 9th Floor
06500 Mexico D.F., Mexico
Tel: 52/5/566-5422; 52/5/592-2655
Fax: 52/5/592-2266

The American Measuring Tool Manufacturers Association (AMTMA)

1025 East Maple Road
Suite 110
Birmingham, MI 48009-6414

Tel: (810) 642-3312
Fax: (810) 646-5316

The American Production and Inventory Control Society (APICS®)

500 W. Annandale Road
Falls Church, VA 22046-4274

Tel: (703) 237-8344
     (800) 444-2742
Fax: (703) 237-1071

The American Society of Heating, Refrigerating and Air-Conditioning Engineers, Inc.

1791 Tulie Circle, NE
Atlanta, GA 30329

Tel: (404) 636-8400
Fax: (404) 321-5478

The American Society of Mechanical Engineers (ASME)

Headquarters
345 East 47th Street
New York, NY 10017-2392

Tel: (212) 705-7722

Telex: (710) 581-5267
Telefax: (212) 705-7674

Service Center
22 Law Drive
P.O. Box 2300
Fairfield, NJ. 07007-2300

Tel: (201) 882-1170

Fax: (201) 882-1717

1-800-843-2763 ext. 951
(1-800-THE-ASME)

1-800-321-2633 ext. 951
(1-800-321-CODE)

Technical Affairs
Telefax: (212) 705-7671

American Society of Plumbing Engineers (ASPE)

3617 Thousand Oaks Blvd., Suite 210   Tel: (805) 495-7120
Westlake Village, CA 91362-3649   Fax: (805) 495-4861

The American Society for Quality Control (ASQC)

611 East Wisconsin Avenue   Tel: 800-248-1946
P.O. Box 3005   (USA, Canada & Mexico)
Milwaukee, WI 53201-3005   (414) 272-8575
                             Fax: (414) 272-1734

American Society of Safety Engineers (ASSE)

1800 East Oakton Street   Tel: (708) 692-4121 Ext. 231
Des Plains, IL 60018-2187   Fax: (708) 296-3769

American Society for Training and Development (ASTD)

P.O. Box 1443   Tel: (708) 683-8100
1640 King Street   Fax: (703) 683-1523
Alexandria, VA 22313

American Statistical Association (ASA)

1429 Duke Street   ✍ Note
Alexandria, VA 22314-3402   Canadian readers may also wish to
                             contact: The Statistical Society of
Tel: (703) 684-1221   Canada
Fax: (703) 684-2037

E-mail: asainfo@asa.mhs.compuserve.com

The American Welding Society (AWS)

550 N.W. LeJeune Road   Tel: (305) 443-9353
Miami, FL 33126   1-800-443-WELD (9353)
                         Fax: (305) 443-7559

The Association of Records Managers and Administrators, Inc. (ARMA International)

4200 Somerset Drive   Tel: (913) 341-3808
Suite 215   1-800-422-2762 (U.S.)
Prairie Village, KS 66208   1-800-433-2762 (Canada)

                         Fax: (913) 341-3742

The Association for Services Management International (AFSM International)

1342 Colonial Boulevard *Administrative Offices:*
Suite 25   1-800-333-9786
Fort Myers, FL 33907-9948 (813) 275-7887

U.S. and Canada: Fax: (813) 275-0794
Membership:
1-800-444-9786

The Association of Standards and Testing Materials (ASTM)

1916 Race Street   Tel: (215) 299-5400
Philadelphia, PA 19103-1187 Fax: (215) 977-9679

The Automotive Industry Action Group (AIAG)

26200 Lahser Road   Tel: (810) 358-3570
Suite 200   Fax: (810) 358-3253
Southfield, MI 48034

The Computer Security Institute (CSI)

600 Harrison Street   Membership Hotline: (415) 905-2470
San Francisco, CA 94107
                        Conferences and Seminars: (415) 905-2626
Tel: (415) 905-2370
BBS: (415) 905-2480   CompuServe
Fax: (415) 905-2234   71702.402@compuserve.com
Fax: (415) 905-2218

Electronic Industries Association (EIA)

2001 Pennsylvania Ave., N.W. Tel: (202) 457-4900
Washington, DC 20006   Fax: (202) 457-4985

Electrostatic Discharge Association, Inc.

200 Liberty Plaza   Tel: (315) 339-6937
Rome, NY 13440   Fax: (315) 339-6793

Industrial Fasteners Institute (IFI)

1717 East Ninth Street Tel: (216) 241-1482
Suite 1505   Fax: (216) 241-5901
Cleveland, OH 44114-2879

Information Technology Association of America (ITAA)

1616 N. Fort Myer Drive   Tel: (703) 522-5055
Suite 1300   Fax: (703) 525-2279
Arlington, VA 22209-1306

Institute of Electrical and Electronics Engineers (IEEE)

IEEE Headquarters   IEEE Customer Service
345 East 47th Street   445 Hoes Lane
New York, NY 10017-2394   P.O. Box 1331
Tel: (212) 705-7900   Piscataway, NJ 08855-1331

"Ask*IEEE" document   Tel: 1-800-678-IEEE (1-800-678-4333)
delivery service: or   (908) 981-0060
Tel: 1-800-949-IEEE   Fax: (908) 981-9667
     (1-800-949-4333)   E-mail: member.services@ieee.org
or   (415) 259-5040
E-mail: askieee@ieee.org

The Institute for Interconnecting and Packaging Electronic Circuits (IPC)

7380 N. Lincoln Avenue   Tel: (708) 677-2850
Lincolnwood, IL 60646-1705   Fax: (708) 677-9570

The Institute of Internal Auditors (IIA)

International Headquarters   Tel: (407) 830-7600
249 Maitland Avenue   Fax: (407) 831-5171
Altamonte Springs, FL 32701-4201

The Instrument Society of America (ISA)

P.O. Box 12277   Tel: (919) 549-8411
Research Triangle Park, NC 27709   Fax: (919) 549-8288

International Society of Certified Electronic Technicians (ISCET)

2708 West Berry Street   Tel: (817) 921-9101
Fort Worth, TX 76109   Fax: (817) 921-3741

The International Safe Transit Association (ISTA)

43 East Ohio Street   Tel: (312) 645-0083
Suite 1022   Fax: (312) 645-1078
Chicago, IL 60611

The International Statistical Applications Institute (ISAI)

2183 S Cooper Street Tel: 1-800-532-7718
Wichita, KS 67207-5834   (316) 777-4425
Fax: (316) 689-6889

The Manufacturers' Alliance for Productivity and Innovation (MAPI)

1200 Eighteenth Street, N.W. Tel: (202) 331-8430
Washington, DC 20036   Fax: (202) 331-7160

The National Association of Purchasing Management (NAPM)

P.O. Box 22160   Tel: 1-800-888-6276
Tempe, AZ 85285-2160 Fax: (602) 752-7890
Fax on Demand:
1-800-329-6276

National Computer Security Association (NCSA)

10 South Courthouse Ave. CompuServe: GO NCSAFORUM
Carlisle, PA 17013   75300.2557@compuserve.com

Tel: (717) 258-1816   Virus Helpline: 1-900-555-NCSA
Fax: (717) 243-8642   ($1.90/min. Must be 18 or older)

National Conference of Standards Laboratories (NCSL)

Serving the World of Measurement

NCSL—Business Office NCSL BBS (Electronic Bulletin Board):
1800 30th Street   (303) 440-3385
Suite 305 B
Boulder, Colorado 80301 Character format: TTY using 8,N,1
Tel: (303) 440-3339   System Operator: Wilbur Anson
Fax: (303) 440-3384

National Conference on Weights and Measures (NCWM)

P.O. Box 4025   Tel: (301) 975-4012
Gaithersburg, MD 20885 Fax: (301) 926-0647

National Electrical Manufacturers Association (NEMA)

2101 L Street, N.W.   Tel: (202) 457-8455
Washington, DC 20037 Fax: (202) 457-8473

The National Fire Protection Association (NFPA)

1 Batterymarch Park   Tel: 1-800-344-3555
P.O. Box 9101   (617) 770-3000
Quincy, MA 02269-9101   Fax: (617) 984-7057

The National ISO 9000 Support Group

Serving North America

9964 Cherry Valley   Tel: (616) 891-0161
Building #2   Fax: (616) 891-9114
Caledonia, MI 49316   BBS:(616) 891-9433

Richard Clements—Chairman

National Safety Council

Council Headquarters   Council Headquarters: 1-800-621-7619
and Central Region Office   Mid-Atlantic Region: 1-800-633-2208
1121 Spring Lake Drive   Northeastern Region: 1-800-432-5251
Itasca, IL 60143-3201   Southeastern Region: 1-800-441-5103
                            Western Region: 1-800-544-1030
                            Texas Safety Assoc.:   1-800-332-8397

Regulatory Affairs Professionals Society (RAPS)

12300 Twinbrook Parkway   Tel: (301) 770-2920
Suite 630   Fax: (301) 770-2924
Rockville, MD 20852

Society for Human Resource Management (SHRM)

606 North Washington Street   Tel: (703) 548-3440
Alexandria, VA 22314-1997 USA   Fax: (703) 836-0367
Tel: (800)283-7476   TDD: (703) 548-6999
                                 Telex: 6503902491

TAPPI (Previously known as the Technical Association of the Pulp and Paper Industry)

Technology Park / Atlanta   Tel: (404) 446-1400 ext. 265
P.O. Box 105113   1-800-332-8686 (U.S.)
Atlanta, GA 30348-5113   1-800-446-9431 (Canada)
                         Fax: (404) 446-6947
                         Toll-free fax number from Mexico:
                             958000100805

Appendix B
Publications You Should Know about

With interest in quality rising over the last few years, several monthly magazines have appeared on the scene. I'm sure that there are many I am not aware of, but here is a listing of some publications you should know about.

Quality Magazines

Quality
Monthly magazine
Circulation Dept.
Chilton Publishing Co.
P.O. Box 2150
Radnor, PA 19080-9279

Quality Progress
Monthly magazine
P.O. Box 3005
Milwaukee, WI 53201-9402

ISO 9000 News:
The International Journal of ISO
9000 Forum
c/o Standards Council of Canada
1200-45 O'Connor
Ottawa, Ontario Canada
K1P 6N7
Tel: (613) 238-3222;
Fax: (613) 995-4564
1-800-267-8220

Quality Systems Update
CEEM Information Services
10521 Braddock Road
Fairfax, VA 22032
Tel: 800-745-5565; 703-250-5900
Fax: 703-250-5313

Quality Digest
Monthly magazine
P.O. Box 882
Red Bluff, CA 96080-9904

Compliance Engineering:
The Magazine for International
Regulatory Compliance
Published quarterly
629 Massachusetts Ave.
Boxborough, MA 01719
(508) 264-4208

Other Related Magazines or Books

U.S. / Latin Trade:
The Magazine of Commerce in
the Americas
Published monthly by
New World Communications, Inc.
One Biscayne Tower
2 South Biscayne Boulevard
Suite 2950
Miami, FL 33131

Tel: (305) 358-8373

ISO 9000—Need to Know
Information for Canadian
Manufacturers and Service
Companies
Canadian Manufacturers'
Association
75 International Blvd., Suite 400
Toronto, Ontario Canada
M4W6L9

Tel: (416) 798-8000 ext. 223,
Attention ISO 9000 Order Desk

ISO 9000–Related Quality NIST/SCI Publications

Available from:

National Technical Information Service (NTIS)
5285 Port Royal Road
Springfield, VA 22161, USA
Tel: (703) 487-4650; 800-553-6847 (orders only)
Fax: (703) 321-8547

Questions and Answers on Quality, the ISO 9000 Standard Series, Quality
System Registration, and Related Issues
NISTIR 4721 / PB 92-126465

More Questions and Answers on the ISO 9000 Standard Series and Related
Issues
NISTIR 5122 / PB 93-140689

Directory of International and Regional Organizations Conducting
Standards-Related Activities
NIST SP 767 / PB 89-221147

Standards Activities of Organizations in the United States
NIST SP 806 / PB 91-177774

The ABC's of Standards-Related Activities in the United States
NISTIR 87-3576 / PB 87-224309

The ABC's of Certification Activities in the United States
NISTIR 88-3821 / PB 88-239793

Laboratory Accreditation in the United States
NISTIR 4576 / PB 91-194495

Directory of Private Sector Product Certification Programs
NIST SP 774 / PB 90-161712

Directory of Federal Government Certification Programs
NBS SP 739 / PB 88-201512

Directory of Federal Government Laboratory Accreditation / Designation Programs
NIST SP 808 / PB 91-167379

Directory of State and Local Government Laboratory Accreditation / Designation Programs
NIST SP 815 / PB 92-108968

Appendix C
Sources for Ordering Standards

Copies of standards can be obtained from the respective standards-issuing organization and/or these sources. Prices vary.

Organization	Standards Provided
The American National Standards Institute (ANSI) 11 West 42nd Street, 13th Floor New York, NY 10036, USA Tel: (212) 642-4900 Fax: (212) 398-0023 (212) 302-1286 (Orders Only) Telex: (212) 42 42 96 ANSI UI	• ANSI and ANSI approved industry standards • International and foreign standards • Select draft CEN/CENELEC standards • Select draft ISO standards (DIS)
Document Center 1504 Industrial Way, Unit 9 Belmont, CA 94002, USA Tel: (415) 591-7600 Fax: (415) 591-7617	• Federal standards and specifications • Industry standards • International and foreign standards • Military standards and specifications
Global Professional Publications 15 Inverness Way East P.O. Box 1154 Englewood, CO 80150-1154, USA Tel: (800) 854-7179 (303) 792-2181 Fax: (303) 792-2192	• Federal standards and specifications • Industry standards • International and foreign standards • Military standards and specifications

General Services Administration (GSA)
Federal Supply Service Bureau
Specifications Branch
490 East L'Enfant Plaza, SW
Suite 8100
Washington, DC 20407, USA
Tel: (202) 755-0325
        (202) 755-0326
Fax: (202) 205-3720

- Federal standards and specifications

Informacion Tecnologica y Consul-
toria (INFOTEC)
Avenida San Fernando No. 37
Apartado Postal 22-860
Tlalpan, 14050, Mexico D.F.
Tel: +52 (56) 06-00-11
        +52 (56) 06-16-20
Fax: +52 (56) 06-03-86

INFOTEC is a nonprofit, private-sector organization devoted to providing a broad range of technical information. I understand it has many Mexican standards (NOMs) available in its library, and states that any others can generally be obtained within 48 hours.

Information Handling Services®
(IHS)
(for IHS subscribers only)
Inverness Business Park
15 Inverness Way East
P.O. Box 1154
Englewood, CO 80150, USA
Tel: (800) 241-7824
        (800) 525-7052
        (303) 790-0600 (International)

- Federal standards and specifications
- Industry standards
- International and foreign standards
- Military standards and specifications
- Select European standards (CEN/CENELEC)

International Organization for
Standardization (ISO)
Case Postale 56, CH-1211
Geneve 20, Switzerland

Tel: 41-22-749-0111
Fax: 41-22-733-3430

- ISO standards

National Standards Association
(NSA)
1200 Quince Orchard Boulevard
Gaithersburg, MD 20878, USA
Tel: (800) 638-8094
     (301) 590-2300
Fax: (301) 990-8378
Telix: 44 6194 NATSTA GAIT

- Aerospace standards
- Federal standards and
  specifications
- Industry standards
- Military standards and
  specifications
- NATO standards

Naval Publications and Forms
Center
Attn: NPODS
5801 Tabor Avenue
Philadelphia, PA 19120-5099, USA
Tel. (215) 697-2667
Fax: (215) 697-5914

- Dept. of Defense (DoD) adopted
  documents
- Naval publications
- Military manuals and other
  related forms

Standardization Document Order
Desk
Naval Publications Printing Service
700 Robbins Avenue, Building 4,
Section D
Philadelphia, PA 19111-5094, USA
Tel: (215) 697-2179
Fax: (215) 697-2978

- Federal standards and
  specifications
- Military standards, specifications,
  and handbooks

Standards Sales Group (SSG)
9420 Reseda Boulevard, Suite 800
Northridge, CA 91324, USA
Tel: (800) 755-2780 (orders only)
     (818) 368-2786
Fax: (818) 360-3804

- International and foreign
  standards, publications, and other
  reference materials
- Translation service
- U.S./foreign general regulatory
  compliance information

Appendix D
U.S. SIC Codes

When applying for registration, you will need to know what your company's SIC code is. This chart will allow you to determine to which major SIC code group you belong.

U.S. Standard Industrial Classification (SIC) Codes

0100	Agriculture—crops	2500	Furniture and fixtures
0200	Agriculture—livestock	2600	Paper and allied products
0800	Forestry	2700	Printing and publishing
0900	Fishing, hunting, and trapping	2800	Chemicals and allied products
1000	Metal mining	2900	Petroleum and coal products
1200	Coal mining	3000	Rubber and plastics products
1300	Oil and gas extraction	3100	Leather and leather products
1400	Mining and quarrying of non-metallic minerals except fuels	3200	Stone/clay/glass/concrete products
1500	General building contractors	3300	Primary metal industries
1600	Heavy construction, except building	3400	Fabricated metal products
1700	Special trade contractors	3500	Industrial machinery and equipment
2000	Food and kindred products	3600	Electrical/electronic equipment
2100	Tobacco products	3700	Transportation equipment
2200	Textile mill process	3800	Instruments and related products
2300	Apparel and other textile products	3900	Miscellaneous manufacturing
2400	Lumber and wood products	4000	Railroad transportation

(continued)

4200	Trucking and warehousing	5800	Eating and drinking places
4400	Water transportation	5900	Miscellaneous retail
4500	Air transportation	6000	Depository institutions
4600	Pipelines, except natural gas	6400	Insurance agents, brokers, and service
4700	Transportation services	7300	Business services
4800	Communications	7500	Auto repair, services, and parking
4900	Electric/gas/sanitary services	7600	Miscellaneous repair services
5000	Wholesale trade/durable goods	8100	Legal services
5100	Wholesale trade/nondurable goods	8200	Educational services
5300	General merchandise stores	8700	Professional services
5400	Food stores	9200	Justice, public order, safety
5500	Automotive dealers and service stations	9500	Environmental quality and housing

Appendix E
References

ANSI/NCSL Z540-1, *"General Requirements for Calibration Laboratories and Measuring and Test Equipment,"* 1994.

ASQC Chemical and Process Industries Division—Chemical Interest Committee, *ANSI/ASQC Q90, ISO 9000 Guidelines for Use by the Chemical and Process Industries*, Milwaukee, WI.: ASQC Quality Press.

ASME NQA-1-1989, "Quality Assurance Program—Requirements for Nuclear Facilities."

Bellcore "Quality System Generic Requirements," TA-NWT-001252, Issue 1, February 1992.

Maureen Breitenberg, *More Questions and Answers on the ISO 9000 Standard Series and Related Issues*, U.S. Dept. of Commerce/Technology Administration—National Institute of Standards and Technology (February 1993).

"Certifying Railroads"—News, *Quality Progress* (July 1993).

W. Edwards Deming, 1982. *Quality, Productivity, and Competitive Position* (published by Massachusetts Institute of Technology, Center for Advanced Engineering Study, Cambridge, MA).

W. Edwards Deming, 1986. *Out of the Crisis* (published by Massachusetts Institute of Technology, Center for Advanced Study, Cambridge, MA).

Ian G. Durand, Donald W. Marquedant, Robert W. Peach, and James Pyle, "Updating the ISO 9000 Quality Standards: Responding to the Marketplace Needs," *Quality Progress* (July 1993, pp. 23–28).

"ISO: What Does It Stand for Anyway?", *Quality Systems Update*, CEEM Information Services (January 1993).

ISO 5807:1985, "Information processing—Documentation symbols and conventions for data, program and system flowcharts, program network charts and system resources charts"

ISO 9000-1:1994, "Quality Management and Quality Assurance Standards—Part 1: Guidelines for selection and use"

ISO 9000-2:1993, "Quality Management and Quality Assurance Standards—Part 2: Generic guidelines for application of ISO 9001, ISO 9002, and ISO 9003"

ISO 9001:1994, "Quality Systems—Model for Quality Assurance in Design/Development, Production, Installation, and Servicing"

ISO 9002:1994, "Quality Systems—Model for Quality Assurance in Production, Installation, and Servicing"

ISO 9003:1994, "Quality Systems—Model for Quality Assurance in Final Inspection and Test"

ISO 9004-1:1994, "Quality Management and Quality System Elements—Part 1: Guidelines"

ISO 9004-2:1991, "Quality Management and Quality System Elements—Part 2: Guide to quality management and quality systems elements for services"

ISO 10011-1:1990, "Guidelines for Auditing Quality Systems—Part 1: Auditing"

ISO 10011-2:1991, "Guidelines for Auditing Quality Systems—Part 2: Qualification criteria for auditors"

ISO 10011-3:1991, "Guidelines for Auditing Quality Systems—Part 3: Managing audit programs"

ISO 10012-1:1992, "Quality Assurance Requirements for Measuring Equipment—Part 1: Metrological confirmation system for measuring equipment"

ISO/DIS 10013, "Guidelines for Developing Quality Manuals"

Theodore B. Kinni, "Playing Games," *Quality Digest* (July 1993).

Ken Kivenko, "Improve Performance by Driving out Fear," *Quality Progress* (October 1994, pp. 77–79).

Donald Marquedant, Jacques Chove, K.E. Jensen, Klaus Petrick, James Pyle, and Donald Strahle, "Vision 2000: The Strategy for the ISO 9000 Series Standards in the '90s," *Quality Progress* (May 1991, pp. 25–31).

MIL-HDBK-350, "A Guide for MIL-STD-1520C Corrective Action and Disposition System for Nonconforming Material," 7 June 1991.

MIL-STD-100E, "Engineering Drawing Practices," 30 September 1991.

MIL-STD-1520C, "Corrective Action and Disposition System for Nonconforming Material," 27 June 1986.

MIL-STD-1521B, "Technical Reviews and Audits for Systems, Equipments, and Computer Software," 4 June 1985.

MIL-STD-2155 (AS), "Failure Reporting, Analysis, and Corrective Action System," 24 July 1985.

MIL-STD-45662A, "Calibration Systems Requirements," 1 August 1988.

"Paper trail can leave companies vulnerable," *Quality Systems Update*, Fairfax, VA: CEEM Information Services (October 1993).

Peach, Robert W., *The ISO 9000 Handbook*, Fairfax, VA: CEEM Information Services, 1992.

"Product standards—conformity assessment," *Business in Europe*, prepared by the U.K. Department of Trade and Industry (DTI) and the Central Office of Information, April 1993.

Quality Systems Requirements (QS-9000), Chrysler, Ford Motor Company, General Motors, September 1994.

Richard C. Randall, *GE Electronic Services—ISO 9000 Questions & Answers*, General Electric Company (April 1992).

The Rath & Strong Personal Initiative Survey (released in February 1994), Lexington, MA, Rath & Strong Management Consultants.

Peter R. Scholtes, *The Team Handbook*, Madison, WI, Joiner Associates Inc., April 1992.

U.S. Department of Transportation —*"Federal Motor Carrier Safety Regulations"* (FMCSR), Part 391.

Mary Walton, 1986. *The Deming Management Method*, Perigee Books.

"When it comes to training, Bio-Rad wins, hands down," *NQA Update*, Vol. 2, No. 1, March 1994.

Index